The
Garland Library
of
War and Peace

The
Garland Library
of
War and Peace

Under the General Editorship of
Blanche Wiesen Cook, *John Jay College, C.U.N.Y.*
Sandi E. Cooper, *Richmond College, C.U.N.Y.*
Charles Chatfield, *Wittenberg University*

The Church of the Brethren and War
1708-1941

by
Rufus D. Bowman

with a new introduction
for the Garland Edition by
Donald F. Durnbaugh

Garland Publishing, Inc., New York & London
1971

The new introduction for this
Garland Library Edition is Copyright © 1971, by
Garland Publishing Inc.
24 West 45 St., New York, N.Y. 10036

Library of Congress Cataloging in Publication Data

Bowman, Rufus David, 1899–
    The Church of the Brethren and war, 1708–1941.

    (The Garland library of war and peace)
    Bibliography: p.
    1. Church of the Brethren--History. 2. War and
religion. I. Title. II. Series.
    [BX7815.B6 1972]   261.8'73   75–147667
    ISBN 0–8240–0425–6

Printed in the United States of America

Introduction

The Church of the Brethren has held a consistent official peace witness since its founding in 1708 in Schwarzenau, Germany. Most of its members came from the Palatinate, ravaged repeatedly in the late seventeenth century by French invasions. They were thus receptive to the peace emphases of the two religious movements which principally formed them — Radical Pietism and Anabaptism. For much of Brethren history the peace conviction can be characterized as biblically non-resistant. Unlike the pacifists of liberal Protestantism of the nineteenth and twentieth centuries, non-resistant Christians saw little possibility of the abolition of war but adamantly refused to participate in warfare in any way. In this the Brethren were very much like the Mennonites, the direct descendants of the sixteenth century Anabaptists, whom they resembled in many ways.[1]

In the early twentieth century the Brethren became more involved in society and more concerned about social activism. Their position came to be much like that of the Society of Friends, who had a far

---

[1] The distinction between non-resistance and liberal pacifism is well discussed in Guy F. Hershberger, War, Peace, and Nonresistance, 3rd rev. ed. (Scottdale, Pa.: Herald Press, 1969), 172-208. See also Reinhold Niebuhr, Moral Man and Immoral Society (New York: Charles Scribner's Sons, 1932).

5

*more positive view of government than did the
Mennonites. Emerging from their cultural isolation as
German sectarians in rural areas, the Brethren were
increasingly related to urban society. Denominational
leaders received their education in eastern and mid-
western universities. Local congregations moved from
the "free ministry" of untrained elders who worked
through the week as farmers or craftsmen to the
employment of seminary-educated professional
pastors. The Church of the Brethren became a
denomination similar to other Protestant bodies,
although retaining some of its previous sectarian
heritage.*[2]

*This shift explains why large numbers of young
Brethren accepted non-combatant military service in
World War I, in contrast with their community's
record during the Revolutionary and Civil wars. The
church leadership found itself unable to counsel men
to take an absolutist, non-registrant position. Their
concern was for "constructive citizenship." Having
accepted the benefits of society, they saw no possibility of complete exemption from military service.*

*A considerable number of Brethren men did,
however, face court-martial for refusal to wear the
uniform or to obey military orders. The long delay by
the United States Government in spelling out the
options for non-combatant service and other administrative confusion and inequity further complicated*

[2]*See Donald F. Durnbaugh, ed.,* The Church of the Brethren: Past
and Present *(Elgin, Ill.: Brethren Press, 1971), 23-25.*

6

the issue.

On January 9, 1918 a special conference of the Church of the Brethren was convened at Goshen, Indiana, to spell out the Brethren peace position and to provide clear guidelines for Brethren caught in conscription. The statement began with a lengthy discussion of biblical references and a reiteration of the pacifist stand. The crucial section of the recommendation read: *"We further urge our brethren not to enlist in any service which would, in any way, compromise our time-honored position in relation to war; also that they refrain from wearing the military uniform. The tenets of the church forbid military drilling, or learning the art or acts of war, or doing anything which contributes to the destruction of human life or property."*[3]

The "Goshen Statement" was widely circulated among the Brethren membership. Soon copies came into the hands of military authorities as draftees used them to explain their refusal to cooperate. In July, 1918, Brethren leaders in Washington, D.C., were informed by the War Department that the Judge-Advocate-General was ready to prosecute the officers of the Church of the Brethren and the authors of the Goshen statement for treasonable intent in obstructing the operation of the draft law. Faced with this ultimatum, the church withdrew the statement, avoiding the prosecution, but at the cost of serious compromise of its peace witness.

[3] Ibid., *160.*

INTRODUCTION

Some of the young Brethren men who experienced the church's ambivalence during World War I determined to devote their lives to strengthening Brethren pacifism and working for international peace. Of this number, four have received national recognition. They are Andrew W. Cordier (1901-), Dan West (1893-1971), M.R. Zigler (1891-) and Rufus D. Bowman (1899-1952).

Dr. Andrew W. Cordier was from 1927-1944 head of the department of history and political science at Manchester College, a Brethren-related school in Indiana. In 1941 he became the first chairman of the Brethren Service Commission, organized to administer the World War II program for conscientious objectors and to carry out aid for war sufferers. As is well known, he went on to become the highest ranking American official at the United Nations and Under-Secretary for General Assembly Affairs. He later resumed his educational career as dean of the School of International Affairs and acting President (1968-1970) of Columbia University.

Dan West served for nearly three decades on the national staff of the Brethren church in the area of peace education and leadership training. He stumped the country giving prophetic messages for peace, attracting many to his concept that a peacemaker must follow a simple and disciplined style of life. As a relief worker in Spain in 1937-38 he was faced with the agonizing task of doling out emergency nutrition to the starving. He conceived there the idea of sending livestock to war sufferers and refugees as a way of providing continual supplies of food. The initial recipient of a cow or goat would pledge to pass on the first female offspring, so that a chain of aid would grow in geometric progression. The idea was realized during World War II as the Heifer Project, Incorporated and began sending livestock to the needy around the world. American farmers, church groups, and service clubs were attracted by the earthy practicality of the scheme, and it won broad support. In 1970 the agency sent 113 shipments worth three-quarters of a million dollars to 34 countries.[4]

M.R. Zigler served as a YMCA secretary with the Marine Corps during World War I and decided that he was going to devote his life to the cause of peace: "I promised some of them that went across and died that I should work for peace and good will the rest of my days."[5] *This pledge he kept as he filled major denominational posts for the Brethren in North America between 1919 and 1948. He was active in ecumenical circles and is often given credit for sparking many of the organizations created by American Protestants such as Church World Service and CROP (Christian Rural Overseas Program).*[6] *1948 he went to the Continent as European director*

[4]Kermit Eby, The God In You (Chicago: University of Chicago Press, 1954), 43-54.

[5]Quoted in Roger E. Sappington, Brethren Social Policy: 1908-1958 Elgin, Ill.: Brethren Press, 1961), p. 195.

[6]Harold E. Fey, Cooperation in Compassion: The Story of Church World Service (New York: Friendship Press, 1966).

9

INTRODUCTION

*of the Brethren Service Commission and repre-
sentative to the World Council of Churches. In these
capacities he reiterated on the highest church levels
his conviction that "if the churches of the world
would unite for the cessation of war, the men of
government would listen."*[7]

The Life of Rufus D. Bowman

*Rufus D. Bowman is unique among these four
Brethren peace leaders in that he not only powerfully
shaped the Brethren position on war but also wrote
the most complete history of it. He was probably the
most trusted, best respected, and best beloved of all
Brethren churchmen during the period 1930-1950
and, next to Zigler, the most influential in forming
the policies of the denomination. His activities
spanned the careers of pastor, church executive, and
educator.*[8]

[7]M. R. Zigler, "To Work for Peace," Messenger *(Church of the
Brethren: November 21, 1968), 2-5.*

[8]*There is no full biography. There is a biographical sketch in* Who
Was Who in America: 1951-1960 *(Chicago: A.N. Marquis, 1963), 94.
See also: Desmond W. Bittinger, "Introduction" in R.D. Bowman,* The
Church of the Brethren and War *(Elgin, Ill.: Brethren Publishing House,
1944), 7-10; Paul H. Bowman, "Rufus David Bowman: The Man,"*
Gospel Messenger *(October 18, 1952), 12-13; J. W. Lear, "President
Rufus David Bowman, D.D.,"* Bethany Biblical Seminary Bulletin, XXV
*(July-September, 1937), 3; John W. Lowe, Jr., "Rufus David Bowman:
A Brethren Witness for Peace,"* Brethren Life and Thought, XVI
*(Spring, 1971), forthcoming; D. Merrill Mow, "Rufus D. Bowman:
Apostle," (unpubl. paper, 1952, Bethany Theological Seminary
Library). There are also memorial addresses on taped recordings in the
Seminary library.*

INTRODUCTION

Born in the Shenandoah valley of Virginia where there have been strong concentrations of Brethren since the colonial period, Bowman was educated in the public schools of Bridgewater, Virginia. He stayed in his home region for his college years, graduating from Bridgewater College (a school founded by Brethren) in 1923. (The institution conferred the Doctor of Divinity degree on Bowman in 1937.) He received a Bachelor of Divinity degree from Yale in 1926, having married Eva Craun the year previously.

His first pastorate was in Roanoke, Virginia. He had unusual success in building up a strong congregation before he was called in 1929 to become the general secretary of the Board of Christian Education in Elgin, Illinois, the denominational headquarters. Five years later he returned to the pastoral ministry in Washington, D.C. where he worked effectively until 1937. In that year he was called to be the President and Professor of Practical Theology and Christian Education at Bethany Biblical Seminary in Chicago (now Bethany Theological Seminary). While continuing his duties as seminary president, he pursued graduate study at Northwestern University and received his Ph.D. in 1944. As an educator, Bowman earned national recognition. He served on the executive committee of the American Association of Theological Schools and in the summer of 1952 was elected president of the Association of Seminary Professors in the Practical Field. Rufus Bowman served as president of the seminary until his sudden

11

*death on August 19, 1952 while returning by train
from a speaking engagement.*

*As a churchman, he gave major leadership in the
areas of education, missions, publications, administration, and peace. He was on the General Education
Board from 1937-1952. He was chairman of the
General Mission Board for years, serving on a delegation of this board to visit the Brethren missions in
China and India in 1948-1949. He sat on a blue-
ribbon committee of fifteen in 1945-1947 which
completely reorganized the administrative structure
of the denomination, and was named first chairman
of the General Brotherhood Board, the top administrative agency created under the new plan. He chaired
the board of the publishing house, and played a major
role in arbitrating difficult labor-management
problems there. He represented the Brethren at the
Federal (later National) Council of Churches of Christ
in the USA. Bowman was twice elected moderator of
the annual conference of the Church of the Brethren
(1940 and 1947), the highest honor at the disposal of
the denomination.*

*Throughout this busy period his major interest was
in the area of peace. He chaired a Brethren committee
from 1935-1941 formed to provide legal counsel for
conscientious objectors and served on the Advance
Committee on Peace of the Church of the Brethren
during the same time span. In 1936 he attended
international peace conferences in Cambridge,*

England and Geneva, Switzerland.[9] *He was repeatedly called upon to represent the Brethren in
contacts with the federal government and his files
contain many letters which he wrote to government
leaders.*

*As a Brethren leader in peace activities he worked
closely with other churches, especially with the other
peace churches — the Mennonites and the Friends. He
was present at the meeting in Newton, Kansas, in
1935 when the term "historic peace churches" was
coined. The result of this conference was the decision
to make common cause in negotiations with the
government. During his Washington pastorate, Bowman had cooperated with the Friends-sponsored
Emergency Campaign for Peace. He was on the
national council of the Fellowship of Reconciliation,
the leading pacifist organization. He worked locally in
Chicago with many theologians and churchmen of
different religious backgrounds to organize support
for pacifists.*

*Bowman himself has told as a participant the story
of the combined efforts of Friends, Mennonites, and
Brethren in bringing their peace concerns to President
Franklin D. Roosevelt in 1937 and 1940. The earlier
meeting was designed to place the peace position of
the three groups on record. In 1940 with war in
Europe already raging and American involvement*

[9] *A report of his reactions to this trip was printed in the denomin-
ational journal: Rufus D. Bowman, "The Church of the Brethren
Facing the Peace Crisis," Gospel Messenger (October 31, 1936), 5-6;
(November 7, 1936), 5-6.*

13

likely, they were concerned with establishing a form of alternative service acceptable to the government which would be consistent with the peace testimony of their constituencies. According to Bowman, FDR gave them a much longer interview than anticipated and praised their initiative: "I'm glad you have done it. That's getting down to a practical basis. It shows us what work the conscientious objectors can do without fighting. Excellent! Excellent!" [10]

The peace churches failed in getting a program for conscientious objectors under civilian direction as they wished. Nor did they get complete exemption for absolutist pacifists. They did succeed in laying the groundwork for a more satisfactory arrangement for pacifists than had been the case in World War I. This provided for cooperation between the churches and the government in enabling civilian work "of national importance" during war time, outside the military. There were many problems in the Civilian Public Service system which was created, such as lack of government support for dependents. Rufus Bowman played a major role in establishing this experiment in church-state relations, and reports on it fully in his book.

Cooperating with the government while holding firmly to a peace witness is consistent with Bowman's own peace philosophy. He wrote often in Brethren publications about peace, but perhaps nowhere is his

[10] Rufus D. Bowman, The Church of the Brethren and War: 1708-1941 (Elgin, Ill.: Brethren Publishing House, 1944), 272ff.

14

INTRODUCTION

*view better expressed than in the last article he ever
wrote, published posthumously. It was about the
Brethren martyr, John Kline, killed near his Virginia
home in 1864 for his pacifist and anti-slavery views.
The article reflects Bowman's spirit fully as much as
it does that of Kline, with whom Bowman closely
identified:* "No one in the history of the Church of
the Brethren has been a greater inspiration to me than
John Kline. His life and spirit shine like a lighthouse
in the church. His humble spirit, his complete
devotion to Christ and his magnificent service to his
fellow man, capture the admiration of us all." *Many
there were in the Church of the Brethren who could
say the same of Bowman. There are indeed similar-
ities between the two Virginians of different generations.*

*The article consists of Bowman's interpretation of
the message of Kline for the contemporary Church of
the Brethren. His main points, with some of the
commentary follow:*

We should keep our peace position Biblical. . . .
From Schwarzenau until today there has been one
consistent thing in the peace position of the
Brethren. That is that war is wrong because of the
spirit and teachings of Jesus. . . . The Brethren
believe that war cannot be reconciled with the
spirit and teachings of Christ. . . .

We should keep our peace testimony clear in an age

15

of power culture.... *Are we keeping our peace convictions clear in a militarist state? ... Do we have courage enough to apply the gospel of Jesus to communism and discover that the answer to communism is not to fight it, but to live the revolutionary aspect of the teachings of Christ? ...*

We should interpret to our people the highest type of patriotism. ... *As a people we believe that our supreme citizenship is in the kingdom of God, however, we love our country and want to work for its highest welfare. We encourage our people to vote, we work for good government and to help create a Christian public opinion which will result in legislation in harmony with the eternal law of God. ...*

We should give a testimony for out faith through unselfish service to mankind. ... *We hold that peacemaking is a faith and a way of life and we must live in the spirit of our faith. The relief of suffering both in war and peace is a record of the Brethren and the spirit by which we want to live. ...*

We should bring to our Christian service the utmost courage and devotion. ... *Is it possible for the Church of the Brethren to be the Church of the Brethren in a power culture? The answer is yes, if*

INTRODUCTION

we are willing to lose our lives. Let us stand upon the heritage of our fathers and go forward in the application of our peace principles to the problems of our days. . . ."[11]

Recent Literature on the Brethren and War

Rufus D. Bowman's monograph on the Brethren and war remains the most complete study yet written, although additional details before 1900 can be found in the massive study by Peter Brock, Pacifism in the United States.[12] *The dissertation from which Bowman's book was distilled covers as well the first years of World War II, whereas the book concludes in 1941.*[13] *Bowman had hoped to write the full story of the Brethren in World War II but his abrupt death frustrated this plan. Questionnaires from all of the Brethren who were in CPS camps during World War II are found in Bowman's files as material for the projected study. The history of the Brethren and alternative service is told in Leslie*

[11] Rufus D. Bowman, "John Kline Speaks to the Church," Gospel Messenger (September 6, 1952), 10-11, 14. The address was delivered at the dedication of a monument for Kline, New Broadway, Virginia.

[12] Peter Brock, Pacifism in the United States (Princeton: Princeton University Press, 1968), 167-178, 267-270, 404-413, 797-821, 907-911 and elsewhere. For the Civil War period, see also Samuel Horst, Mennonites in the Confederacy (Scottdale, Pa.: Herald Press, 1967).

[13] Rufus D. Bowman, An Historical and Interpretative Study of the Church of the Brethren and War, (unpubl. Ph.D. dissertation, Northwestern University, 1944).

Eisan's Pathways of Peace.[14] *A broader interpretation of the same period is given in a dissertation by Lorell Weiss, a pastor, professor, and longtime Brethren Service Commission staff worker.*[15] *Don Royer, a Brethren professor who was imprisoned during the war as a non-cooperator, studied the shifts in Brethren attitude toward war using the techniques of sociological research.*[16]

The most detailed study of Brethren peace and relief activities in the twentieth century is Roger Sappington's Brethren Social Policy.[17] *This goes beyond Bowman's work in utilizing denominational archival materials and brings the story up to 1958. There is as yet no complete history of the Brethren Service Commission (although it is dealt with in Sappington's book); this agency carried the peace program of the Brethren from 1941 until its dissolution in a restructuring of the denominational offices in 1968.*[18]

[14] Leslie Eisan, Pathways of Peace *(Elgin, Ill.: Brethren Publishing House, 1948).*

[15] Lorell Weiss, Socio-Psychological Factors in the Pacifism of the Church of the Brethren during the Second World War. *(unpubl. Ph.D. dissertation, University of California, 1957).*

[16] Don Royer, *"The Acculturation Process and the Peace Doctrine of the Church of the Brethren in the Central Region of the United States," (unpubl. Ph.D. dissertation, University of Chicago, 1955).*

[17] *See footnote 5. It is a condensation of a broader work: "The Development of the Social Policy in the Church of the Brethren: 1908-1958" (unpubl. Ph.D. dissertation, Duke University, 1959).*

[18] *See Lorell Weiss,* Ten Years of Brethren Service (1941-1951) *(Elgin, Ill.: Brethren Service Commission, 1951).*

18

INTRODUCTION

Another important story for which there are only scattered references is the development of the department of peace studies at Manchester College since 1948 under Dr. Gladdys E. Muir (1895-1967) and others. This was the first such academically oriented program in American higher education and the first department to offer a major in peace.[19]

Two significant initiatives by the Church of the Brethren in the broader peace concern are exchange and dialogue with the Russian Orthodox Church and the theological conferences in Europe on the Lordship of Christ. The former was initiated in 1963 and has developed into a program of exchanges of delegations and conferences in Europe and North America on current peace issues.[20] *The latter series of conferences in Western Europe has been called the Puidoux Peace Conferences from the small Swiss town where the first meeting took place in 1955. These involve theologians from the historic peace churches and European Landeskirchen. They have been called the first serious discussion between the*

[19] *Besides scattered references in college and denominational literature, see Allen C. Deeter, "Educational and Career Inventory of Peace Studies Students, Manchester College, 1948-1970," (unpubl. paper supported by a grant from the Central States College Association under Project Grant No. 7-E179X, United States Office of Education). See also* Bulletin of the Peace Studies Institute *(Manchester College, January 1971).*

[20] *See among other articles, Dale W. Brown, "Baugo and Zagorsk: Extremes in Encounter,"* Christian Century *(January 8, 1964), 52, 54, 56 and Leland Wilson, "A Bridge Built by Dialogue,"* Messenger *(April 25, 1968), 10-11, 20-21. The exchange was hotly criticized by fundamentalist Carl McIntire in his publication* Christian Beacon.

INTRODUCTION

two groups since the sixteenth century.[21]

Two important articles published in a Brethren journal for opinion and scholarship survey Brethren attitudes toward war and attempt to construct typologies. They are Robert McFadden's "Perspective in Pacifism" and Richard B. Gardner's "Brethren and Pacifism." McFadden argues from a position of nuclear pacifism, Gardner from that of "critical Anabaptism."[22]

The past several years have seen several Brethren-authored books on the topic. Donald F. Durnbaugh's The Believers' Church *places the Brethren and their peace witness in a broader perspective;*[23] Six Papers on Peace *is a symposium by Brethren of different backgrounds and persuasions.*[24] *Art Gish compares student radicalism with the religious radicalism of the Anabaptists and calls for renewal through radical discipleship in* The New Left and Christian

[21] Donald F. Durnbaugh, "The Puidoux Conferences: Ten Years of Theological Peace Discussion Among Members of the Historic Peace Churches and Others," Brethren Life and Thought, XIII *(Winter, 1968)*, 30-40.

[22] Robert McFadden, "Perspective in Pacifism," Brethren Life and Thought, VI *(Spring 1961), 36-52; Richard B. Gardner, "Brethren and Pacifism: An Analysis of Contemporary Brethren Approaches to Peace and War,"* Brethren Life and Thought, VIII *(Autumn 1963), 17-37.*

[23] Donald F. Durnbaugh, The Believers' Church: The History and Character of Radical Protestantism *(New York: Macmillan, 1968)*.

[24] Ralph E. Smeltzer, ed., Six Papers on Peace *(Elgin, Ill.: Church of the Brethren General Board, 1969). The authors are: William G. Willoughby, Robert C. Johansen, C. Wayne Zunkel, Kenneth L. Brown, William Schule, and William R. Faw.*

20

INTRODUCTION

Radicalism.[25] *Dale W. Brown, professor of historical theology at Bethany Theological Seminary, presents an excellent concise history of Brethren attitudes toward war in his* Brethren and Pacifism. *The body of the book is a discussion of the main questions faced by pacifists today, presenting personal answers and positions. It deals as well with the increasing movement among Brethren youth to reject cooperation with the Selective Service system because of the favored position given to Brethren.[26] There is evidence of a renewed interest and vitality in the Brethren peace witness brought on by the challenge of an undeclared and bloody war in Southeast Asia.*

Donald F. Durnbaugh
Professor of Church History
Bethany Theological Seminary

---

[25] *Arthur G. Gish,* The New Left and Christian Radicalism *(Grand Rapids, Mich.: William B. Eerdmans, 1970).*

Dale W. Brown, Brethren and Pacifism *(Elgin, Ill.: Brethren Press, 1970).*

ABOVE: The village of Schwarzenau in Wittgenstein. At or near this spot on the banks of the Eder River the first baptisms took place in 1708. Photo by H. Spenser Minnich in 1924. BELOW: The mother church at 6613 Germantown Avenue, Philadelphia. Property of the brotherhood by action of Conference in 1943. Photo supplied by B. F. Waltz.

THE CHURCH OF THE BRETHREN AND WAR

THE CHURCH OF THE BRETHREN AND WAR

1708-1941

by

RUFUS D. BOWMAN, Ph. D.

President of Bethany Biblical Seminary

BRETHREN PUBLISHING HOUSE

Elgin, Illinois

Printed by the
BRETHREN PUBLISHING HOUSE
Elgin, Illinois

DEDICATED

to

MY WIFE, EVA CRAUN BOWMAN

Whose devoted companionship has made life a joyous adventure, whose constant helpfulness lifted the laborious writing of this volume into a happy privilege, and whose encouragement enabled the author to transform a dream into a living reality

INTRODUCTION

To accept the New Testament as one's creed and the spirit of Christ it portrays as one's inspiration and guide requires courage. If done conscientiously it demands a willingness to venture beyond the usual patterns of conduct and the usual easier interpretations of Scripture. The New Testament calls its followers to climb to the peaks of spiritual worship and to walk far in the broad plains of Christian service.

Followers of the New Testament Christ have a high standard by which their lives must be measured; they must pattern them after his life, and accept seriously his challenge, "Be ye therefore perfect, even as your Father in heaven is perfect." How far they will go on social issues and where they will take their stand cannot be determined by what society will approve, or even by what society will accept, but rather it must be determined by what the New Testament reveals that Christ taught and what he himself stood for. To gauge one's life by this standard takes courage in any age and in some ages it calls for sacrifice and martyrdom.

The Church of the Brethren was founded by courageous souls on the assumption that its followers would live by this rigorous New Testament standard. From Alexander Mack and Christopher Sower down to this present age Brethren have been courageous and many have been willing to suffer. Moreover, their interpretation of the spirit of the New Testament has called them to the forefront on many social issues. Among these have been slavery, the use of intoxicants and tobacco, and the issue of simple, honest, nonviolent living.

The story of *The Church of the Brethren and War, 1708-1941* is one that needed to be written; our brotherhood has been waiting for it. The book makes it clear that our church has stood for peace with continuing courage and steadfast zeal during every American war, and worked for peace during each interim between wars. The story of this steadfastness and progress as revealed in this book should give courage to every Church of the Brethren member in our day and in succeeding days; it should make him proud of the record of his church, and kindle within him new resolves to carry forward this great message of peace and goodwill until all men everywhere, in the name of our great Peacemaker, Christ, can at last be free.

No other one in the Church of the Brethren could write this story so well as Dr. Rufus D. Bowman, president of Bethany Biblical Seminary in Chicago. He comes from the staunch Brethren stock whose homes had been founded on the limestone soil of the Valley of Virginia. In him are combined two Brethren-building names, Bowman and Miller (B. F., father; Mary Elizabeth, mother). He was educated in Bridgewater College, from which he received an A.B. degree in 1923 and a D.D. degree in 1937. He received his B.D. degree from Yale Divinity School in 1926 and his Ph.D. degree from Northwestern University in 1944. In 1925 he was married to Eva Margaret Craun, who has been a faithful helpmeet to him; and three children, Mack Daniel, Jane Esther, and Judy Margaret, now grace their home. His fields of work have been varied but in each of them he has rendered outstanding Christian service. Ordained to the ministry in 1921, he took up his first pastorate at the First church in Roanoke, Virginia, 1926-29, served as general secretary of the Board of Christian Education, Elgin, Illinois, 1929-34, then served as pastor of the Washington City church 1934-37. Since 1937 he has been president of Bethany Biblical Seminary and under his leadership Bethany has taken forward steps both in standardization and in the service it has rendered to the

Church of the Brethren. He has served as moderator of Annual Conference and for some years has been chairman of the General Mission Board and chairman of the Board of Directors of the Brethren Publishing House at Elgin, Illinois.

In addition to this he has served on several commissions to visit the President of the United States, and has interviewed members of the President's Cabinet and important members of the Congress to clarify before them the peace position of the Church of the Brethren, together with the similar positions of other pacifist church bodies. In these capacities he had no little influence in helping to give form to the present Selective Service legislation as it applies to those who are conscientiously opposed to war. These experiences enable him to write from firsthand knowledge much of the recent history contained in this book.

Dr. Bowman is one of the great preachers of the Church of the Brethren. His message is clear, deeply spiritual and courageous. His thinking on spiritual issues and on the New Testament doctrines is penetrating and direct. He takes his stand fearlessly but kindly for the things that are taught there. His love for his church is unparalleled and his interest is that his church might serve humanity to "the ends of the world."

The Church of the Brethren and War, 1708-1941 is simply and directly written. Even though it contains much documentary material, it is written in such a style that it flows with the freedom of work eagerly undertaken and willingly done. As a history of a specific and important phase of our church life it is outstanding and authoritative and as a general history of our church it has value. This book should find its way into many libraries outside of our fellowship as well as within our church. It should be read by every member of the Church of the Brethren, that this central theme in our purpose might be strengthened: "Glory to God in the highest and on earth peace, good will among men."

Desmond W. Bittinger

PREFACE

This study, *The Church of the Brethren and War,* deals with one of the most important problems in the history of the denomination. It aims to show why the Brethren historically have been opposed to war, to trace the development of the Brethren position on war from the founding of the church in 1708 to the outbreak of World War II, and to interpret any significant changes that have taken place in the attitude of the Brethren toward the war problem. The study is conducted within the general area of church and state relationships and is confined to the Brethren and the war issue. The Brethren are seen as a minority religious group whose opposition to war has brought them into many conflicts with the state. How the state has dealt with the Brethren in the various war periods is clearly analyzed. The movement of this church group from non-co-operation to co-operation with the state in working out mutual problems unfolds as a gradual process over more than two hundred years.

This volume does not attempt to give a complete history of the Church of the Brethren, but offers historical data necessary to clarify the development of the Brethren's position on war. It does not set forth a full discussion of other historical peace churches, but mentions these churches as they bear upon the Brethren ideal and practice. It does not compare the Brethren position on war with that of other denominations in general. Neither does it attempt to deal with the whole problem of church and state. It presents one denomination as a religious minority group in its relationships to the state regarding war.

The substance of this volume was accepted as a dissertation to the Graduate School of Northwestern University in partial fulfillment of the requirements for the Doctor of Philosophy degree. The dissertation was en-

titled An Historical and Interpretative Study of the Church
of the Brethren and War, and covered the period from the
founding of the denomination in 1708 at Schwarzenau,
Germany, through several years of World War II.   This
book, however, deals with the Brethren and war from 1708
to 1941, leaving the record of the Brethren and World
War II for a later presentation.

In making this study, personal letters, interviews and
questionnaires were used as instruments of investigation.
More important still, the author made a thorough investigation of Brethren literature bearing on this problem.   The
historical libraries at Bethany Biblical Seminary, Chicago,
Illinois, and the Brethren Publishing House, Elgin, Illinois,
were exceedingly valuable.   In addition, a month was spent
in the East studying in historical libraries.   In the library
at Juniata College, Huntingdon, Pennsylvania, the writer
found the historical collection of Abraham H. Cassel which
contained original letters and writings of Christopher
Sower, the Brethren printer in colonial America.   The
libraries of the Germantown Historical Society and the
University of Pennsylvania were likewise rich in original
materials.   However, the Pennsylvania Historical Society,
Philadelphia, offered the most valuable collection for this
research.   The books dealing with the early settlers of
Pennsylvania, the publications of the Pennsylvania Historical Society, the Pennsylvania Archives and Colonial
Records were found there, and in addition, copies of German newspapers, calendars and broadsides of Christopher
Sower.   The writer employed a German refugee, Frank F.
Fliess, who had taught English in Berlin, to help in trans-
lating the Christopher Sower publications.   All of his writings which could be discovered were investigated for their
materials bearing on the war problem.   Many articles on
peace were translated which have been unknown among

the Brethren. With rare exceptions the English and the punctuation of copied documents have been retained.

The Congressional Library at Washington, D. C., was especially valuable in giving information on the laws affecting the Brethren in the various war periods. A number of days were spent at the National Service Board for Religious Objectors collecting and studying the materials relating to the conscientious objectors and Selective Service. A visit was likewise made to the headquarters of Selective Service. Two principles were paramount in canvassing the literature relating to the Brethren and war: thoroughness in the research, and as far as possible the discovery of original materials.

The author desires to give grateful acknowledgement to Dr. Frank N. McKibben of Garrett Biblical Institute and Northwestern University, Evanston, Illinois, who served as director of this study as a doctoral thesis; to Miss Lois Amy Eller of Bethany Biblical Seminary for untiring efforts in typing and correcting this work; and to Mrs. Eva Craun Bowman for sharing with her husband the burden of creating this volume every step of the way. The writer also offers wholehearted thankfulness to all who were so gracious in giving of their time for interviews, for the writing of personal letters and the answering of questionnaires. The secretaries of the Brethren Service Committee, Elgin, Illinois, and of the National Service Board, Washington, D. C., gave of their time in unlimited measure in helping the writer to secure the needed information. The librarians at the various historical libraries mentioned earlier took a personal interest in this research.

The following publishers have granted permission for copyrighted material to be used: Hastings House, New York City, *We Won't Murder*, by Paul French; Harper and Brothers, New York City, *The Story of Religion in*

America, by William Warren Sweet; Vanguard Press, New York City, *Is Conscience a Crime?* by Norman Thomas; Liveright Publishing Corporation, New York City, *The Conscientious Objector,* by Walter Kellogg; Charles Scribner's Sons, New York City, *History of the Christian Church,* by Williston Walker, and *Religion in Colonial America,* by William Warren Sweet; Easton Daily Express, Easton, Pennsylvania, *The Story of the Pennsylvania Germans,* by William Beidleman (copies available from the publishers at fifty cents each plus mailing charges); Macmillan Company, New York City, *A Service of Love in Wartime,* by Rufus Jones; Brethren Publishing Company, Ashland, Ohio, *Christianity Versus War,* by D. C. Moomaw; Funk and Wagnalls, New York City, Volume IX of the *Schaff-Herzog Religious Encyclopedia;* Mr. C. Henry Smith, Bluffton, Ohio, *The Mennonites in America,* by C. Henry Smith; The Mennonite Historical Society, Goshen, Indiana, "Spiritual Changes in European Mennonitism," in the *Mennonite Quarterly Review* for January 1941; Mr. Kirby Page, La Habra, California, "20,870 Clergymen on War and Economic Justice," in *The World Tomorrow,* for May 10, 1934.

If any uncredited use of copyrighted materials has been made it was a matter of oversight rather than of intent, and the author and publishers will make such satisfaction as may be adjudged right.

Finally, the author wishes to express his own undying appreciation for the church fathers of yesterday whose sturdy character and strong convictions against war bequeathed to their children a heritage worthy of their loyal devotion.

Rufus D. Bowman

Oak Park, Illinois
May, 1944,

TABLE OF CONTENTS

The Position of the Church of the Brethren Regarding the State

How the State Dealt With the Brethren as a Religious Minority Group

The Brethren Philosophy Regarding the Relationship of Church and State

Pertinent Problems

CHAPTER I

WHO ARE THE BRETHREN?

A study of the Church of the Brethren and war calls for information about the Brethren. What kind of a church is being studied? Some understanding of the main characteristics of the denomination will make this investigation more meaningful. The Church of the Brethren is one of the historic peace churches. The Brethren have been a minority religious group through the years and are today one of the smaller denominations in America. The membership at the present time is one hundred seventy-nine thousand with one thousand nineteen churches.[1] These churches are scattered through thirty-eight states.

CONFUSION REGARDING THE CHURCH NAME

The official name of this church body is "Church of the Brethren."[2] Before 1908 the official name was "German Baptist Church." The change was made because the word "German" was becoming "misleading and in many places detrimental to our church work."[3] Because the form of baptism was immersion, the early Brethren were sometimes called "Taufers"[4] or "Tunkers"[5] by their contemporaries. The designation "Tunkers" was gradually changed to "Dunkers" for euphonic reasons. "Dunkers" was the name most commonly applied to the Brethren in the early history of the church in America and it has persisted in usage to some extent until today. The name "Dunkers" was vulgarized into "Dunkards" by those who spoke of the

---

[1] *Yearbook, 1943*, Church of the Brethren, p. 14.
[2] This name was adopted by the Annual Conference of 1908. *Minutes of the Annual Meetings of the Church of the Brethren, 1778-1909*, p. 873.
[3] *Ibid.*, p. 872.
[4] The word "Taufer" comes from the German verb "taufen" meaning "to baptize or christen."
[5] The word "Tunker" comes from the German verb "tunken" meaning "to dip."

Brethren disparagingly. 'I'his nickname still follows the church and is used by many who know nothing of the earlier meaning of contempt.

In this study the official name, "Church of the Brethren," is used, and the members are usually referred to simply as "the Brethren."

GERMAN IN ORIGIN

The Brethren are German in origin. The original members all came from Germany. The church in its early history was a religious expression of the German mind. The German people have been known for their patience, for their obedience to and their respect for their leaders.[6] It is difficult to get a revolution in Germany. Obedience is expected in political life. The German people have stubborn determination, do not give up easily, and are willing to die for a cause which grips them.

These German characteristics throw light upon the history of the Church of the Brethren. The Brethren people have been essentially law-abiding, obedient and patient. The Brethren people through the years have followed their church leaders and have trusted them. The Brethren historically have not been a protesting people in their relations to government unless great religious and moral issues were at stake which affected their peaceful living and freedom of worship. In such cases no amount of sacrifice was too great. The Mennonites and Brethren have a common German heritage and have manifested many characteristics which are alike. The Society of Friends was a religious expression of the British mind, essentially independent and nonconformist. These churches have worked together through a united opposition to war.

---

[6] For a fuller discussion of this subject see Emil Ludwig's article, "The German Mind," in the *Atlantic Monthly*, February, 1938, pp. 255-263.

FOUNDING OF THE CHURCH

The story of the founding of the church gives further help in understanding the denomination.

The Church of the Brethren was founded at Schwarzenau, Germany, in 1708. Alexander Mack, the founder, was born in 1679, at Schriesheim, Germany. He came from a "very respectable and wealthy family," and his father was a miller by occupation and "possessed a very profitable mill and a handsome patrimony and several vineyards at Schriesheim."[7] The extent of Mack's education is not clear from the records, but that he was a man of learning and culture is clear from his writings. He was a member of the Reformed Church but became dissatisfied with the religious conditions in Germany. The formalism, corruption, persecution and lack of piety in the state churches caused him to become a seeker for truth. Alexander Mack, Jr., says that there was "great decay of true Christianity almost in every place."[8]

Mack started to study the New Testament and church history. The more he studied the New Testament, the more convinced he became that he must separate from the state church. He studied apostolic Christianity and the teachings of Jesus and felt that these should become the standard for the Christian's faith and conduct. The following statement from the Memoirs of Alexander Mack collected by James Quinter summarizes the matter.

Becoming dissatisfied with the religious system in which he had been brought up, and being anxious to ascertain the mind of the Lord as revealed in the Scriptures, to this source was his mind directed in searching for old paths. He became convinced, by his reading of the Scriptures, that an immersion in water was the New Testament baptism, and a believer the only proper subject for the ordinance, and that the doctrines and practices defended in the fol-

---

[7] Alexander Mack, *A Plain View of the Rites and Ordinances*, p. iv.
[8] *Ibid.*, p. viii.

lowing work are such as believers should receive and obey. Accordingly he and his wife and six others, in the year 1708, were immersed in the river Eder, and covenanted together to walk in all the commandments and ordinances of the Lord.[9]

In his searching for a better way, Mack came under the influence of a noted Pietist, Christopher Hochmann. Mack and Hochmann formed a close friendship. Together they went up and down the Rhine Valley on preaching tours. They preached in many parts of Germany, and also visited Holland. They naturally met many religious leaders and became acquainted with various sects. These men studied their Bibles together and for the most part shared the same views. They wondered for a while if they could find a group which practiced the New Testament as they understood it. Being disappointed in this, they began to study church history diligently to see how the various churches practiced the New Testament doctrines. The conviction grew that Christians should practice the doctrines of the New Testament as they were given by Jesus.

Because of persecutions these seekers for light and many others gathered at Schwarzenau, where freedom of worship was granted for a while. Here an earnest group carried on intensive Bible study and prayer. Alexander Mack became convinced that in order to practice in an adequate way the New Testament doctrines, a church organization should be formed. On this point Hochmann differed. Hochmann agreed with Mack on the doctrines to be lived but as a devout Pietist and an individualist he felt that a church organization was unnecessary. The men parted company but remained good friends. Alexander Mack, Jr., from material gathered from his father and Peter Becker, tells the story of the founding of the church.

To those persecuted and exiled persons the Lord pointed out a place of refuge, or a little "Pella," in the land of Wittgenstein, where

---

[9] *Ibid.*, p. v.

at that time ruled a mild count, and where some pious countesses dwelt. Here liberty of conscience was granted at Schwarzenau, which is within a few miles of Berlenburg. And from this cause, though Wittgenstein is poor and rough country, many people, and those of various kinds, collected at Schwarzenau, and this place, which had been but little esteemed, became so much changed that in a few years it became a place extensively known.

Those who were brought together there from the persecutions, though they were distinguished by different opinions, and also differed in manners and customs, were still, at first, all called Pietists, and they among themselves called each other Brother. But very soon it appeared that the words of Christ, Matthew 18, where he says, "If thy brother shall trespass against thee, go and tell him his fault between thee and him alone," etc., could not be reduced to a common Christian practice, because there was no regular order yet established in the church. Therefore some returned again to the religious denominations from which they had come out, because they would not be subjected to a more strict Christian discipline; and to others it appeared that the spiritual liberty was carried too far, which was thought to be more dangerous than the religious organizations they had left.

Under these circumstances, some felt themselves drawn powerfully to seek the footsteps of the primitive Christians, and desired earnestly to receive in faith the ordained testimonies of Jesus Christ according to their true value. At the same time, they were internally and strongly impressed with the necessity of the obedience of faith to a soul that desires to be saved. And this impression also led them at the time to the mystery of water baptism, which appeared unto them as a door into the church, which was what they so earnestly sought. Baptism, however, was spoken of among the Pietists in different ways, and the manner in which it was sometimes spoken of caused pain to the hearts of those who loved the truth.

Finally, in the year 1708, eight persons consented together to enter into a covenant of a good conscience with God, to take up all the commandments of Jesus Christ as an easy yoke, and thus to follow the Lord Jesus, their good and faithful shepherd, in joy and sorrow, as his true sheep, even unto a blessed end. These eight persons were as follows, namely, five brethren and three sisters. The five brethren were George Grebi, from Hesse Cassel, the first;

Lucas Vetter, likewise from Hessia, the second; the third was Alexander Mack, from the Palatinate of Schriesheim, between Manheim and Heidelberg; the fourth was Andrew Bony, of Basle, in Switzerland; the fifth, John Kipping, from Bareit, in Wurtemberg. The three sisters were Johanna Noethiger, or Bony, the first; Anna Margaretha Mack, the second; and Johanna Kipping, the third.

These eight persons covenanted and united together as brethren and sisters into the covenant of the cross of Jesus Christ to form a church of Christian believers. And when they had found, in authentic histories, that the primitive Christians, in the first and second centuries, uniformly, according to the command of Christ, were planted into the death of Jesus Christ by a threefold immersion into the water-bath of holy baptism, they examined diligently the New Testament, and finding all perfectly harmonizing therewith, they were anxiously desirous to use the means appointed and practiced by Christ himself, and thus, according to his own salutary counsel, go forward to the fulfillment of all righteousness.[10]

The Church Missionary and Evangelical

The church in Germany was missionary and evangelical. Again the story is well told by Alexander Mack, Jr.

After this the said eight persons were more and more powerfully strengthened in their obedience to the faith they had adopted, and were enabled to testify publicly in their meetings to the truth; and the Lord granted them this special grace, so that still more became obedient to the faith, and thus, within seven years' time, namely to the year 1715, there was not only in Schwarzenau a large church, but, here and there in the Palatinate, there were lovers of the truth, and especially was this the case in Marienborn, where a church was gathered; for the church in the Palatinate was persecuted, and its members then came to Marienborn. And, when the church here became large, it was also persecuted. Then those that were persecuted collected in Crefeld, where they found liberty under the king of Prussia.[11]

Character of the Early Brethren in Germany

D. W. Kurtz, who studied and traveled in Germany, made personal investigations of the possible sources of informa-

---

[10] *Ibid.*, pp. ix-x.
[11] *Ibid.*, pp. x-xi.

tion bearing upon early Brethren history. Practically no records were left of this movement there. For historical data it is necessary to depend upon the records left by the Brethren after they came to America. However, D. W. Kurtz found in the archives of Laasphe five letters written by the daughter of Count Henry, who lived at Schwarzenau, describing the life and habits of these people. She wrote—

They spend their time in Bible study, in prayer, and in deeds of kindness and charity.[12]

The history of the Brethren in Germany is a history of persecutions. A discussion of the causes, nature and effects of these persecutions upon the church is reserved for another chapter. The Brethren came to America for religious liberty. Twenty-five years after the church started, the record in Germany was closed. Other historical information will be given in connection with the Brethren and the war problem.

FIRST PRINCIPLES OF THE CHURCH OF THE BRETHREN

Peace

The late Ex-Governor Brumbaugh of Pennsylvania, himself a minister in the Church of the Brethren, and generally regarded as the greatest historian of the Brethren, gives "no exercise of force in religion" as the fundamental first principle in Brethren doctrine.[13] The formation of this principle was influenced by the coercion of minority groups by the German state. Brumbaugh outlines the elements included in this doctrine of "non-coercion."

(1) To compel anyone to join or to leave the church of Christ is an exercise of force. Children are compelled, with no show of reason or desire on their part, to join the church. Hence infant baptism is at variance with their faith. The church is at the outset logically arrayed against infant baptism.

---

[12] D. W. Kurtz, *Nineteen Centuries of the Christian Church*, p. 162.
[13] M. G. Brumbaugh, *Two Centuries of the Church of the Brethren—Bicentennial Addresses*, p. 21.

(2) To compel by law an individual to take an oath is not only contrary to the teaching of Jesus, but it is a violation of the sacred rights of a people whose religious tenets decry all force. Hence the church is at the outset logically opposed to taking the oath.

(3) War is a violent interference with the rights of others. It imposes unwilling burdens upon people. It is, therefore, wrong, and the church at the outset is logically opposed to war.

(4) The injunction of Christ is one thing, the power of prince or ecclesiastic another. The might of the state has no right to interfere with the religious belief of the individual. Hence at the outset the church logically opposed state religions, sustained freedom of conscience, and exalted allegiance to God above allegiance to rulers.

(5) In matters of faith each individual is free to follow his own convictions. Hence they resented all persecution and themselves never persecuted a single soul.[14]

In another treatise Brumbaugh says, "The Church of the Brethren never sanctioned, never encouraged, never participated in war. Peace as a fundamental principle was and always has been honored by the members."[15] Kurtz says, "The first principle laid down by the founders of the church in 1708 was the doctrine of peace."[16] He holds that peace meant three things for the Brethren: opposition to war, no force in religion, and "no litigation in pagan courts." The church since its foundation has had an unbroken testimony against war.

No Creed but the New Testament

The Church of the Brethren has never written a creed. In fact, it has purposefully avoided creeds. The church leaders have held that creeds are dangerous, man-made and difficult to change. The church started out by taking the New Testament as its basis with the attitude of seeking for light. The unyielding creeds of the state churches certainly influenced the Brethren not to adopt a creed. Fur-

---

[14] *Ibid.*, p. 21.
[15] M. G. Brumbaugh, *A History of the Brethren,* pp. 537-538.
[16] D. W. Kurtz, *Ideals of the Church of the Brethren,* p.8.

ther, it seems that there were at Schwarzenau a great number of different persons and groups brought together because of persecutions. There were many discussions and differences of opinion.[17] There was much confusion. When Mack gathered his small company together they decided to put away all creeds and follow the New Testament. This is still the position of the church. Almost unconsciously through the years the Brethren have taken the position that the New Testament is the members' guide, and efforts should be made constantly to discover new light. This has been a wholesome factor in stimulating study on the part of ministers and teachers. The Brethren use the Old Testament and appreciate its value, but the New Testament has always been regarded as being superior to the Old. The Church of the Brethren may be called a New Testament church rather than a theological church based upon an unyielding creed. The Brethren are practical rather than theoretical. The Brethren through the years have held in common with other evangelical churches the great doctrines, such as God, Christ and immortality. The early Brethren started out to live according to the Sermon on the Mount. No one can claim that the Brethren have maintained complete consistency with this position, but the early intention is clear.

The nearest the Brethren ever came to having a creed was the "Confession of Faith" by Christopher Hochmann, written in 1702. Hochmann was in prison and in order to secure his release Count zur Lippe-Detwold required him to write out his "Confession of Faith." It was published in Germany in 1702 and reprinted in 1703. The document was well known to Alexander Mack and it is probable that it was used as a handbook of beliefs and ordinances for the church at Schwarzenau.[18] The early Brethren in

[17] Mack, *op. cit.* p. ix.
[18] Brumbaugh, *A History of the Brethren,* pp. 72-83.

America prized it so highly that Christopher Sower printed it at Germantown in 1743.[19]   It was never accepted as a creed but its influence was great upon the thought of the early Brethren.

Benjamin Franklin gives an illuminating statement about the Brethren having no creed.

Those embarrassments that the Quakers suffered, from having established and published it as one of their principles that no kind of war was lawful, and which, being once published, they could not afterward, however they might change their minds, easily get rid of, reminds me of what I think a more prudent conduct in another sect among us, that of the Dunkers. I was acquainted with one of its founders, Michael Wohlfahrt,[20] soon after it appeared. He complained to me that they were grievously calumniated by the zealots of other persuasions, and charged with abominable principles and practices to which they were utter strangers. I told him this had always been the case with new sects, and that to put a stop to such abuse I imagined it might be well to publish the articles of their belief and the rules of their discipline. He said that it had been proposed among them, but not agreed to for this reason: "When we were first drawn together as a society," said he, "it had pleased God to enlighten our minds so far as to see that some doctrines which were esteemed truths were errors, and that others which we had esteemed errors were real truths. From time to time he has been pleased to afford us further light, and our principles have been improving and our errors diminishing. Now we are not sure that we are arrived at the end of this progression and at the perfection of spiritual or theological knowledge, and we fear that if we should once print our confession of faith, we should feel ourselves as if bound and confined by it, and perhaps be unwilling to receive further improvement, and our successors still more so, as conceiving what their elders and founders had done to be something sacred—never to be departed from."

This modesty in a sect is perhaps a single instance in the history of mankind, every other sect supposing itself in possession of all

---

[19] Julius F. Sachse, *The German Sectarians of Pennsylvania, 1742-1800*, p. 78.
[20] It is known that Michael Wohlfahrt was an active leader of the Ephrata Sabbatarian Dunkers but the Ephrata Society retained the practice of having no creed, like the Brethren from whom it had separated. It is likely that Franklin referred to the whole group of Brethren.

truth, and that those who differ are so far in the wrong; like a man traveling in foggy weather, those at some distance before him on the road he sees wrapped up in the fog as well as those behind him, and also the people in the fields on each side, but near him all appears clear, though, in truth, he is as much in the fog as any of them. To avoid this kind of embarrassment, the Quakers have of late years been gradually declining the public service in the Assembly and in the magistracy, choosing rather to quit their power than their principle.[21]

The Ordinances as a Means of Grace

From the beginning the Brethren have practiced trine immersion baptism. The communion service, usually held twice a year, includes feet-washing, the brotherhood meal, the bread and the cup. The communion services are services of fellowship, worship and consecration. The anointing service is practiced for the sick. These symbols reflect the original idea of the Brethren to carry out the actual practices set forth by Jesus and the apostolic church. Alexander Mack in his book, "A Plain View of the Rites and Ordinances," emphasizes baptism and the Lord's Supper (meaning what is now called the communion service). The Brethren have always held that these symbols should be practiced as a means of grace in order to express in life the principles for which they stand. The constant practice of these symbols for over two hundred years can be understood only as one senses the New Testament character of the church, the fellowship and worship experiences of the communion and the fact that in the sufferings of the church the table of the Lord has brought peace.

No exercise of force in religion, including no participation in war, no litigation and taking the oath, freedom of conscience and tolerance toward those of differing opinions; no creed but the New Testament; and the practice of the church ordinances as a means of grace were the most

---

[21] *The Autobiography of Benjamin Franklin:* The World's Greatest Literature, pp. 149-150.

outstanding principles upon which the Church of the Brethren was founded.

OTHER IDEALS WHICH DEVELOPED IN THE CHURCH EARLY

Brotherhood

At Schwarzenau they called themselves "Brethren."[22] At the beginning they were a fellowship. The church was early called "German Baptist Brethren," then "Church of the Brethren." Alexander Mack emphasized love for each other. Matthew 18 was taken as the basis for settling differences between members. This great forgiveness chapter has been used by the church as the standard for human relationships. All members are supposed to be instructed before baptism to live according to Matthew 18. Fellowship is one of the outstanding characteristics of the Brethren. There is a like-mindedness. The members frequently visit together from thirty to forty minutes after a church service. Since the denomination is small most of the church leaders know each other as friends. The two most frequent emphases among the Brethren regarding the doctrine of the church are its New Testament character and the church as a fellowship.

The Good Life

The early Brethren were greatly influenced by Pietism. Although they differed from the Pietists in creating a church organization, Pietism had a direct effect upon the formation of Brethren ideals. F. E. Mallott, Professor of Church History at Bethany Biblical Seminary, says, "The Brethren are Biblical, mystical Pietists.[23] Religion is emphasized as practical living based upon the New Testament. This ideal led the Brethren to develop the doctrine of "nonconformity with the world." This doctrine has negative aspects but it can be understood in terms of persecution and

---

[22] Kurtz, *Ideals of the Church of the Brethren*, p. 16.
[23] Statement by F. E. Mallott, personal interview, December 2, 1942.

corruption in government and society. The Brethren for years did not vote and hold office, which was a part of the idea of separateness. With the beginning of the twentieth century the Brethren were becoming active participants in community life and were voting and holding office.

The ideal of the good life manifested itself in terms of simple living. The early Brethren were opposed to extravagancies, luxuries, the wearing of jewelry, dancing and card playing. Brethren homes were the centers of fellowship. Special forms of dress were developed in colonial days as a means of keeping separate from the world. There is no record that any distinctive dress was worn by the Brethren when they came from Germany. They gradually adopted the Quaker hat and bonnet because these had become a symbol of the peace-believing people.[24]. This manner of dress persisted with some modification as a mark of separateness and simplicity. While the majority of the Brethren have lost the distinctive garb, there are still quite a number of devout and sincere members who hold to it faithfully.

The Brethren from the beginning refused to allow members to engage in the liquor traffic. There are recorded Annual Conference decisions as early as 1821 asking members not to make and use strong drink. The church has also taught against the use of tobacco. The Annual Conference of 1827 passed the following statement regarding the raising of tobacco:

Considered, that members should have nothing to do with such things, by which so much mischief is done, and so many men (and women too) are led captive, as is the case with tobacco.[25]

Today some of the members smoke but the writer has no personal knowledge of any minister in the Church of the Brethren who uses tobacco.

[24] Brumbaugh, *History of the Brethren,* p. 547.
[25] *Minutes of the Annual Meetings, op. cit.,* p. 52.

Another strong teaching has been the sanctity and permanence of marriage. Alexander Mack declared that the "Lord God himself instituted matrimony in Paradise.[26] The church has always advised against divorce and taught the sacred character of the marriage bond. While some divorces are happening in Brethren homes the influence of the church's teaching is still strongly felt.

THE BRETHREN A RURAL PEOPLE

In America the Brethren settled mostly on farms. They were good farmers and knew good land. They were thrifty, industrious and frugal. They founded sturdy homes and frequently had large families. Economic reasons sometimes governed their moving into another county or state, but when they moved they aimed to start a Brethren community and begin a church. Brethren people developed Brethren communities and were rather clannish in their fellowship. Their like-mindedness and group solidarity may be explained in part by what happened to them from the outside world. For many years they did not believe in life or property insurance. When a neighbor's barn burned they rebuilt it. When a widow was in need, they helped her. They cared for their needs and did not bother the state. Today with many Brethren heavily insured, some are beginning to wonder whether the trust and mutual helpfulness of a group is not the best protection after all. The Brethren now have a number of strong city churches but the denomination is still predominantly rural.

Morgan Edwards gives the following description of the Pennsylvania Brethren within a generation of their coming to America:

They use great plainness of language and dress, like the Quakers; and like them will never swear nor fight. They will not go to law; not take interest for the money they lend. They commonly wear

---

[26] Mack, *op. cit.*, pp. 55-56.

their beards; and keep the first day Sabbath, except one congregation. They have the Lord's Supper with its ancient attendants of love feast, washing feet, kiss of charity, and right hand of fellowship. They anoint the sick with oil for recovery, and use the trine immersion, with laying on of hands and prayer, even while the person baptized is in the water; which may easily be done as the party kneels down to be baptized, and continues in that position till both prayer and imposition of hands be performed. . . . Every brother is allowed to stand up in the congregation to speak in a way of exhortation and expounding, and when by that means they find a man eminent for knowledge and aptness to teach, they choose him to be a minister, and ordain him with imposition of hands, attended with fasting and prayer, and giving the right hand of fellowship. They also have deacons; and ancient widows for deaconesses; and exhorters, who are licensed to use their gifts statedly. They pay not their ministers unless it be to the way of presents; though they admit their right to pay; neither do the ministers assert the right; esteeming it more blessed to give than to receive. Their acquaintance with the Bible is admirable. In a word they are meek and pious Christians; and have justly acquired the character of the Harmless Tunkers.[27]

DEMOCRATIC ORGANIZATION

The Church of the Brethren has the democratic form of government. The membership has the power to rule the church. Practically, however, the Brethren people follow their leadership. The highest governing body is the Annual Conference. The decisions of the Annual Conference are supposed to be followed by the local churches but there is no organized effort to enforce them. Consequently, churches follow the decisions with varying degrees of support. Annual Conferences are often attended by five to twenty thousand members. Members look forward to these meetings. They are just big family gatherings. They have been one of the greatest unifying factors in the life

---

[27] Morgan Edwards, *Materials Toward a History of the Baptists in Pennsylvania*, Vol. I, Pt. IV, pp. 66-67. This work is in the rare book collection of the Pennsylvania Historical Society, Philadelphia.

of the denomination. Common ideals, fellowship and consecration to a program, rather than theology or legislation, hold the denomination together.

Much of the work of the church is now being done through general boards and committees. The General Education Board supervises the six Brethren colleges and one seminary; the Board of Christian Education has charge of the local educational program, including peace and temperance education. The General Ministerial Board supervises ministers and recommends them for placement. The General Mission Board plans for home and foreign missions. The Brethren Service Committee deals with the relief and reconstruction program, refugee work and especially the church's relationship to the government in the program for conscientious objectors. These organizations have their separate meetings but also meet several times yearly in a united body known as the Council of Boards. It is important to see this organizational picture because the most forward-looking work of the church is being planned by these boards and committees. The following page gives a graph of the general church organization.

The democratic organization set forth in the diagram may be explained as follows:

1. Delegates from the local churches and districts comprise the voting body of the Annual Conference. While Standing Committee (the district delegates) makes the nominations for vacancies on general boards and committees, reviews the business of the Conference, and may originate new business, the voting body of Conference is the final authority. The delegates usually participate freely in the discussions.

2. No sessions of the general Annual Conference are closed. The business sessions are usually attended by a large number of the laity. Speaking on the problems un-

THE CHURCH OF THE BRETHREN

One Thousand Nineteen Forty-eight

Local Districts Churches

The Annual Conference

General Attendance of the Laity

Delegates from Local Churches

Delegates from Districts or The Standing Committee

The Council of Boards

| General Mission Board | Board of Directors of Brethren Publishing House | General Ministerial Board | Board of Christian Education | General Education Board | Brethren Service Committee | Council of Men's Work | Council of Women's Work | National Youth Cabinet |

der consideration is not limited to delegates.   Any man, woman or young person may ask for the floor.

3. The general boards and the Brethren Service Committee are appointed by Annual Conference and must report yearly to that body.   A report is given both to Standing Committee, where detailed questions are often asked, and to the General Conference.   The councils of Men's and Women's Work and the National Brethren Youth Cabinet are elected by their respective bodies and approved by Conference.   The delegates from local churches and districts have a share in making appointments and in appraising the work.

4. The items of business for Annual Conference are printed in the "Gospel Messenger" and the program booklets so that the delegates and members may have the opportunity to study them.

5. The delegates from local churches and districts carry the report of the Annual Conference back to their various constituencies.

6. Business for Annual Conference may originate through any local church bringing a query through district conference, through Standing Committee, through the Council of Boards, or through any general board or committee.

7. The humblest member, if he thinks the local church has not treated him fairly, may get a hearing by coming to Standing Committee.   The writer has been on Standing Committee when such cases were heard with sympathy and understanding.

A NEW SENSE OF MISSION

There has been a change of direction in the Church of the Brethren from exclusiveness to co-operation.   The church is overcoming its timidity and feeling of inferiority and is being captured by the spirit of adventure.   The church is getting a new sense of mission. There have been other periods when the church was awakened, like the beginning in Germany, and the rise of foreign missions and education. The new awakening now is the sense of mission regarding a program for conscientious objectors in their relationship to the government, the opportunity to help humanity in ways of peace, relief and reconstruction, and the chance to pioneer in helping to solve the difficult problem of church and state. Some outstanding Brethren leaders are saying that the church should accept the challenge given to the historic peace churches by the late Arthur E. Holt.

Leonard Bacon said that when the revivalist came to American religious life, leadership passed from the Congregationalists and Presbyterians to the Methodists and Baptists, and if the Methodists and Baptists and Congregationalists and Presbyterians who are here will pardon me, I'm rather inclined to think that with these multiplying wars, leadership is going to pass from those groups to the historic peace groups. I think they've got the eloquence to which the world will listen.[28]

This chapter has aimed to furnish some acquaintance with the Church of the Brethren as a background for further study. The writer has given this picture of the church out of a thorough canvass of Brethren literature, and twenty years of active service in the church. There have been inconsistencies in the church and some unfortunate divisions which will be mentioned in connection with the consideration of the war problem.

---

[28] Address delivered at a conference on The Conscientious Objector in the Second World War, held in Chicago, November 15, 1941, and printed in *America's Pacifist Minority*, p. 96. This booklet was distributed by the Mid-West Fellowship of Reconciliation, Chicago, Illinois, and is a report of the above-mentioned conference.

CHAPTER II

THE POSITION OF THE FOUNDERS OF THE CHURCH
OF THE BRETHREN ON WAR

Founders Believed War Contrary to Teachings of Jesus

The founders of the Church of the Brethren took the position that war was contrary to the life, spirit, and teachings
of Jesus and that it was wrong for them to fight. This historical position is well summarized by the Annual Conference of 1932:

One of the fundamental tenets of the Church of the Brethren
since its origin in 1708 has been the acceptance of the New Testament as its rule of faith and practice. Our church fathers have consistently taught and declared in private life as well as in official
pronouncements that Christianity and war are incompatible. They
believed in and taught the gospel of peace and goodwill. They
founded their faith in the spirit and teachings of the Bible as exemplified in the life and teachings of the Prince of Peace.[1]

First Brethren Community Nonresistant

Further light on the position of the founders is given by
Elder James Quinter in the "Memoirs" collected of Alexander Mack, Sr., the founder of the church. Speaking of
the early Brethren community in Germany he says, "With
all the Christian profession of the times, this community,
with its nonresistant principles, with its self-denying doctrines, and with the sole object in view of glorifying God
and in bringing forth the fruits of obedience to his commandments, was not tolerated."[2] According to these "Memoirs" the original Brethren community practiced nonresistance. Alexander Mack, Jr., in writing the story of the
founding of the church tells us that these earliest leaders

---
[1] *Annual Meeting Minutes, 1932,* p. 47.
[2] "Memoirs of Alexander Mack." Preface to *A Plain View of the Rites and Ordinances,* p. v.

were seeking for "truth and righteousness, as they are in Jesus," and that "very soon it appeared that the words of Christ, Matthew 18, where he says, 'If thy brother shall trespass against thee, go and tell him his fault between thee and him alone,' etc., could not be reduced to a proper Christian practice, because there was no regular order yet established in the church."[3]   Thus, the proper carrying out of the great forgiveness chapter of the Bible played a part in the founding of the church.

EARLY CHURCH CONFERENCE UPHELD NONRESISTANCE

The Annual Conference of 1785, held at Big Conewago, Pennsylvania, in answer to a letter written by Valentine Power, a member of the church who seemed to hold some differing views about war and was seemingly confused by the words of 1 Peter 2: 13-14, defined the position of the church on both war and its relationship to the state. Because of its importance a large section of the statement is quoted.

Now we see that Christ always, in all his sufferings, endured them, and that with great patience, and never resisted and defended himself; but as Peter says, "He committed himself to him that judgeth righteously." We see further that our loving Savior, though innocent, was attacked in a murderous manner by just such men as brother P. has mentioned in his letter; but the Savior stood fast in the covenant of faithfulness, as the brother stated. In a murderous manner he was attacked, and Peter was quick and ready to draw his sword according to the legal justice of God, and struck a servant, and smote off his ear. But what says the Savior: "Put up again thy sword unto his place; for all they that take the sword shall perish with the sword." Here, indeed, was the greatest necessity for self-defense, but all this time the Savior resisted not; but he suffered patiently, and even healed the one whose ear was smote off, acting as it is written: "The righteous shall live by faith": and again, "I believe, therefore I speak," etc. Thus our Savior had said before, "That we resist not evil"; for so he believed and thus he

---

[3] *Introduction by Alexander Mack, Jr., Ibid.,* pp. viii-ix.

spake, and thus he did. So we hope the dear Brethren will not take it amiss when we, from all these passages of Scripture, and especially from the words of Peter, can not see or find any liberty to use any (carnal) sword, but only the sword of the Spirit, which is the word of God. . . .

But that the higher powers bear the sword of justice, punishing the evil and protecting the good, in this we acknowledge them from the heart as the ministers of God. But the sword belongeth to the kingdom of the world, and Christ says to his disciples: "I have chosen you from the world," etc. Thus we understand the beloved Peter, that we are to submit ourselves in all things that are not contrary to the will or command of God, and no further.[4]

There is no evidence that this is a change of the church's original position. We may assume rather that it is an expression of it. This was only sixty-six years after the first Brethren came to America, fifty-six years after the founder himself reached Pennsylvania. Alexander Mack, Jr., was living and knew well the mind of his father. Christopher Sower, Jr., the great Brethren printer of colonial America, had been dead one year. A number of the young people who came to America with their parents were the leaders of the church. The above decision was written by the children who had been schooled at the firesides of the first Brethren in Europe and America. The position was Biblical and centered in Jesus. The commandments of Christ, they said, aimed "throughout at nonresistance."

Church Founders Took No Part in War

Another evidence of the church's original position is that the early Brethren in Germany and America did not participate in war. Actions are often more powerful than statements. In Germany the Brethren communities were separated from the activities of the state and during the American Revolution the failure of the Brethren to fight brought misunderstanding and persecution. The experi-

---

[4] *Minutes of the Annual Meetings, 1778-1909*, pp. 9-10.

ences of Elder John Naas in Germany may provide illumination. John Naas was a leader of the Brethren at Creyfeld. Next to Alexander Mack he was counted the ablest
leader of the Church of the Brethren in Germany. He was
a man of great physique and commanding personality.
Creyfeld, in the province of Marienborn, was under the
control of the king of Prussia. John Naas would frequently
go on preaching tours in the surrounding country. It so
happened that on one of these preaching tours he met the
recruiting officers of the king of Prussia, who were canvassing for members of the king's bodyguard. A. H. Cassel
gives this story beautifully:

So one day, as it happened, they came in contact with these recruiting officers, when Naas was immediately seized and taken up
to enlist; but he refused, upon which they put him to various tor-
tures to compel him, such as pinching, thumbscrewing, etc. But
he still resisted, until at length they took him and hung him up with
a cord by his left thumb and right great toe, in which ignominious
posture they meant to leave him suspended until he would yield to
their wishes. But he still continued steadfast and immovable, so
that they began to despair of accomplishing anything by torture,
and that he might die by leaving him longer suspended. So they
took him down again, and dragged him along by force to the king's
audience, stating all how they had tried, by persuasion and by torture, to accomplish their designs, to no purpose, and thinking him
too desirable an object to let pass, they had brought him to his audience to dispose of as he thought proper.

The king, then eyeing him closely, said he would like to have him
very much; "Tell me, why will you not enlist with me?"

"Because," said he, "I have already, long ago, enlisted into one of
the noblest and best of enrolments, and I would not, and indeed
could not, become a traitor to Him."

"Why, to whom, then? Who is your captain?" asked the aston-
ished king.

"My captain," said he, "is the great Prince Immanuel, our Lord
Jesus Christ. I have espoused his cause and therefore cannot, and
will not, forsake Him."

"Neither will I then that you should," answered the noble king, whilst reaching into his pocket to present him with a handsome gold coin as a reward for his fidelity, and bid him adieu.

He then went his way, greatly rejoiced at his honorable dismissal, and joined his companion Priesz. They continued their labors for awhile, until the persecution became so fierce that they fled with the others from the mother church to Serustervin, in West Friesland, from whence they emigrated to America in the fall of 1719, stopped awhile with the Brethren at Germantown, and then settled in Amwell, New Jersey, when he and old brother Rudolph Harley founded the church.[5]

A further insight into the position of the founders of the Church of the Brethren may be gained from an incident which happened after Mack came to America. A preacher of unusual eloquence came to Germantown and many of Mack's members were attending his services. Some of them persuaded Mack to hear him. After the meeting his faithful members gathered around to see what their leader thought. "Oh, he might do very well for an army chaplain but not at all for a minister to a peace-loving people. I advise you not to hear him."[6]

Soon after that the visiting minister joined the army as a chaplain and Mack's prediction was fulfilled.

HOCHMANN'S INFLUENCE UPON MACK

It was stated earlier that Alexander Mack and Christopher Hochmann studied the Bible and traveled together prior to the starting of the church. Without doubt Hochmann exerted a tremendous influence upon Alexander Mack. Robert Friedmann, an authority on both Pietism and Anabaptism, says:

The mystic Ernst Christoph Hochmann von Hohenau was himself a strong pacifist and he might have been a decisive factor for Alexander Mack. Yet he never became a member of the Mack group. For a mystic pacifism is the natural attitude and needs no further explanation.

---

[5] Article by A. H. Cassel in The Brethren Family Almanac, 1871, p. 24.
[6] Brumbaugh, A History of the Brethren, p. 94.

By and large, a nonresistant attitude is nothing special for any group which takes the Bible seriously. Did not such "pacifists" exist through all centuries? Also the Anabaptists did not root somewhere else but in this one book. And its study was even more increased in lay circles in the time of Pietism. This Pietism was always pacifistic or better, nonresistant as far as it was a lay movement of and not only an oppositional movement of the younger clergy against the sterile old orthodoxy. For instance, we find in Wurtemberg in the eighteenth century Pietists without visible contacts with earlier groups which show almost identical features with Mennonites and Brethren.[7]

THE POSITION OF THE FOUNDERS REGARDING THE STATE

The position of the early Brethren regarding the state is so closely related to their point of view on war that the two should be considered together. The Church of the Brethren broke with the state in Germany because the church and state were united, and separation from the established church meant breaking with the state. The earliest known statement regarding the state which was influential in forming Brethren thought was the "Confession of Faith" of Christopher Hochmann. The following quotation gives the point of view:

Concerning high power. I believe that it is a divine ordinance, to which I willingly submit in all civil matters according to the teachings of Paul (Romans 13: 1, 7). On the other hand, however, with all true evangelical (believers) I accord no power to those who struggle against God's Word and my conscience or the freedom of Christ: for it is said: We ought to obey God, etc. (Acts 5: 29), and if anything should be charged against God and my conscience I should rather suffer unjust force than act contrary to this. . . .[8]

Hochmann believed that civil government was divinely sanctioned by God and that Christians should submit to civil

---

[7] Letter from Robert Friedmann, January 23, 1943, Goshen College, Goshen, Indiana. Roland Bainton, Professor of Church History, Yale Divinity School, recommends Robert Friedmann as an authority on both Anabaptism and Pietism and a scholar who devoted fifteen years to Anabaptist research while in Austria. Letter from Roland Bainton, January 15, 1943.

[8] *Glaubens Bekenntniss*, bey Ernst Christoph Hochmann. Bedruckt bey Christoph Sauer, Germantown, Pennsylvania, 1743. A copy in German is in the Pennsylvania Historical Society Library, Philadelphia. An English translation is in *A History of the Brethren*, by M. G. Brumbaugh, pp. 75-88.

authority when the actions of government did not disobey
God's Word and the individual's conscience. When government conflicted with conscience and Christ, then the believer, he held, should "obey God rather than man" even
if it meant suffering. This point of view was quite characteristic of later Brethren thought. Alexander Mack held
much the same view.

And believers are also taught by Paul, Romans 13: 1, 7, that every
soul shall be subject, for the Lord's sake, to human regulations,
made by those in authority, and to render them all their dues,
tribute, custom, fear and honor; for all governments are ordained
of God, to punish evil-doers and protect the good, i. e., if they will
fulfill their office according to the will of God.[9]

The position is believed by the Brethren to be Biblical.
In fact, it is based upon quite a literal interpretation. Although the early Brethren broke with the government, they
believed in the necessity of government, and that they
should render unto government their dues, pay their taxes,
and obey sane laws. They were dissenters only when the
laws of government conflicted with their understanding
of the New Testament. The statement of Mack based upon
Romans 13 that "all governments are ordained of God, to
punish evildoers and protect the good," was a point of confusion among the Brethren. They wanted their convictions to be entirely Biblical. Since Paul said that "the
powers that be are ordained of God" (Romans 13: 1) the
Brethren felt that they must believe it. But they could not
see how all governments, some of which were persecuting
the Brethren, were ordained of God. Alexander Mack believed he solved the problem by stating that governments
are ordained of God, "if they will fulfill their office according to the will of God." Christopher Hochmann stated
that he would "accord no power to those who struggle
against God's word." The Brethren through the years de-

---
[9] Mack, *op. cit.*, p. 41.

veloped the interpretation that the fact and necessity of government are ordained of God but individual governments may not be. But what about governments "to punish evil-doers and protect the good"? What kind of punishment does this mean and what kind of protection? It is not explained. It indicates, however, that the early Brethren may have thought that governments had to do some things which the Brethren according to their nonresistant principles could not do. This interpretation is borne out by later developments in the life of the church.

POSSIBLE FACTORS WHICH INFLUENCED THE POSITION OF THE FOUNDERS ON WAR

It is important for this study to discover as far as possible what made the Church of the Brethren a peace church. It is necessary first to notice the conditions of the times.

Political and Religious Conditions in Germany

The Church of the Brethren was born under the most trying political and religious conditions. The Lutheran Reformation freed northwestern Europe from papal rule. Germany could be governed by the Germans. But the country was not united. It was divided into small provinces governed by princes. The religion of each province was dictated by the prince who ruled. The Catholic and Protestant princes were intolerant of dissenters. Many were becoming dissatisfied with the formalism and corruption of the established churches. Persecution, bitterness between Catholics and Protestants, jealousies between princes, plunder, and war all came to a head in the Thirty Years' War (1618-1648) in which the German people suffered untold misery. William Warren Sweet gives an excellent summary of the results of this war.

To account for this large migration of Germans to the New World it will be necessary to recall some of the effects of the Thirty Years' War (1618-1648). There is little doubt that this war was one of the most cruel and brutal in modern history. Seventy-five per cent of the population throughout Germany were killed, while the property loss was even greater, and it is an accepted fact, based upon carefully gathered statistics, that the war set back German material development by two hundred years. Southern Germany, or the Palatinate, was the region which suffered most. But so fertile was the soil and so great was the recuperative power of the people, because of their industry and agricultural skill, that soon after each invasion the country was transformed from a desert into a garden, only to attract other plunderers. But as though the sufferings of the Thirty Years' War were not enough, Louis XIV of France, on three different occasions (1674; 1680; 1688) in the last quarter of the seventeenth century, sent his armies into the Palatinate to burn and to plunder. The greed and cruelty of the French, we are told, exceeded even that of the "Landsknechte" of the Thirty Years' War, who drove nearly 500,000 Palatinates from their burning houses and devastated fields.

Added to the terrible conditions produced by the wars and invasions were the religious persecutions. The Treaty of Westphalia (1648), which marked the end of the Thirty Years' War, provided for some degree of toleration. Catholics, Lutherans and Reformed were to have equal rights in the Empire, though the individual princes could still restrict the religious freedom of their subjects. But neither Catholics, Lutherans nor Reformed respected the rights of the smaller sects, such as the Mennonites, Dunkers, and German Quakers. Thus religious persecution, the tyranny of petty rulers, destructive wars and general economic distress produced the background out of which came German emigration to the American colonies.[10]

The Treaty of Westphalia (1648) gave equal rights to the Catholics, Lutherans and Reformed but the rights of the smaller sects were not protected. Dissenters or separatists were persecuted almost everywhere. Whether any measure of religious freedom was granted in a province depended entirely upon the character and goodwill of the ruling prince.

The conditions of the times undoubtedly affected the point of view of the founders. They saw the suffering, the

---

[10] Sweet, *The Story of Religion in America,* pp. 32-34.

cruelty, the destruction and the economic disaster caused by war. They naturally hated the very thought of it. Brumbaugh in his Alexander Mack Memorial Address summarized the founder's attitude as follows:

> There is another thing for which he (Mack) stood. I pointed out, a moment ago, that at the Treaty of Westphalia the bloody wars were presumably ended. But this treaty, resulting in a branch of ecclesiastics, banding together to persecute the others brought about a new period of carnage in Germany, so that the people of the Rhine Valley had to live under the immediate presence of the horrors of war for more than two hundred years, and Mack, along with other pious men, could not understand how any follower of Jesus Christ could himself be the instrument of persecution. Mack lived the doctrine of nonswearing, the doctrine of peace, the doctrine of goodwill to all men, and as he read these things in the life of the Nazarene, he inaugurated them into the doctrine of the church, so that all things which the Church of the Brethren hold most dear came out of the heart of Mack and have been observed through more than two hundred years as he himself formulated them.[11]

The union of church and state in the provincial governments was not the only religious factor. The state churches were corrupt. Their creeds were unyielding, they persecuted the nonconformists and there was a general lack of piety. Worship was cold and formal. This caused a movement for deeper spiritual life.

Attitude Toward the New Testament

The political and religious conditions made the Brethren hate war, but their attitude toward the New Testament was the most significant factor in making the Church of the Brethren a peace church. From the beginning the New Testament was taken as their rule of faith and practice. As they studied the New Testament it became clear to them that war and Jesus were incompatible. The Church of the Brethren is one of the historic peace churches because the

---

[11] Brumbaugh, Address delivered at the unveiling of the Alexander Mack memorial tablet, Germantown, Pennsylvania, April 9, 1911. Printed in the *Gospel Messenger,* May 13, 1911.

founders felt that war was wrong according to the teachings of Jesus. That this was the most fundamental reason for the church's peace position has been and is shared by leading Brethren. This was the conviction of M. G. Brumbaugh.[12] This is the position of D. W. Kurtz as expressed in the following:

They discovered in the New Testament and in the life of the Apostolic Church some ideals that are basic for the Christian life. These are peace; temperance; the spiritual (or simple) life, as against worldliness and luxury; brotherhood; and a religion of the good life, fellowship and harmony with Christ, as against mere creeds and cultus of the churches from which they came.[13]

In answer to the question, "What made the Church of the Brethren a peace church?" four leading interpreters of Brethren life and thought answered as follows:

Floyd E. Mallott: The early Brethren started out to live according to the Sermon on the Mount. They were practical rather than theoretical. The Brethren are Biblical, mystical Pietists.[14]

Charles D. Bonsack: Our attitude of accepting the New Testament as our creed made us a peace church. One can hardly read the New Testament without being peaceminded.[15]

J. E. Miller: Our slant as to the Bible, giving it a prominent place. We adopted the theory of progressive revelation, taking the New Testament as a newer and better revelation than the Old.[16]

George N. Falkenstein, one of the oldest ministers of the Church of the Brethren, and a long-time student of Brethren history, in answer to the writer's question about the extent to which local conditions influenced early Brethren attitudes toward war, said:

Now, returning to the matter of local conditions, at the time our church fathers organized the church, I think the influence of such conditions can easily be overemphasized. They found these fundamental doctrines in the New Testament and so thorough were their

---

[12] Brumbaugh, *A History of the Brethren*, p. 558.
[13] Kurtz, *Ideals of the Church of the Brethren*, p.8.
[14] Personal interview, December 2, 1942.
[15] Personal interview, December 30, 1942.
[16] Personal interview, December 31, 1942.

studies, and so strong were their convictions that they covenanted they would follow the New Testament wherever it would lead them.[17]

I have a very deep conviction that our church fathers made a conscious effort to re-establish primitive Christianity, based on the teachings of Jesus in the New Testament, and the practice of the apostolic church.[18]

The Influence of the Pietists

Pietism in Germany was a revolt against the "dead orthodoxy of the established churches," an assertion of the primacy of the feeling in Christian experience, a vindication for the laity of an active share in the upbuilding of the Christian life, and the assertion of a strict ascetic attitude toward the world.[19] Pietism stressed prayer, devotion, and moral conduct, and held that Christianity consisted in a life of spirituality. The original Brethren were not Pietists in a strict sense but they believed in the life of spiritual devotion for which Pietism stood. The founders of the church were separatists and were called Pietists only in the general sense that all refugees at Schwarzenau were referred to as Pietists.[20] However, there is a direct line of influence from the Pietists. While the concern here is chiefly with the influences upon the early Brethren's war position, yet this position was vitally related to their total outlook upon life. Any influence which helped to fashion the faith of the early Brethren affected their attitude toward war.

The direct connection of the early Brethren with Pietism came through Christopher Hochmann. This noted Pietist studied at the University of Halle and was awakened under the influence of Francke. Francke, one of the strongest Pietists, was a pupil of Spener. Spener, the founder of Piet-

[17] Letter from George N. Falkenstein, December 30, 1942.
[18] Letter from George N. Falkenstein, January 13, 1943.
[19] Williston Walker, *A History of the Christian Church*, p. 496.
[20] Mack, *op. cit.*, p. ix.

ism, held that Christianity is genuine only when it shows itself in life. "He shifted the center of interest from the maintenance of orthodox doctrine to conduct and practical piety."[21]   Spener, Francke and Hochmann emphasized a personal religion of the heart based upon a devotional study of the Bible.

In 1697, Hochmann went to Giessen and entered into relations with Gottfried Arnold,[22] who was a friend of Spener and for a time a professor at Giessen. In his great work, "Unparteiische Kirchen und Ketzer-Historie," Arnold introduced the idea that "no man is to be deemed a heretic because his own age so deemed him."[23]   He was the first man to write an impartial church history on the heretical sects that separated from the Catholic Church. He held that the heretics have their place in Christian thought. Another work of Gottfried Arnold, "A Genuine Portraiture of the Primitive Christians," was known to the early Brethren. Alexander Mack quoted from it on pages 18 and 54 of his book, "A Plain View of the Rites and Ordinances." Since Arnold advocated doctrines like nonswearing, trine immersion, baptism of adults only, feet-washing, the salutation, anointing, and nonresistance, it is entirely possible that he influenced the position of the early Brethren on war.[24]

Alexander Mack in discussing immersion quoted Jeremias Felbinger.[25] Felbinger, who lived fifty years earlier than Arnold, probably influenced the latter in his interpretation of the Scriptures. Felbinger in 1660 translated the New Testament into German. This made the New Testament available to the common people and was an impetus to the development of Pietism. Felbinger's "Christian Hand

---

[21] *Schaff-Herzog's Religious Encyclopedia*, **IX**, p. 56.
[22] *Ibid.*, p. 999.
[23] Walker, *op. cit.*, p. 501.
[24] Brumbaugh, *A History of the Brethren*, p. 14.
[25] Mack, *op. cit.*, p. 23.

Book" touches upon many of the Brethren doctrines, like baptism, feet-washing and the problem of the oath.

The Pietists emphasized many of the doctrines held by the early Brethren. There was a direct line of influence from Spener and Felbinger through Francke and Arnold to Hochmann and Mack. It is also quite likely that Mack through his travels and study of church history came into vital contact with these Pietistic leaders.

Possible Influence of the Waldenses

The influence of the Waldenses upon the Brethren was not direct. In fact, it can only be said that there was a possible influence. H. R. Holsinger in his "History of the Tunkers and the Brethren Church," speaks of the Waldenses as exerting a probable influence upon early Brethren thought.[26] There seem to be two reasons why this might be true: First, Alexander Mack in his study of church history may have become acquainted with the Waldenses. Second, there is a striking similarity between the doctrine held by the Waldenses and the early Brethren. The Waldenses, founded by Peter Waldo, in 1176, held that the Bible, and especially the New Testament, is the sole rule of belief and life.[27] They rejected oaths and all shedding of blood, and observed the Lord's Supper. One cannot prove any connection between the Waldenses and the Brethren but the similarity in doctrine makes it possible.

The Influence of the Mennonites and Quakers

Here the relationship can be more easily determined but it is still indirect. There are three reasons why it is probable that the Mennonites and Quakers influenced the attitude of the early Brethren on war. First, all three groups held to the same nonresistant principles, opposed slavery, and refused to take the oath. Second, the Mennonites and

---

[26] Holsinger, *History of the Tunkers and the Brethren Church*, pp. 27-29.
[27] Walker, *op. cit.*, p. 252.

Quakers originated prior to the Church of the Brethren
and it is likely that the early Brethren were acquainted
with the doctrines of these groups. The Mennonite Church
was started by Menno Simons in the Netherlands around
1535. Because of persecutions there were migrations to
Germany and later to America. The Quakers originated in
England around 1646 under the leadership of George Fox.
They were evangelical and during the first ten years of
their history Quaker missionaries had preached in Germany, Austria and Holland. William Penn had made missionary journeys to the Palatinate and Holland in 1672 and
1677. Third, the Mennonites and Brethren had associations
together in Europe. The Mennonites were in Creyfeld and
it is likely that Christopher Hochmann visited them as
early as 1705. Friedmann states:

> Into this circle entered the German mystic Hochmann von
> Hohenau (d. 1721), a man of unusually powerful spirituality, who
> deeply influenced everyone with whom he came in touch. In Crey-
> feld he was well received by the Mennonites, who gladly gave him
> the opportunity to preach several times in their meetinghouse. He
> also visited the congregations in the Palatinate several times,
> preaching his spiritualistic message of a purely inward Christianity.
> Like all extreme spiritualistic personalities, he was opposed to
> "forming sects"—as he puts it, but his activity nevertheless even-
> tually prompted one of the strong and aggressive movements of the
> time, that of the *Dompelaars* or Dunkers.[28]

It is thought also that Alexander Mack traveled among
the Mennonites seeking a people who held his ideals of
life.[29] Agreeing with their nonresistant principles but
differing with their form of baptism, he turned toward the
formation of a separate church organization.

A further contact with the Mennonites came when persecution drove the Brethren to Creyfeld. Alexander Mack,
Jr., informs us that when the members in the Palatinate

---

[28] Robert Friedmann, "Spiritual Changes in European Mennonitism, 1650-1750."
Reprint from *Mennonite Quarterly Review*, January 1941, p. 10.
[29] Henry C. Smith, *The Mennonites of America*, p. 179.

were persecuted, they went to Marienborn, and when the church at Marienborn was persecuted the members went to Creyfeld. Friedmann describes their reception in Creyfeld.

These people met persecution at many places in the Rhineland but in 1715 found a refuge in Creyfeld like so many others before them. There the Mennonites were deeply impressed by this pietistic but very dynamic group, and many brethren including several preachers turned to them. It is characteristic of the spirit of toleration in those days that one of the ministers, Gossen Goyen, who administered baptism in the new way of immersion, nevertheless was allowed to continue as a Mennonite preacher. In 1719 a great part of the Creyfeld Dompelaar group, including several former Mennonites, joined the German Baptist emigrants from Schwarzenau and came to Pennsylvania bringing with them their ascetic and emotional spirituality. (There they founded what is now known as the Church of the Brethren.) In Creyfeld, as a result of the loss of leadership due to emigration, the movement died out a few years later.[30]

The Quakers were in Creyfeld, too. They had preached among the Mennonites between 1670 and 1683 and had won adherents to their faith. From Creyfeld the first Mennonite group came to America in 1683 and settled at Germantown, Pennsylvania.[31] From Creyfeld the first Brethren came to America in 1719 and settled likewise in Germantown, Pennsylvania.[32] C. Henry Smith, an outstanding historian of the Mennonites, says:

So great is the similarity between these two denominations that we can but conclude that the Dunkards must have borrowed many of their religious practices and doctrines from the Mennonites. Both reject infant baptism, oppose the bearing of arms and the taking of oaths. Some of their religious practices are similar; the kiss of peace, the use of the prayer head-covering and bonnet for the women, and feet-washing at the communion service.[33]

---

[30] Friedmann, *op. cit.*, p. 11.
[31] Smith, *op. cit.*, p. 104.
[32] Brumbaugh, *A History of the Brethren*, pp. 191-192.
[33] Smith, *op. cit.*, pp. 178-179.

How the State Dealt With the Early Brethren as a Minority Group

We have already seen that the peace of Westphalia did not grant religious freedom to minority groups, and that the treatment of minority groups within any county in Germany depended upon the attitude of the ruling prince. The original Brethren fled to Schwarzenau because there Prince Henry (Heinrich Albert, 1658-1723) granted some measure of religious freedom. Schwarzenau is in the county of Wittgenstein in the province of Westphalia. Wittgenstein is a mountainous district between the Rhine and the Weser river systems and admirably adapted as a quiet refuge for dissenters. The headquarters of Prince Henry were at Laasphe. Not far away was Berleberg, another refuge for Pietists, ruled over by Hedwig Sophia and her son, Count Casimir. Historians claim that Hedwig Sophia was very kind to the Pietists and that she befriended them.

The Brethren have been under the impression for years that Prince Henry was friendly and somewhat sympathetic toward Pietism. D. W. Kurtz, who examined the records carefully in Germany and talked to German historians, corrects this impression. He states:

When I was in Laasphe and Schwarzenau, I stayed with Dr. Guder, the family physician of the royal family, the direct descendants of Prince Henry. Dr. Guder was a great reader and like most educated persons in Germany, was acquainted with the family history of the rulers. He told me that Prince Henry was not a Pietist, but was far from it—he was a rather cruel man, and very selfish. His descendants all spoke of him as such. This was verified by Rev. Hinsberg, who helped me in the archives at Laasphe. They all said that they were greatly surprised at Brumbaugh's statement that Henry was pietistically inclined. On the other hand, Henry made money out of these Pietists by charging a head-tax for their privilege of being in his province. When I mentioned to the reigning prince that Henry was so kind to our people, the family looked at each other in great surprise. I was completely convinced from these local historians that Brumbaugh's picture of Henry is not correct. The professor of church history at Marburg, to whom I gave Brumbaugh's book to read, also confirmed this local picture of Henry. They all told me that Henry was a very selfish man and charged a head-tax for his protection. Now, I do not claim that there is absolute proof, but all of the Germans were opposed to Brumbaugh's picture of Henry.[34]

It is probable that Alexander Mack's money went to Henry, for the Memoirs of Mack inform us that his wealth, "handsome patrimony, fine vineyards, and profitable mill," were all taken from him by paying the fines of Brethren.[35]

The record of Christopher Hochmann is one series of prison experiences. He was imprisoned at Detmold in 1702, Hanover in 1703, Nurenberg in 1708, and at Halle in 1711.[36] His record was one of imprisonment and release but with no stopping of his evangelistic fervor.

The Schwarzenau congregation in 1720 was persecuted and Alexander Mack led the members to Westervain in West Friesland. The conditions of their leaving Schwarzenau is a matter of interest. Kurtz saw the original records in the Schloss Wittgenstein in Laasphe. He found at least a half dozen letters and complaints sent to Prince Henry charging him with disloyalty to the empire for permitting godless and blaspheming persons to live in the land. Kurtz says that "each time Henry's answer was that no such persons were in his land, that the ones referred to were quiet, God-fearing people, who spent their time in deeds of love and kindness, did no harm at all, and were in the truest sense, Christians and Protestants."[37] The records show that the Count at Wetzlar, a relative of Henry, brought suit against him for religious toleration. Whether Henry asked the Brethren to leave because of the pressure upon him cannot be determined, although it is probably what

---

[34] Letter from D. W. Kurtz, January 16, 1943.
[35] "Memoirs of Alexander Mack," *op. cit.*, p. v.
[36] *Schaff-Herzog's Religious Encyclopedia*, p. 999.
[37] Kurtz, Article in the *Gospel Messenger*, August 7, 1909, pp. 498-499.

happened. Henry answered the charge against him by stating that no such people were there any more, that about forty families, about two hundred people, had left, and that no one except Catholics, Lutherans, and Reformed remained.[38]   Outside pressure probably caused Henry to tell the Brethren to leave.

Kurtz found a letter written by Seebach, a Pietist, who said that in 1719 the soldiers came to Schwarzenau and took the children of the Wiedertaufer out of the hands of the mothers and baptized them by force.[39]   In this act the soldiers and church officials united.   This may have influenced the Brethren to leave Schwarzenau.

The church at Creyfeld was also persecuted.   In 1714 six members of the Reformed Church united with the Creyfeld church through baptism.   The government called the six men for trial and threw them into the Düsseldorf prison where they had to remain four years.   Arrests, fines and imprisonments were common.   Alexander Mack, Jr., summarizes the persecution of the early Brethren with these words:

But as they found favor with God and men on the one hand, so (on the other hand) there were also enemies of the truth, and there arose here and there persecutions for the Word's sake.   There were those who suffered joyfully the spoiling of their goods, and others encountered bonds and imprisonment; some for a few weeks only, but others had to spend several years in prisons.   Christian Libe was some years fastened to a galley, and had to work the galling oar among malefactors; yet, by God's special providence, they were all delivered again with a good conscience.

Since the persecution in the form of poverty, tribulation and imprisonment, by which they were oppressed, made them only the more joyful, they were tried in another manner, by men of learning seeking to confound them with sharp disputations and subtle questions, of which the forty searching questions of Eberhard Ludwig

[38] *Ibid.*, p. 499.
[39] Early Brethren were sometimes called "Wiedertaufers."

Gruber, which with their answers, will be annexed to this treatise, will sufficiently inform the reader.[40]

THE COMING TO AMERICA FOR RELIGIOUS LIBERTY

William Penn had traveled in Europe and had invited the Mennonites to come to Pennsylvania. Mennonites had gone from Creyfeld to America. The persecutions at Creyfeld made the Brethren look toward this country. They desired religious liberty. The advertisements of William Penn's agents and the Frankfort Land Company probably exerted some influence upon the Brethren. Peter Becker brought the first group to Pennsylvania in 1719. Alexander Mack and the members at Westervain came over in 1729 at the urgence of the Brethren in America. Religious freedom and economic motives combined to bring the first Brethren to this country.

THE FIRST INCONSISTENCY

A thing happened in the Creyfeld church which was inconsistent with the position of tolerance which the Brethren had taken. A young brother of the name of Hacker married the daughter of a Mennonite businessman and the ceremony was performed by the bride's father. Christian Libe, a Brethren minister at Crefeld, stirred up opposition because this young man had married outside of the church. John Naas, the elder of the church, pled for tolerance, but Libe was a very strong personality and solicited enough help so that he forced the excommunication of Hacker. The results were disastrous. Hacker brooded over the matter until he died. The church was so disturbed that it did not recover until the group came to America. Elder Naas became discouraged and withdrew to Switzerland until he came to America with his family in 1733. Libe himself gave up religious work within a few years. This was a

---

[40] Alexander Mack, Jr., Introduction to *A Plain View of the Rites and Ordinances*, p. xi.

serious disruption in the church. It did not represent the attitude of the early Brethren as a whole. It was the work of a dominating personality and an example of intolerance.

SUMMARY

The founders of the Church of the Brethren believed that war was contrary to the life and teachings of Jesus. The original Brethren community practiced nonresistance and the first Brethren took no part in war. Alexander Mack's pacifism was probably influenced by Christopher Hochmann, the noted Pietist.

The early Brethren believed in the necessity of government and held that they should obey sane laws. They broke with the state because the church and state were united in the persecution of dissenters.

The peace position of the Church of the Brethren was influenced by the following factors:

1. The political and religious conditions in Germany which made them hate war.

2. Taking the New Testament as their guide for living which led them to see that war and the ethics of Jesus were incompatible.

3. The direct influence of outstanding Pietists upon early Brethren thought and the fact that these Pietists taught nonresistance.

4. The similarity in doctrine between the Waldenses and Brethren makes it possible that Alexander Mack was acquainted with the ideals and practices of this sect.

5. The influence of the Mennonites and Quakers upon early Brethren thought. These churches originated prior to the Brethren and have the same peace ideals. Alexander Mack was acquainted with their doctrines. He traveled among the Mennonites before he founded the Church of the Brethren.

The original Brethren lived at the mercy of the ruling princes. The law granted no religious freedom. Prince Henry, who ruled over Schwarzenau, tolerated the Brethren because they paid him head taxes. The churches at Schwarzenau, Marienborn, and Creyfeld were persecuted. The sufferings imposed by a united church and state drove the Brethren in Germany from one place to another and made conditions of living there intolerable. The response of the Brethren to this situation was emigration to America.

Chapter III

THE CHURCH OF THE BRETHREN'S ATTITUDE TOWARD WAR IN COLONIAL AMERICA AND DURING THE REVOLUTIONARY WAR

The period under consideration in this chapter is from the coming of the first Brethren to America in 1719 to the close of the Revolutionary War in 1783. This is a very important period in the development of the Brethren peace position for the entire church was transported to a new land and these nonresistant people faced new conditions. Twenty-five years after the church originated, the record in Germany was closed and the Brethren became a frontier group in America. What did they find here?

RELIGIOUS LIBERTY IN COLONIAL PENNSYLVANIA

William Penn, an English Quaker, received from the crown of England in March 1681 the grant of the province of Pennsylvania in settlement of a debt which the government owed to his father. Penn, who was a young man of thirty-seven, set about to find settlers for his colony. A tremendous flow of Quakers started from the British Isles. Penn and Benjamin Furley, his counselor, compiled a booklet entitled "Some Account of the Province of Pennsylvania in America."[1] It was printed by the Frankfort Land Company, issued in English, German and Dutch and circulated throughout Holland and parts of Germany. The earlier travels of Penn and this book, which gave a glowing account of Pennsylvania, stimulated the great German emigration to this country.

The Mennonites came to America at the invitation of William Penn. Francis Daniel Pastorius led the first colony of Mennonites from Creyfeld to Pennsylvania in 1683.

---

[1] Sachse, *Falckner's Curieuse Nachricht von Pennsylvania, A. D. 1700*, pp. 8-9.

They arrived at Philadelphia but soon followed an Indian trail through what is now perhaps Germantown Avenue to an elevated spot about six miles north of Philadelphia. They settled there and founded historic Germantown.

The naturalization papers of these Mennonites give evidence regarding the freedom to be accorded the Germans:

Naturalization Papers of Francis Daniel Pastorius and of Sixty-two High and Low Germans

Germantown

From

William Penn, Esq.

Dated 7th May, A.D., 1691

"I do declare, and by these presents confirm them the said inhabitants before named, to be Freemen of this government, and that they shall be accordingly held and reputed in as full and ample manner as any person or persons residing therein. And that they, the said Freemen, have liberty and freedom hereby to trade and traffic in this colony or in any of the King's Dominions and plantations, as other good subjects may lawfully do without any matter Lett, Hinderance or Molestation Whatsoever."

Recorded in the Rolls' Office at Philadelphia,
The thirteenth Day of the third Month, 1691.

Patent Book A, folio 275.

Exq Da: Lloyd Deputy.[2]

The Brethren came to Pennsylvania in response to the general invitation of William Penn which went out to all Germans but more particularly through the influence of the Mennonites with whom they had been associated at Creyfeld. While without doubt economic motives helped to bring the Brethren and Mennonites to America, religious liberty was the primary cause. Penn made it clear that religious freedom would be granted in his province. His frame of government was organized before the Brethren

---

[2] The original is in the Cassel Library, Juniata College, Huntingdon, Pennsylvania.

set sail. They came under the promise of religious freedom and, as William Warren Sweet says, "were advocates of religious liberty from principle."[3] The following is a section of Penn's "Charter of Privileges to the Provinces and Counties of Pennsylvania," approved in the Assembly. October 28, 1701:

Because no people can be truly happy, though under the greatest enjoyment of Civil Liberties, if abridged of the freedom of their consciences as to their religious profession and worship; and Almighty God being the only Lord of Conscience, Father of Lights and Spirits, and the author as well as object of all divine knowledge, faith and worship, who only doth enlighten the mind and persuade and convince the understanding of people, I do hereby grant and declare that no person or persons, inhabiting in his Province or Territories, who shall confess and acknowledge One Almighty God, the Creator, Upholder and Ruler of the World, and profess him or themselves obliged to live quietly under the civil government, shall be in any case molested or prejudiced in his or their person or Estate because of his or their conscientious persuasion or practice, nor to be compelled to frequent or maintain any religious worship, place or ministry contrary to his or their mind, or to do or suffer any other act or thing contrary to their religious persuasion. And that all persons who also profess to believe in Jesus Christ to be the Savior of the world, shall be capable (notwithstanding their other persuasions and practices in point of conscience and religion) to serve this government in any capacity, both legislatively or executively.[4]

This was the charter of Pennsylvania for seventy-five years. Penn wrote to the Provisional Council, January 14, 1718, saying:

Observe the law for liberty of conscience which I take to be a Fundamental one in Pennsylvania; and was one great encouragement for the Quakers to transport themselves thither, and to make it what it now is, for which they merit the favor of my family, as well as on many other accounts, and shall always have it when in my power; and this I desire you will let the people know.[5]

Penn was given unrestricted possession of his province

---

[3] Sweet, *Religion in Colonial America,* p. 323.
[4] *Colonial Records,* 1700-17, II, p. 57.
[5] *Colonial Records,* 1717-36, III, p. 64.

and was allowed to apply his ideas of government. Nevertheless, the settlers were subjects of the British crown. The Provincial Council became alarmed at the large German immigration and on September 17, 1717, passed an ordinance requiring all newcomers to take an oath of allegiance to the king and his government. Provision was made for the Mennonites, who could not take oaths according to conscience, admitting them "upon their giving any equivalent assurance in their own way and manner."[6] The first Brethren were admitted under the general consideration given to the Mennonites. By the time Alexander Mack and his followers landed in 1729 a declaration of loyalty to King George was demanded. Freedom of religion promised under Penn and loyalty to the king were factors which did not always prove compatible, as later history proves.

CHARACTERISTICS OF THE CHURCH OF THE BRETHREN IN COLONIAL AMERICA

Geographical Distribution

Four years after the Brethren landed in America, the first church was organized at Germantown, Pennsylvania, on Christmas Day, 1723. Peter Becker was elder. On September 7, 1724, a new church was organized at Coventry, Pennsylvania, in Chester County. On November 12, 1724, the Conestoga church in Lancaster County was started with Conrad Beissel as minister. The coming of Alexander Mack in 1729 was a great stimulus to the Brethren. John Naas, who landed with his family in 1733, located at Amwell, New Jersey. Other congregations were established until prior to the Revolution there were about twenty organized churches with about eight hundred members. Most of the churches were in Pennsylvania, but there were a few organized churches in Maryland, one in New Jersey,

---

[6] *Ibid.* p. 29.

and a few scattered Brethren settlers in Virginia. The Brethren up to the time of the Revolutionary War were limited to four colonies, with the great majority of them being in Pennsylvania.

A German Language Church

It has already been noted that the original Brethren were all Germans. Their early activities were restricted to the German population. They spoke the German language throughout the colonial period. They brought their social ideas and customs from the old world. Their German language and customs created a barrier between them and their English-speaking neighbors. The Brethren were often misunderstood and criticized. Their answer to criticism was the forming of a compact and somewhat exclusive church fellowship.

The Two Christopher Sowers

Christopher Sower, Senior and Junior, were the most outstanding Brethren of colonial America. The Sower family came from Germany in 1724. In 1738 a thriving printing business was established at Germantown. In 1739 "Der Hoch-Deutsch Americanische Calender" was issued, which continued for forty-nine years. In the same year "Der Hoch-Deutsch Pennsylvanische Geschicht Schreiber," the first German newspaper in America, appeared, which was continued until the Revolutionary War destroyed the Sower printing business. In 1743 Sower published the royal quarto Bible, the first German Bible to be published in America. This was his monumental work. Christopher Sower, Sr., died in 1758 and his son fell heir to his printing business.

Christopher Sower, the Second, carried on the German newspaper started by his father. He issued a second edition of the Bible in 1763, and a third in 1776. He published

the "Geistliche Magazin," the first religious magazine printed in America. The third edition of the Sower Bible had
been printed and the leaves had been placed in the loft
of the Germantown meetinghouse to dry when the battle
of Germantown took place. The soldiers took the leaves
and scattered them under their horses for bedding. When
the battle was over Sower gathered as many of these sheets
together as he could to complete a few Bibles.

Christopher Sower, the Second, had been trained by
Christopher Dock, the great Mennonite teacher. Sower
believed in education and became a leader in founding the
Germantown Academy. He served twenty years as a
trustee and five years as chairman of the board of trustees.
He championed the cause of education among the Brethren
people. His publications had a great influence among the
Pennsylvania Germans. Sweet says:

> The Sowers were undoubtedly the most influential Germans in
> the colonies, and Germantown, through their activities, was the cul-
> tural center for the colonial Germans.[7]

The leaders of the Brethren in Germany and the leaders
in colonial America believed in education. Ludwig Hoecker
as early as 1748 started a Sabbath school at Ephrata and
maintained it for thirty years before Robert Raikes founded
his first Sunday school.[8] The school continued until the
battle of Brandywine in the Revolutionary War demanded
the room for hospital purposes. After that the school was
never opened. The Revolutionary War caught the Brethren
publisher at the height of his influence when the prospects
were for an educational dawning among the Brethren
people as a whole.

Conrad Beissel and His Ephrata Society

It is important to mention this because the Ephrata Society has been so often mistaken for the Church of the Breth-

---

[7] Sweet, *The Story of Religion in America*, p. 154.
[8] Brumbaugh, *A History of the Brethren*, p. 464.

ren in early Pennsylvania history. Conrad Beissel, the founder of the society, was baptized by Peter Becker and was for four years minister of the Conestoga church. He had highly mystical tendencies which led him to break with the Brethren and start the Ephrata Cloister in 1732. Here the "brothers" and "sisters" lived in separate houses, practiced a kind of monasticism, and celibacy. This group was called the "Seventh Day Baptists." Beissel controlled the cloister thirty-six years until his death in 1768. After that the society rapidly declined. Since its members had been recruited from Brethren ranks, many of them returned to Brethren churches. "The Chronicon Ephratense," which gives the history of this community, is valuable for the light it sheds on the colonial period, and the experiences of the society during the Revolutionary War are a legitimate part of this treatise.

Early Relationships With the Mennonites and Friends

In the settlement of Peter Becker and his followers at Germantown, associations between the Brethren and Mennonites were immediately renewed. In the spread of these churches, the Mennonites and Brethren settled in many of the same communities. Mennonite historians claim that the Brethren proselyted among them.[9] At least it can be said that there was a feeling of kinship between the two groups. The records do not indicate such a definite relationship with the Quakers in the early colonial period, possibly because the Quakers were English-speaking people. The relationship came when the Germans united their efforts with the Friends to keep the peace-loving people in control of the government.

THE COLONIAL PERIOD

To an understanding of the characteristics of the Breth-

---

[9] Smith, *The Mennonites of America*, p. 178.

ren in colonial times, should be added a look at the colonial period itself. It was a pioneer period of new settlements and the formation of governments. There were wars with the French and Indians (1689-1763), until France gave up her empire in America to England (1763). The thirteen colonies were organized. In this period Thomas Jefferson was born; George Washington became a leading general; Benjamin Franklin won distinction as a printer, and Jonathan Edwards published his work on the freedom of the will. In this period the Stamp Act was passed, the first Continental Congress was called in Philadelphia in 1774, and the Declaration of Independence was adopted in 1776. The Revolutionary War, led by General Washington, was fought, ending with the treaty of peace signed in February, 1783. This was followed by the formation of the Union, the adoption of the United States Constitution, and the election of George Washington as the first president. It was a pioneer period of struggles, hardships, Indian massacres, wars, and forming new governments. How did the peace attitude of the Brethren fare in colonial America?

THE BRETHREN AND WAR DURING THE COLONIAL PERIOD

The Brethren did not keep good records. There are no recorded Annual Conference minutes until 1778. Other sources yield information regarding the Brethren and war.

Statement of Robert Proud

"The History of Pennsylvania," published in 1798, by Robert Proud, characterizes the Brethren in this fashion:

Those people, in Pennsylvania, called Dunkards, Tunkers, or Dumplers, are another species of German Baptists. They are singular in some of their opinions and customs; and perhaps more so in their manner of living, and personal appearance, than any others of that name in the province, particularly those who reside at a place, called by them, Ephrata, in Lancaster County.

They also hold it not becoming a follower of Jesus Christ to bear arms, or fight; because, say they, their true master has forbid his disciples to resist evil; and because he also told them not to swear at all, they will by no means take an oath; but adhere close to his advice, in the affirmation of yea and nay.

As to their origin, they allow of no other, than that, which was made by Jesus himself, when he was baptized by John in Jordan. They have a great esteem for the New Testament, valuing it higher than the other books; and when they are asked about the articles of their faith, they say they know of no others but what are contained in this book; and therefore can give none.[10]

This historian gives evidence that the Brethren during the colonial period would not fight and that their convictions were rooted in the teachings of Jesus.

Christopher Sower on Peace

In an article entitled "About War and Peace," published in "Der Hoch-Deutsch Americanische Calendar" in 1749, Christopher Sower, Sr., gives his point of view regarding peace.

At present it seems as if the great and the little warriors will have peace for awhile. The end will show how long it will last. For they make and give peace as the world gives it. But Christ gave his disciples a peace which remains eternal and not such as is given by the world. John 14: 27: for there is a peace in our hearts which nobody can take. The children of this world might have peace for a somewhat longer time, in each country, at each place, and in each house if they would only listen a little to the chastising spirit of God and might resist haughty ideas and just think; I will not be too fond of myself, I will suffer a little, and suffer a little more, and suffer still a little more, and so on. This would be the beginning of how at last to learn to stand and suffer very much and to remain at peace. However that is not the way of man, but that is the way of Christ's disciples and successors. They could not have been this way if His spirit had not 'dwelt' in them. For He says: Without me you cannot do anything, John 15: 5. Therefore they long so much for Him, that they may have Him, the 'Peace King,' in their hearts and keep Him there. So the great and the little 'world children' may argue, quarrel, beat, shoot, stab or destroy,—Christ's peace will remain in the hearts of His children although they have to live in the midst of all

[10] Robert Proud, *The History of Pennsylvania*, pp. 345-347.

this. But he who cannot suffer little or great things, will soon lose peace and be in quarrel and fight, war and trouble.[11]

Again it is easily seen that the early Brethren position on war was based upon the spirit and teachings of Jesus.

The Sowers on Peace With the Indians

Not much has been recorded regarding the Brethren's attitude toward war with the Indians. Enough, however, can be gleaned to discover the point of view. Christopher Sower in his newspaper of 1756 speaks about a conference with the Indians and advocates the giving of money so that these Indians may be satisfied and bound to the province by an annual income. Christopher Sower, Senior and Junior, were both working on the papers at this time and the point of view expressed in the following paragraphs may be taken as representing the convictions of father and son.

As it is not only the maxim of the Quakers, but also the faith-principle of many others, that one should not strike with the sword but put it in the sheath, that one should do good things to the enemy, that one should look for peace . . . and for a long time many Germans have offered that—if it were possible to make a lasting peace with the Indians without bloodshed—the Germans would contribute according to their fortunes—to many poor people's lives being saved on both sides, etc. It is made known herewith that all those who have or will still get the same opinion shall give . . . what they want to contribute voluntarily.[12]

As it is not a secret any longer why the Indians don't keep peace . . . and that evidently no real peace can be expected from the Indians unless they are made peaceable, many peace-loving people have resolved to contribute to a voluntary tax, that the Indians may have—for all the years—a certain sum for their needs.

Different kinds of people volunteer for this tax: Some think if you make war on the Indians, you have to sacrifice many white people. To save those lives, it would be better to satisfy the Indians.

Others believe Christ's doctrine requires that one should do good

---

[11] *Der Hoch-Deutsch Americanishe Calendar, 1749,* p. 34. Translated from the copy in the Pennsylvania Historical Society, Philadelphia, Pa.
[12] *Pennsylvanische Berichte,* 1756, August 16, p. 4. Translated from the original copy in the Pennsylvania Historical Library, Philadelphia.

things to the enemies, and one should live in peace with all men. They would like already on earth to wander with a peaceful mind with the 'Peace-Prince,' that in 'Eternity' they might appear before Him in peace and live in Him and with Him.

Besides, there are a few people who believe and say: One should slay all the dogs, but they want to remain at home. Such people don't have the spirit of God and are not inclined to forgive seventy times seven.[13]

About two years later the Christopher Sowers wrote:

It appears the Indians did not trust their friends. The white people would be wise if—when they come to the Indians—they dealt modestly and in a friendly manner with them, that no cause and no opportunity might be given for a new hostility and war.[14]

These great Brethren publishers wanted peace with the Indians. They wanted the Indians treated fairly. They advocated a voluntary tax to care for the Indians' needs. They believed that peace with the Indians would come by doing good to them. The thought of the Sowers was doubtless representative in a large measure of the Brethren as a whole.

The Brethren Sufferings at the Hands of the Indians

U. J. Jones, another historian of Pennsylvania, recorded the massacre of Brethren by the Indians at Morrison's Cove. He wrote in a critical vein but in doing it showed the faith and spirit of the Brethren regarding war. Jones said:

They are strict nonresistants; and in the predatory incursions of the French and Indians, in 1756-63, and, in fact, during all the savage warfare, they not only refused to take up arms to repel the savage marauders and prevent the inhuman slaughter of women and children, but they refused in the most positive manner to pay a dollar to support those who were willing to take up arms to defend their homes and their firesides, until wrung from them by the stern mandates of the law, from which there was no appeal.

They did the same thing when the Revolution broke out. There was a scarcity of men. Sixty able-bodied ones among them might

[13] *Ibid.*, 1756, November 27, p. 3.
[14] *Pennsylvanische Berichte*, 1758, Feb. 18, p. 4. Translated from the original copy in the Pennsylvania Historical Library, Philadelphia.

readily have formed a cordon of frontier defense, which could have prevented many of the Indian massacres which took place between 1777 and 1780, and more especially among their own people in the Cove. But not a man would shoulder his rifle; they were non-resistants! They might, at least, have furnished money, for they always had an abundance of that, the hoarding of which appeared to be the sole aim and object of life with them. But no; not a dollar! They occupied neutral ground, and wished to make no resistance. Again; they might have furnished supplies. And they did furnish supplies to those who were risking their lives to repel the invaders, —but it was only when the almighty dollar accompanied the demand.

After the massacre of thirty of them, in less than forty-eight hours, Colonel Piper, the lieutenant-colonel of Bedford County, made a strong appeal to them. But it was of no avail; they were nonresistants, and evidently determined to remain such.

Of the peculiar religious tenets of these primitive people we do not profess to know anything; hence our remarks are unbiased. We are solely recording historical facts.[15]

Again the author stated:

On their first expedition they would have few scalps to grace their belts, had the Dunkards taken the advice of more sagacious people, and fled, too; this, however, they would not do. They would follow but half of Cromwell's advice; they were willing to put their "trust in God," but they would not "keep their powder dry." In short, it was a compound they did not use at all.

The savages swept down through the Cove with all the ferocity with which a pack of wolves would descend from the mountain up-on a flock of sheep. Some few of the Dunkards, who evidently had a latent spark of love of life, hid themselves away; but by far the most of them stood by and witnessed the butchery of wives and children, merely saying, "Gottes wille sei gethan." How many Dunk-ard scalps they carried to Detroit cannot now be, and probably never has been clearly ascertained,—not less than thirty, according to the best authority. In addition to this they loaded themselves with plunder, stole a number of horses, and under cover of night the triumphant warriors marched bravely away.[16]

[15] U. J. Jones, *History of the Early Settlement of the Juniata Valley*, pp. 208-209.
[16] *Ibid.*, p. 212.

The author added an interesting note at the bottom of a page. The words "Gottes wille sei gethan" ("God's will be done") were repeated by the Brethren so often during the massacre that the Indians retained a vivid recollection of them. During the war with Britain some of the old Indians were anxious to discover from the Huntingdon volunteers whether the "Gotswiltahns" still lived in the Cove. They did not forget the people who refused to fight back.

Jones gave one exception to the Brethren spirit of non-resistance. Two Indians, an old man and a young warrior, stopped at Neff's Mill. Neff was a Dunker. He took his loaded rifle, aimed through the window and deliberately shot the old Indian. Neff and the young Indian engaged in battle until Neff shot him through the head. The author commented critically, "For the part Neff took in the matter he was excommunicated from the Dunkard Society."[17] However, this shows the strictness of the Brethren in applying their ideal of nonresistance.

The Brethren Almanac of 1876 gives the experiences of Dr. Thomas Eckarly and his two brothers. They were peace-loving Brethren who came from Pennsylvania and settled on the Cheat River near Morgantown, West Virginia. They lived for several years unmolested although a destructive war was being waged around them. Dr. Eckarly left the Cheat River for a trading post on the Shenandoah. On his return he stopped at Fort Pleasant on the South Branch. The inhabitants, in war fever, arrested him on suspicion of being a spy and in confederacy with the Indians. He attested his innocence and was finally allowed to proceed to his home with armed guards who were to make an examination of his habitation. When they reached his home his cabin was in ashes, the mutilated bodies of his loved ones were

---

[17] *Ibid.*, p. 216.

upon the ground, and the hoops upon which the Indians dried their scalps were hanging in the yard.

The Annual Conference on War

The most outstanding official statement of the church's position on war during this period was made by the Annual Meeting of 1785, held at Big Conewago, Pennsylvania. It is quoted at length in Chapter II and therefore is not reproduced here. The statement is Biblical, centering in the teachings of Christ. The statement intimates that questions had arisen among some members regarding taking the sword. There were some honest doubts within Brethren ranks about the church's position. The doubts seem to have arisen through the literal interpretation of certain passages of the New Testament. The words of 1 Peter 2: 13-14 were quoted: "Submit yourselves to every ordinance of man for the Lord's sake; whether it be to the king, as supreme; or unto governors, or unto them that are sent by him for the punishment of evildoers, and for the praise of them that do well."

The Annual Conference after due consideration went on record saying that the words of Peter did not mean submitting to higher powers to do violence, or the shedding of blood, that Peter himself exhorted that "we ought to obey God rather than man," and that submission to higher powers meant only in so far as it was the will of God. This was an interpretation which put the will of God above loyalty to the state. The Brethren held that they could not "find any liberty to use any carnal weapon,"[18] and closed the pronouncement by saying, ". . . That no brother should permit his sons to go to the muster ground, much less that a brother go himself."[19] *Muster* meant military training for the citizens. The Brethren were to absent themselves from these military practices.

---

[18] *Minutes of the Annual Conference, 1778-1909*, p. 10.
[19] *Ibid.*, p. 10.

Associators and Non-Associators

In the early days of the Revolution there was little united action. Each colony organized its own militia and furnished its own arms. In 1775 the Assembly of Pennsylvania asked that all able-bodied white male inhabitants "associate" for the common defense. Those who had scruples against these military organizations were called non-associators.

Associators Requested to Bear a Tender Regard Toward Non-Associators

The Assembly of Pennsylvania recognized that there were many Quakers, Mennonites and Dunkers in the province and on June 30, 1775, took the following action:

> The House taking into consideration that many of the good people of this Province are conscientiously scrupulous of bearing arms, do hereby earnestly recommend to the Associators for the Defense of their Country, and others, that they bear a tender and brotherly regard toward this class of their fellow-subjects and Countrymen; and to these conscientious people it is also recommended, that they cheerfully assist, in proportion to their abilities, such associators as cannot spend their time and substance in the public service without great injury to themselves and families.[20]

The Assembly recommended goodwill toward the non-associators but asked that the nonresistant people help in other ways to carry on the war.

Criticism Developing

As the war progressed the increased patriotism and the difficulties in financing the military campaigns caused the development of a feeling against the non-associators. The records of the House of Representatives of Pennsylvania, September 27, 1775, give a memorial from the military association of the city of Philadelphia. This memorial protests against the leniency shown toward those who profess to be conscientiously opposed to bearing arms. It

---

[20] *Votes of the House of Representatives of Pennsylvania, 1767-1776,* VI, p. 594.

claims that a considerable share of the property of the province is held by people claiming a "tender conscience in military matters." It urges that a plan be worked out requiring every inhabitant to contribute toward the Revolutionary cause either with his person or property.[21]

Quakers Petition the Assembly

The Quakers realized the feeling which was developing against the non-associators. They addressed the Assembly on October 26, 1775, in an appeal for peace and preservation of liberty of conscience.[22] They recounted the liberty granted by William Penn and urged that it be preserved.

The Mennonite and Brethren Petition

The Mennonites and Brethren likewise seeing the seriousness of the situation addressed the House of Representatives of Pennsylvania on November 7, 1775, in the following statement:

An address of Declaration signed by divers persons in behalf of the Societies of Menonists and German Baptists in this Province, was presented to the House, and follows in these words.

In the first place we acknowledge to the most high God, who created heaven and earth, the only good Being, to thank him for all his great Goodness and manifold mercies and love through our Saviour Jesus Christ, who is come to save the souls of men, having all Power in Heaven and on Earth.

Further, we find ourselves indebted to be thankful to our late worthy Assembly, for their giving so good an advice in these Troublesome Times to all Ranks of people in Pennsylvania, particularly in allowing those, who, by the Doctrines of our Saviour Jesus Christ, are persuaded in their consciences to love their enemies, and not to resist evil, to enjoy the liberty of their consciences, for which, as also for all the good things we enjoyed under their care, we heartily thank that worthy Body of Assembly, and all high and low in office, who have advised to such a peaceful measure, hoping and confiding that they, and all others entrusted with Powers in this hitherto

---

[21] *Ibid.*, p. 599.
[22] *Ibid.*, pp. 634-636.

blessed Province, may be moved by the same spirit of grace, which animated the first Founder of this Province, our late worthy Proprieter William Penn, to grant liberty of Conscience to all its Inhabitants, that they may in the great and memorable Day of judgement be put on the right Hand of that just Judge, who judgeth without Respect of Person, and hear of him these blessed words, "Come, ye blessed of my Father, inherit the Kingdom, prepared for you," etc. What ye have done unto one of the least of these my Brethren, ye have done unto me," among which number (i. e., the least of Christ's Brethren) we by his Grace hope to be ranked; and every Lenity and Favour shewn to such tender consciences, although weak, Followers of this one blessed Saviour, will not be forgotten by him on that great day.

The advice to those who do not find Freedom of conscience to take up arms, that they ought to be helpful to those who are in need and distressed circumstances, we receive with cheerfulness towards all men of what station they may be—it being our principle to feed the Hungry and give the Thirsty Drink;—we have dedicated ourselves to serve all men in everything that can be helpful to the preservation of Men's Lives, but we find no Freedom in giving, or doing, or assisting in any thing by which Men's Lives are destroyed or hurt. We beg the Patience of all those who believe we err in this point.

We are always ready, according to Christ's Command to Peter, to pay the Tribute, that we Offend no man, and so we are willing to pay Taxes, and to render unto Caesar those things that are Caesar's, and to God those things that are God's, although we think ourselves very weak to give God his due Favor, he being a Spirit and Life, and We only dust and ashes.

We are also willing to be subject to the higher powers, and to give in the Measures Paul directs us; for he beareth the sword not in vain, for he is the minister of God, a Revenger to execute wrath upon him that doeth evil.

This Testimony we lay down before our worthy Assembly, and all other persons in Government, letting them know that we are thankful as above-mentioned, and that we are not at Liberty in Conscience to take up arms to conquer our Enemies, but rather to pray to God, who has Power in Heaven and Earth, for us and them.

We also crave the patience of all the inhabitants of this country,— what they think to see clearer in the Doctrine of the blessed Jesus Christ, we will leave to them and God, finding ourselves very poor;

for Faith is to proceed out of the word of God, which is Life and Spirit, and a Power of God, and our consciences are to be instructed by the same, therefore we beg for patience.

Our small Gift, which we have given, we gave to those who have power over us, that we may not offend them, as Christ taught us by the Tribute Penny.

We heartily pray, that God would govern all Hearts of our Rulers, be they high or low, to meditate those good things which will pertain to our and their happiness.

Ordered to lie on the table.[23]

This statement is significant for a number of reasons. It shows that these two churches were working together and that their points of view were similar. It makes clear again that the peace convictions of these churches were centered in the New Testament. It shows how precious the liberty of conscience granted under Penn was to these people. It gives the consecration of these nonresistants to do everything possible to preserve life rather than destroy it. The statement presents their willingness to pay the taxes demanded for the war, their anxiety not to offend any one, and their thought that the government may have to do some things which they could not do. The Brethren and Mennonites were clear that war was wrong for them, but they felt that there might be times when, according to the Scriptures, war was necessary for the state.

Non-Associators to Pay an Equivalent

The petition of the Mennonites and Brethren must have had some effect. The next day, November 8, 1775, the Assembly took this action:

That all male white persons between the ages aforesaid (sixteen and fifty years) capable of bearing arms, who shall not associate for the defense of the Province, ought to contribute an equivalent to the time spent by the associators in acquiring military discipline; ministers of the gospel of all denominations, and servants purchased bona fide, and for valuable consideration, only exempted.[24]

---

[23] *Ibid.*, VI, Nov. 7, 1775, p. 645.
[24] *Pennsylvania Archives, Votes of the Assembly,* Series 8, VIII, p. 7351.

There was no exemption from responsibility for supporting the war. On November 24 the Assembly ordered a committee to make an investigation regarding "the contributions made by the people called Menonists, Omish Menonists and Sunday Baptists in Lancaster County . . . and
report to the House at their next meeting, how much of
the said contributions has been paid for the use of the
army."[25]

Criticism Getting Stronger

Criticism of the non-associators developed increasingly.
The Assembly on April 6, 1776, ordered that all arms be
collected from them.[26]   The Supreme Executive Council
of Pennsylvania on April 5, 1777, issued this statement:

As the militia has lately been out, and many of them are disgusted
that the non-associators of this state have not yet been compelled
to contribute anything towards the Association, or in support of the
American Cause, and that some of the associators have screened
themselves from the service of the last campaign; and they com-
plain very heavily that the burden lies entirely on those who are
willing to go forth; there are also great complaints of some of the
militia being obliged to go home without their Pay; the opinion of
Congress is desired whether a Bounty ought not to be given, and
how much.[27]

The Oath Law Passed

In an intense spirit of patriotism the oath of allegiance
was passed, June 13, 1777. The preamble implies that it
was aimed directly at the non-associators. The whole
statement is quoted because no act was passed which had
more tragic consequences upon the Brethren.

Whereas, from sordid or mercenary motives, or other causes inconsistent with the happiness of a free and independent people, sundry persons have or may yet be induced to withhold their service
and allegiance from the Commonwealth of Pennsylvania as a free
and independent state, as declared by Congress:

---

[25] *Votes of the House of Representatives of Pennsylvania*, 1717-1776, VI, p. 653.
[26] *American Archives*, Series 4, VI, p. 889.
[27] *Colonial Records*, 1776-79, II, p. 198.

And whereas, Sundry other persons in their several capacities have, at the risk of their lives and fortunes, or both, rendered great and eminent service in defense and support of said independence, and may yet continue to do the same, and as both these sorts of persons remain at this time mixed, and in some measure indistinguished from each other, and the disaffected deriving undeserved service from the faithful and well affected:

And whereas, allegiance and protection are reciprocal, and those who will not bear the former are not nor ought to be entitled to the benefits of the latter:

Therefore it is enacted, that all white male inhabitants of the state, except the counties of Bedford and Westmoreland, above the ages of fifteen years, shall, before the first day of the ensuing July, and in the excepted counties before the first day of August, take and subscribe before some justice of the peace an oath in the following form:

I............do swear (or affirm) that I renounce and refuse all allegiance to George the Third, king of Great Britain, his heirs and successors; and that I will be faithful and bear true allegiance to the Commonwealth of Pennsylvania as a free and independent state, and that I will not at any time do or cause to be done any matter or thing that will be prejudicial or injurious to the freedom and independence thereof, as declared by Congress, and also, that I will discover and make known to some justice of the peace of said state all treasons or traitorous conspiracies which I now know or hereafter shall know to be formed against this or any of the United States of America.[28]

John Hubley wrote to President Wharton of the Supreme Executive Council in July, 1777, protesting against the Oath of Allegiance, stating that " it was intended for nought but to hinder substantial, good disposed people to elect or be elected; depriving them of their rights of freemen."[29] The Council of Safety on October 21, 1777, ordered army officers to collect from those who had not taken the oath of allegiance, "blankets, shoes and stockings for the use of the army."[30] On this same day the Council of Safety or-

[28] *Pennsylvania Archives*, Series 2, III, pp. 4-5.
[29] *Ibid.*, 1776-77, Series 1, V, p. 427.
[30] *Colonial Records*, 1776-79, II, p. 328.

dered the personal estates and effects of inhabitants seized
who had aided the enemy.[31]   Power was also granted for
the real estate and goods to be sold. These actions brought
on much suffering. The Brethren were opposed to taking
the oath on Biblical grounds just as they were opposed
to war. The historic peace churches faced a very difficult
situation. Misunderstandings of the nonresistant people and
accusations against them were frequent. The decisions as
to the persons who had aided the enemy were often left to
the bias of local officials.

The Brethren Still Did Not Fight

In spite of all this pressure the Brethren did not fight
and it was difficult to get sufficient soldiers in sections
thickly populated with them. R. D. M'Calester wrote to
President Wharton of the Executive Council, Lancaster,
Pennsylvania, on November 12, 1777, stating how hard it
was to fill up his company because of the great number of
Quakers, Mennonites and Dunkers in the county and that
because of so many scrupulous people much hiring was
necessary.[32]   One can see how criticism grew regarding
the Brethren. They did not believe in fighting, they would
neither go nor give their sons to the army, and they would
not take the oath of allegiance.

Christopher Sower a Subscriber to Captain Hill's Company

In the Pennsylvania Historical Society the writer discovered something which has been unknown among the Brethren. Captain Hill during the Revolutionary days organized
a company in the lower District of Germantown for the
protection of the town. For the equipment and other expenses of the company a subscription was taken. Christopher Sower, one of the wealthiest men in Germantown, was
asked to head the list. What did this Dunker elder do?

[31] *Ibid.*, p. 329.
[32] *Pennsylvania Archives*, 1776-1777, Series 1, V, p. 766.

His name was right there heading the list and subscribing one pound and ten shillings. But Sower designated his gift by writing under his subscription, "Für die arme Weibir und Kinder (for the poor wives and children)."[33] No other subscriber made such a designation.

Sower's Poem

Nowhere has Christopher Sower better expressed what he thought about the results of war than in his poem printed in the almanac of 1778.

> Thou once so happy land, by God and nature blessed,
> And teeming with abundant joy,
> But now alas, by sin and wrong and vice depressed,
> Thou seem'st to wither and to die.
> O Land; what art thou now? A scene of dismal woes,
> To wake our pity and our tears;
> Oppressed by rapine, murder and a thousand foes,
> Unknown in by-gone years.
> And desolation, hunger, want stalk in the wake
> Of the avenger's bloody steel.
>
> Earth's pregnant fields lie waste, untouched by
> Who erst, full-peaceful turned the soil;
> The unwilling sword he grasps and dashes in the fight;
> What tears will flow from this turmoil.[34]

Maryland's Law More Liberal

Since there were a few Brethren churches in Maryland it is important to see how the members fared there. The record shows that on reading a petition from the Mennonites and German Baptists, July 6, 1776, the Maryland Convention took the following action:

Resolved that the several committees of observation may, in their discretion, prolong the time or take security for the payment of

---

[33] *Captain Ashmead papers,* Rolls of His Company, 1777-1778, p. 18. Original in the Pennsylvania Historical Society.
[34] *Der Hoch-Deutsch Americanische Calendar,* 1778, Germantown, Pennsylvania. The original copy is in the Cassel Library, Juniata College, Huntingdon, Pennsylvania.

any fine by them imposed for not enrolling in the militia, and may remit the whole or any part of the fines by them assessed; and it is recommended to the committee to pay particular attention, and to make a difference between such persons as may refuse from religious principles, or other motives.[35]

This law was more liberal toward nonresistant people than the Acts of Pennsylvania.

Virginia Laws Do Not Mention Brethren

The Virginia laws during the Revolution do not mention the Brethren. It may be assumed, however, that the few Brethren families who resided there were given consideration similar to that given to the Mennonites and Quakers. The laws were liberal at first, granting exemption from all militia duty for Mennonites and Quakers.[36] During the Revolutionary War, however, the committee of observation in Frederick County presented a petition to the Constitutional Convention on June 19, 1776, requesting that the Quakers and Mennonites be required to pay a sum of money to be assessed by the county court for failure to appear at the militia musters, that they should be drafted in the same proportion as other people, and that they should furnish substitutes if they refused to serve.[37] In October of the following year these suggestions were embodied into law.

THE BRETHREN AND THE STATE DURING THE COLONIAL PERIOD

It has already been stated that the Brethren with their strong peace convictions made no clear-cut statement that it was wrong for the state to use armed force. They paid their taxes, lived quiet peaceful lives and generally were loyal to the state. They protested and refused to obey the state only when laws conflicted with their religious principles. They cherished the freedom granted under the

[35] *The American Archives*, Series 4, VI, p. 1504.
[36] W. W. Hening, *Statutes at Large* (Virginia) 1619-1822, VIII, p. 242.
[37] *The American Archives*, Series 4, VI, p. 1579.

charter of William Penn and for more than twenty-five years lived sheltered lives under the Quaker government.

The leaders of Brethren thought in colonial America were Christopher Sower, Senior and Junior. These men held firmly to the principles of the church. They were not only publishers; they were reformers. And different from most Brethren of their time, they did not hesitate to engage in political controversy when principles were at stake. The Sowers probably engaged in more political activity than any other members of the Church of the Brethren during the first one hundred fifty years of Brethren history.

Christopher Sower, Sr., Worked to Keep the Quaker Government in Power

The political activity of Christopher Sower centered in efforts to keep the Quaker government in power. His purpose was to help preserve peace and the liberties of the Germans. The Quaker government came under severe criticism by various governors of Pennsylvania and many other colonists because of its refusal to sponsor military measures to protect the inhabitants from the Indians. On January 10, 1740, Governor Thomas addressed the Assembly of Pennsylvania in the following way:

I must lament the unhappy circumstances of a country, populous indeed, extensive in its trade, blessed with many natural advantages, and capable of defending itself; but from a religious principle of its Representatives against bearing of arms, subject to become the prey of the first invader, and more particularly of its powerful neighbors, who are known to be well armed, regular in their discipline, inured to fatigue, and from thence capable of making long marches, in alliance with many nations of Indians, and of a boundless ambition.[38]

Governor Thomas made a stirring appeal for the defense of the province. From this time (1740) until the Quakers lost control of the government in 1756, there was trouble

---
[38] *Votes of the Assembly,* Original Edition, III, p. 364.

between the governors and the Quaker Assembly. Many people wanted a change of government. There were loud demands for severe measures against the Indians. Benjamin Franklin and many other outstanding citizens were critical of the Quaker Assembly. How did the Quakers, who represented a minority in the province, keep a majority in the legislature for so long? This was accomplished through the aid of the Germans. And the publications of Christopher Sower were the leading influence among them. It is probably true that the German publisher held the balance of power at least for a few years.

Dr. William Smith, who later became provost of the University of Pennsylvania, estimated the inhabitants of Pennsylvania at 220,000, of whom one half were Germans, and about 40,000 Quakers.[39] Isaac Sharpless, Quaker historian, indicates that the Quakers stood in power through the influence of Christopher Sower and his publications.[40] William Beidelman wrote: "Sower's German paper was the only German newspaper circulated among the Germans for many years, and it controlled their political action throughout."[41] William Smith stated: "The Germans, who had hitherto been peaceful without meddling in elections, came down in shoals, and carried all before them. Near 1800 of them voted in the county of Philadelphia which threw the balance on the side of the Quakers; who having found out this secret, have ever since excluded all other persuasions from the Assembly, constantly calling in the Germans to their aid, by means of this printer."[42] This was the election of 1744.

One can easily see how criticism developed against the Germans and especially against Christopher Sower. The

[39] Isaac Sharpless, *Quakerism and Politics*, p. 131.
[40] *Ibid.*, p. 131.
[41] Beidleman, *The Story of the Pennsylvania Germans*, pp. 82-83.
[42] Cross, *An Answer to a Brief State*, p. 65. Rare Book Collection, Congressional Library, Washington, D.C.

people clamoring for a change of government saw that the Germans were standing in the way of that change. The people who wanted war with the Indians saw that the Germans were supporting the Quakers because they desired peace. More than that, the Germans had not been absorbed very well in colonial life. They held tenaciously to their German language and German papers. Consequently, some people began to say that a change for the better in Pennsylvania demanded that laws be passed restricting the power of the Germans. William Smith advocated, as a way of overcoming the Quaker control of the Assembly, the disfranchisement of all non-English-speaking people, prohibiting the German almanac of Christopher Sower, and making all Quakers ineligible for office by the imposition of an oath.[43]   Others urged the establishment of English schools for the Germans and the sending of English preachers to them. To this Sower replied:

Others hearing the charitable schools have something else in view, that the school masters should be made only of English students, the Germans fear that they might be forced hereafter to hear English ministers preach also and being ignorant in that language they would be obliged to sit in their meetings like geese and hold their tongues like sheep, for which reason they will rather avoid receiving such charitable gifts.[44]

The growing criticism of the Germans caused these people great concern. The Assembly in a message to the governor, September 29, 1755, recognized that there was a design in the "Proprietories and Governor to abridge the people of their privileges," and stated that the governor himself had said that there were too many Germans in Pennsylvania for a dependent colony.[45]   The election of 1755 was hotly contested. The question of a militia law

---

[43] Sharpless, *op. cit.,* p. 46.
[44] *Peter's Papers,* IV, 1755—Nov. 1757. Extracts from the German newspapers published by Christopher Sower. Article quoted is from his newspaper of Feb. 16, 1755. Rare book collection, Pennsylvania Historical Society, Philadelphia.
[45] *Colonial Records,* VI, p. 632.

was the campaign issue. The Brethren felt that their peace principle was at stake. Christopher Sower printed a Broadside entitled "A Very Urgent Warning and Admonition to the Free Inhabitants of Pennsylvania by one who is interested in and anxious about the welfare of the country."[46] This Broadside was distributed among the Germans. The English translation covers seventeen pages and therefore only a few quotations are given:

Dear Countrymen: Liberty is our natural right: a right the maintenance of which the God of nature and virtue requires of you, and He will help you that you may be able to maintain and keep it. Your rulers got their power to protect you, not to subjugate you. Your government is established in such a way that you have got to make half of the decrees and laws. And by nature and the maxims of a constitution you have the whole right of possession of your purse and all that is yours. You alone form the great counter-balance, and you have the power to influence the other part and to take care of it remaining in the proper limits. If it (the other part) transgresses its limits too far, it will be your fault. And it is up to you—through your assembly-men—to call to account the tools of subjugation and to punish them. And the assembly-men can prevent the remaining magistrates and 'super-authorities' from assisting the robbers and plunderers of men under the pretext of right and law. That you may be able to do this, it is necessary for you to exert the greatest caution in the election of your assembly-men. It is not sufficient that you elect an assembly-man, but you must elect honorable, unselfish, experienced people, of whom you know that they have already proved their faithfulness, that they will maintain your liberties and untiringly oppose the enemies of freedom.

The mere name of your Assembly will not protect you. Nero was an absolute and arbitrary emperor and did what he liked, although people under Nero had their governors, tribunes and other officials whom they elected themselves. France is having a parliament; nevertheless her king is a tyrant as great as any Turkish Sultan in the East. And you, too, gentlemen, may have an Assembly and yet, your rulers and government may become as arbitrary as those in

---

[46] The original German Broadside is in the Pennsylvania Historical Society. The translation was made from the original. This Broadside of 1755 was probably issued by Christopher Sower, Sr., but the son was sharing freely in the business at that time.

Constantinople, Rome, or Paris. This will be your miserable state, too, if you ever elected such men whose actions are determined by such maxims—if you promoted such people as I described to you previously, men who by presents or fear may or will be caused and corrupted to give up your rights and privileges.

What they do, what they negotiate, what alliances and intrigues they make—all this will be done at your expense; you will have to pay the great and costly bill, to pay the awful amounts of money— and in addition to this you will have to expect subjugation, violence and privation.

But! Fellow-brethren and fellow-subjects! You still have the power to escape these indescribable evils and misfortunes, by exerting a little carefulness, courage and resoluteness at the next election.

You may be English, German, Low Germans or Swedes! You may belong to the High Church, Presbyterians, Quakers or any other religious groups—by residing here, and by the laws of the country you are free people and no slaves. You are entitled to all the liberties of the English-born people, and have your share in the fundamental laws of the country. You are men who have sense. Let me exhort you again that you may use your common sense, that you may awaken and maintain your liberty. It is up to you alone; You may get rid of your present, evident misfortune. For you cannot expect any remedy for recovery and improvement of the state from the sources from which this sickness originates. Nor can we expect the conservation of our rights and liberties from people who got their offices, their honor, their power, their fortune and their riches from those who are only anxious to destroy such rights and liberties. For people with such pens would like to have your liberties destroyed and would like to become the chief tools of the destruction of your rights.[47]

The Germans responded to this appeal and came to the polls in great numbers. The Quakers won twenty-eight out of thirty-six Assembly seats. However, in the spring of 1756 the governor declared war against the French and Indians, and the Quakers resigned their seats. This was the end of Quaker control, and from this time on the Brethren had to guard their rights increasingly. Christopher Sower, Jr., issued a remarkable Broadside, September 18,

---

[47] *Ibid.*

1765, calling attention to the peaceful government the Germans previously enjoyed, urging the people to cling fast to their precious liberties and to vote for assemblymen who would preserve their privileges.[48] He, like his father, took an interest in political outcomes.

The Oath of Allegiance

It has been noted that the oath of allegiance during the Revolutionary War was aimed directly at the non-associators. This act represented the culmination of the developing hostility toward the nonresistant peoples. The assemblymen knew that the Quakers, Dunkers and Mennonites did not believe in taking the oath. The Brethren stood strongly against it. The Annual Conference of 1778 said that the Brethren who had taken the attest "should recall it before a justice, and give up their certificate, and apologize to their churches, and truly repent for their error."[49]

The next year the Annual Conference considered the oath again and made the following statement:

> On account of taking the attest, it has been concluded in unison as follows: Inasmuch as it is the Lord our God who establishes kings and removes kings, and ordains rulers according to his own good pleasure, and we cannot know whether God has rejected the king and chosen the state, while the king had the government; therefore we could not, with a good conscience, repudiate the king and give allegiance to the state.[50]

The declaration is interesting not only regarding the oath but more especially because it shows the neutrality of the Brethren during the Revolutionary War. Upon arriving in this country they had made a declaration of loyalty to the king. Now they could not reject the king because they did not know which government represented the will of God. They would wait and see.

---

[48] The original German Broadside is in the Pennsylvania Historical Society.
[49] *Annual Meeting Minutes, 1778-1909*, p. 5.
[50] *Ibid.*, pp. 5-6.

The Overruling of the Conscience Is Wrong

One of the most significant declarations of the Brethren during a war period was made by the Annual Conference of 1781. It shows that the Brethren felt it was wrong to pay money to hire substitutes, that at no time should money for this purpose be given voluntarily, but under compulsion it did not seem to them so sinful. They felt the responsibility was on the government then. The Brethren were advised to pay the war taxes in order to avoid offense, but the consciences of those who could not pay them were to be respected. They said, "We deem the overruling of the conscience as wrong."[51]

The Persecution of the Brethren

The money required for war, taxes and substitutes was relatively insignificant in consequence compared to the oath of allegiance and the act granting the right to seize property. Many Brethren lost their property. Some were robbed or beaten, and a few were killed. The Brethren answered persecution as they had done formerly. They fled from it. Many of them moved southward and westward. Some who remained in Pennsylvania moved to new counties.

Christopher Sower, Jr., in the Hands of the Law

The great Dunker publisher was not to escape the consequences of war. He had been at the center of strong political conflicts. He had been fearless in his writings. Naturally, he had a number of enemies. During the Revolutionary War he did not declare himself in opposition to England. Professor Seidensticker of the University of Pennsylvania says that "he was not a Tory and had no connections with the enemy but his principles were against

[51] *Ibid.*, p. 7.

weapons and war."[52] In another work Seidensticker says of Sower: "He did not espouse the cause of England, but on the other hand he felt no love for the violent resistance of the patriots. The calamities that followed in the wake of war, the overthrowing of all past institutions, the uncertainty and want of confidence felt everywhere, the stagnation of trade, the sufferings and misery of the people, were looked upon by him as the scourge with which God chastised the people for their many transgressions."[53] It seems that Sower and the Brethren wished to remain neutral. It is probable that they naturally hesitated to see a well-established government overthrown, under which they had had liberty, and the reigns of government given to their English neighbors who were hostile toward them. But there is no evidence that the Brethren were Tories. They wanted peace and waited for the will of God, as they thought, to work things out.

The story of what happened to Christopher Sower comes from Sower himself. The following is Sower's own account which the writer copied verbatim from the original manuscript:

Having heard that a number of Quakers were banished and carried away to Virginia and being informed that there was yet some hundreds of substantial inhabitants on the list to be taken up and secured amongst which my name also was put down and as there was already a beginning made and some of the Millers and on wisehecon were actually taken from their families I considered what I could do knowing Germantown would always be a disturbed place English and Americans would continually march through it for and backward and having three of my children already living in Philadelphia I bethought myself to go there to live in peace and accordingly went to Philadelphia on the 19th day of October 1777 (Many

---

[52] Address delivered in German by Professor Seidensticker of the University of Pennsylvania before the Pioneer Verein Club of Philadelphia, May 26, 1881. Original copy in the Cassel Library, Juniata College, Huntingdon, Pennsylvania.

[53] Seidensticker, *German Pioneers in Pennsylvania*, pp. 73-83. A book in pen and ink in the Germantown Historical Society.

months before that act was made which forbad to go to Philadelphia) and so I lived there quiet and peasible till 23rd Day of May
1778 when I went back to Germantown and was in my house that
night and the next day till 10 o'clock at night when a strong Party
of Captain McClean's Company surrounded my House and fetched
me out of my bed it being a dark night and they lead me through the
Indian corn fields, when I could not come along so fast as they
wanted me to go they frequently stuck me in the back with their
bayonets and they brought me to Bastian Miller's Barn where they
kept me till next morning. Then they stripped me naked to the
skin and gave me an old shirt and breeches so much torn that I
could barely cover my nakedness. Then cut my beard and hair and
painted me with oil colours, red and black, and so led me along
barefooted and bareheaded in a very hot sunshining day. A friend
of mine seeing me in that condition asked them whether they would
not take the shoes from me if he would give me a pair. The officer
gave his word they should not be taken from me if he would give
me a pair, and so he took the shoes from his feet and the hat from
his head and gave them to me but after we had marched 6 miles a
soldier came and demanded my shoes and took them and gave me
his old slabs which wounded my feet very much. On the 26th at 9
o'clock I arrived at the Camp and was sent to the Provo. My accusation in the Mittimus was "an oppressor of the Righteous and a
spy." On the 27th in the morning God moved the heart of the most
generous General Muhlenberg to come to me and inquire into my
affairs and promised that he would speak to General Washington
and procure for me a hearing and the next day sent me word that I
should make a petition to General Washington, which I did and
through the good hand of Providence and the faithful assistance of
said General Muhlenberg I was permitted to go out of the Provo on
the 29th Day of May. But I was not free it being against my conscience to take the Oath to the States I was not permitted to go
home to Germantown as appears by the following pass. Viz. "Permit the Bearer hereof Mr. Sower to pass from hence to Methatchey
not to return to Germantown during the stay of the enemy in this
state, he behaving as becometh. Given under my hand at the orderly office this thirtieth day of May 1778.

Nich-Gilman Ass. Adj't. Gen.

So I went to Methatchey and staid there until the 23rd of June when
I returned to Germantown and there lived quiet till the 27th of

July when Colonel Smith and Colonel Thompson came to my house and asked me whether I had entered special Bail at the Supreme Court at Lancaster. I told them "No." "Why not?" Said they. "Because I had no notice." "That cannot be," said Thompson, "it was in the newspapers and handbills." I told them I had at that time been in the Provo at Methatchey and had seen none of those papers and nobody had told me of it till after the time was expired. "Have you taken the Oath to the States?" "No"! "Why not?" "Was you so attached to the King?" "No. It was not the attachment to the King but as you have in your Act that they that do not take that oath shall not have the right to buy nor sell and as I find in the Book of Revelation that such a time will come, when such a mark would be given, so I could not take that oath while it stood on that condition." "But you went to the English in Philadelphia," said Smith. I said, "Do you know why?" "No," said he, "nor I don't want to know." Then they told me that they were come to take an Inventory of my Personal Estate and sell it and to rent out my Real Estate. I told them I would submit to all that the Lord permitted them to do, and so Smith stood guard that I might not put anything out of the way and Thompson went out to get appraisers and a clerk and so they began to appraise. I then begged that they should let me keep my bed but Smith gave for answer they had no right to let me have anything besides my clothes and provisions (which last they did not abide by) for when they found a barrel of beef they took it down altho it was provision). I then begged for a few medicines which I had put by for my family's use as they were chiefly of my and my father's preparation and nobody else knew what they were. But Smith said, "Medicines are very valuable, they must be sold." Then I begged for nothing more but my spectacles which was granted. On the 28th they told me that I must quit the house for they must rent it out and so I moved out on the 30th of July. Then they proceeded to sell my effects but before the sale came on my son Daniel endeavored to stop it and applied to Thomas Mattock and asked him whether his father should not have a hearing. "Yes, but we must sell his effects first." He then applied to Mr. Lewis to stop the sale till next court, who endeavored to do it, but they had invented a lie that I or some of my people had secretly crept into the house and had destroyed all the New Testaments and if the sale did not go on all would be destroyed before the said court came on, and so they passed on with the sale of my Personal Estate and rented out my houses and lands for one year and then sold them also contrary to the concession of the Convention in the case of Forfeited Estates that no estate could be sold before the youngest son is of age and so they have not only broken the Testimental rule in selling my Estate but have also published me in almost all newspapers as a Traitor without any cause and without ever giving me a hearing or trial. Although I never was gone a mile from my place of abode and their own attorney Mr. Bradford has himself declared to a friend of mine that "if I had not forfeited my life I had also not forfeited my Estate for they had no more right to my Estate than to my life.[54]

The unfortunate thing was that Christopher Sower's three sons, who were reared in the culture of Philadelphia, did not espouse the cause of their father.   Christopher the Third and Peter Sower aligned themselves with the British when the latter occupied Philadelphia.   When the father went to live with his children through the winter, he was suspected as being a friend of the British.   There were two actions against Sower.   The first one was military when he was taken by officers of the army, confined for six days, presumably at Valley Forge, and released through the intercession of General Muhlenberg with George Washington.   The second was a civil action on the part of the government of Pennsylvania on the charge that Sower was guilty of treason.   The name of Christopher Sower appears in the Pennsylvania archives under the heading, "Persons Gone With Ye Enemy."[55]   A notice was posted by the government that the persons charged with treason had to appear before a justice of the peace by a certain time and give an account.   Sower did not appear because he never saw the notice.   He was held a captive at Valley Forge during the time that he could have cleared himself with the law.   When released by the army officials his property was confiscated.   His personal property was sold at public auction on August 15, 24 and 28, 1778, and his real estate was

---

[54] The original manuscript is in the Cassel Collection, Juniata College, Huntingdon, Pennsylvania.
[55] *Pennsylvania Archives*, Series 6, XIII, p. 546.

sold at the Court House, Germantown, September 18, 1779. The total value of his property was estimated at one hundred fifty thousand dollars.

Sower could have stopped these sales for they were illegal. According to the Pennsylvania law for the sale of confiscated property the youngest son should have been twenty-one. This was not the case. Neither was there a trial to prove Sower's guilt. The publisher remained true to his convictions and resigned to these injustices. His printing press and all of his property were taken. Sower never recovered from this blow. He lived the rest of his life in retirement, a crushed man. He could endure his losses better than to have his name put down as a traitor. He felt that he had done nothing to justify this accusation. Consequently he brought three queries to the Annual Conference of 1780:

As there are debts yet due on Bonds, notes and book debts, who has the best Right to demand them of the people, or the State?

If a man is openly declared a Traitor without a cause, without hearing or trial, when he was not absent and might have been heard, is it just to let him forever lie under that reproach?

Is it right that Colonel Smith be permitted to carry on a lawsuit against my son Daniel and to pocket 50 pounds in hard money to himself when he has paid the State (if he ever has) with a Trifle of Continental?[56]

The answer of the Brethren was not published. Sower died August 26, 1784, at the age of 63 years.

The Effect of Persecution Upon the Church of the Brethren

The loss of the Sower publications took from the Dunkers the leading educational influence among them. The hostility under which these people had lived caused them to develop a greater exclusiveness. The doctrine of nonconformity to the world gripped the church. A special

---

[56] Copied from the original queries in the Cassel Library, Juniata College, Huntingdon, Pennsylvania.

type of dress as a mark of separateness from the world was established. The Revolutionary War settled the matter that this was going to be an English-speaking country. The Brethren saw that an adjustment in language would be necessary through the years. They would be governed, too, by their English neighbors, some of whom were critical of them. The effect of this whole situation was to cause great numbers of the Brethren to move into states to the south and west. And in emigration the Brethren became a frontier people without educational advantages. The Revolutionary War probably set the Church of the Brethren back seventy-five years.

SUMMARY

Religious liberty was granted to the settlers in colonial Pennsylvania through Penn's "Charter of Privileges" of 1701. The Brethren lived for many years under the protection of the Quaker government. They were a German language people living mostly in Pennsylvania. Christopher Sower, Senior and Junior, were the most outstanding leaders of thought among the Brethren.

Attitude of the Brethren Toward War

Robert Proud, the historian, stated that the Brethren thought "it not becoming a follower of Jesus Christ to bear arms." Christopher Sower, Sr., wrote against war and strongly advocated peace with the Indians. He based his peace convictions on the teachings of Jesus. Sower worked to keep the Quakers in power in Pennsylvania because he thought they would preserve the liberties of the people and would not go to war with the Indians. U. J. Jones, another historian, described the sufferings of Brethren at the hands of the Indians and showed that they practiced nonresistance. The Annual Conference of the church in its statement of 1785 placed the will of God above loyalty to the state and refused to permit church members to go to the muster grounds. The church was definitely opposed to participation in war and war activities.

How Brethren Fared During the Revolution

The Brethren were called non-associators by those who organized for the defense of the country. At the outset of the Revolution, the Assembly of Pennsylvania asked the people of the province to have a "brotherly regard" toward those conscientiously opposed to war. It was not long, however, until criticism developed toward the non-associators. Many people felt that the nonresistant inhabitants of Pennsylvania were not doing their share financially toward the support of the war. Consequently, in lieu of military service, they were required to pay an equivalent to the time spent by associators in military practices. The peace people were not exempted from supporting the war economically. All arms were collected from non-associators. In a strong spirit of patriotism the Oath of Allegiance was passed, June 13, 1777. This was aimed directly at non-associators. Since the Brethren did not believe in taking the oath, it worked a great hardship upon them. A little later the Council of Safety ordered the confiscation of personal estates and effects of those who had aided the enemy. The Brethren aimed to be neutral but because they would not fight for the colonies, they were misunderstood. Many of them lost their property, and some of them were persecuted. Christopher Sower, Jr., the great Dunker printer, suffered humiliation, the loss of his printing press and all of his property. With the destruction of the Sower press, the greatest educational light among the Brethren was gone. The church members fled from the effects of the oath and seizure laws and scattered to the south and west.

CHAPTER IV

THE PERIOD BETWEEN THE REVOLUTIONARY AND CIVIL WARS

THE PERIOD OF EXPANSION AND ECLIPSE (1777-1851)

The years from the enactment of the Oath Law in 1777 to the revival of printing in 1851 represent the eclipse of the church. A large part of the church's membership moved into the wilderness. Most of the frontier communities did not have schools. The struggle was for subsistence rather than for culture. Opposition to education and to Sunday schools developed among the Brethren. They opposed the inroads of cultural influences from the outside. The aggressiveness found among leading Brethren in earlier days was gone. The church membership did not vote or hold political offices. They lived to themselves and formed communities of their own. The members were taught to keep themselves separate from the world. Much of the preaching was doctrinal. The church became somewhat legalistic in its requirements for members to conform to the church's rules and practices.

This was also a period of expansion. By 1790 members were scattered from Germantown to Fayette County, Pennsylvania, and south through Maryland, Virginia, Tennessee, and the Carolinas. The Brethren reached Ohio by 1793, Missouri by 1795, Indiana and Illinois by 1809. Reaching on farther west the Brethren touched the Pacific Coast by 1850. Considering the new churches established, the Brethren communities developed and the territory covered, the geographic groundwork was laid for the future Church of the Brethren.

The Revival of Printing and the New Enlightenment

On April 1, 1851, the "Gospel Visitor" appeared, edited by Henry Kurtz. Kurtz had been a minister in the Lutheran Church and after uniting with the Church of the Brethren soon saw the necessity for a church paper. The paper started with some misgivings on the part of many church members but it grew in circulation and influence. In 1856 James Quinter became associate editor. The "Gospel Visitor" brought church news into the widely scattered Brethren communities and helped to keep the church united. It gradually developed interest in Sunday schools and missions. The Annual Conference of 1857 gave permission to have Sunday schools. In 1861 the first Brethren educational institutions were started. From that time on there was a rapid increase in education. The beginning of interest in missions started around this same time. The church had begun to look out of the wilderness.

The reasons for the change within the church, it seems to the writer, are two: first, the influence of more aggressive leadership in the church, centering in the revival of printing; and second, the influence of the Industrial Revolution. The Industrial Revolution broke down community barriers. The outside world invaded Brethren homes. Church members saw their need of education. When the Civil War broke upon the Church of the Brethren, the denomination had an influential church paper which was a great factor in unifying the church, and constructive leadership was creating a vital interest in education and missions.

The Church of the Brethren and Slavery

One of the most serious problems of the period under consideration for the American people was that of slavery. The attitude of the Brethren toward slavery was significant, not only as revealing the point of view of this denomination, but because it had a direct bearing on the situation faced by the Brethren during the Civil War. The Brethren were an antislavery people. They maintained a consistent record in opposition to slavery. The two Christopher Sowers spoke out against it. The Annual Conference of 1797 said "that no brother or sister should have negroes as slaves."[1] The Annual Conference of 1812 called the slave trade "a most grievous evil," that "should be abolished as soon as possible,"[2] while the Conference of the following year claimed that slavery made "merchandise of souls of men."[3] The Brethren in 1835 proclaimed that color should make no difference in receiving members into the church,[4] and in 1853 declared again in Annual Conference that members of the church should have "nothing at all to do with slavery in no shape or form whatever."[5] The records indicate that the Brethren had some difficulty with a few members holding slaves. The church in 1857 decided that members holding slaves should be visited, asked to liberate them, but if unwilling "they should be dealt with according to the Gospel manner of dealing with all gross transgressions."[6] The Church of the Brethren made at least a dozen general pronouncements against slavery prior to the Civil War. The decisions seemed to be stronger the nearer the Civil War approached.

THE POSITION OF THE CHURCH ON WAR

The persecution suffered and the scattering of the Brethren into many states of the Union made no difference in the church's attitude toward war. The only source of information regarding the Brethren's peace convictions during this period is the records of the Annual Conferences. The decis-

---

[1] *Minutes of the Annual Meetings, 1778-1909*, pp. 18-19.
[2] *Ibid.*, p. 30.
[3] *Ibid.*, p. 31.
[4] *Ibid.*, p. 58.
[5] *Ibid.*, p. 136
[6] *Ibid.*, p. 163.

ions of 1778, 1779, 1781 and 1785 have already been noted. In 1790 the Annual Conference stated:

We believe and confess that Christ has forbidden to his followers the swearing of oaths and partaking of war. Hence we must keep to his word and truth, and withdraw ourselves from every brother that returns again to swearing and war. It is impossible for us to break the bread of communion with such a brother, who pretends the higher powers were requiring such of him. For they cannot compel us, if they would, because we are to obey God rather than men. But now, thanks to God, we have such a government that will not require of us what is against our conscience.[7]

The record is clear that shortly after the Revolutionary War members who favored war or took part in its activities were seriously disciplined by the church.

The war with England from 1812 to 1815, sometimes called the Second War for Independence, found the Brethren true to their peace convictions. The church in 1815 decided to help pay the fines of those who were not financially able:

It has been discussed by us concerning the war matter, and it is agreed by all the brethren that a brother's sons who consider themselves according to the teaching of the brethren, "defenseless," and prove themselves to be such and wish to obey the teachings of the brethren; when these shall be hard pressed with the payment of fines they shall be assisted by the brethren according to the teaching of the apostle; let us bear the burden of another; thus you will fulfill the law of Jesus Christ.[8]

The attitude of the Church of the Brethren at this time toward military training is significant. A query came to the Annual Conference of 1817 asking "whether Brethren or their children may go on the muster ground or not." The Brethren made the following answer:

Whether brethren or their children may go to the muster ground or not?

The counsel was, that no member may go there, and prevent also

---

[7] *Ibid.*, p. 14.
[8] *Ibid.*, p. 40.

their children from going on that ground, and not willingly permit it to them as long as they are under the parental authority; should a brother do so, he could not be in full fellowship with the church; for the Savior said to Peter, "Put up thy sword into his place; for all they that take the sword, shall perish with the sword.[9]

Going on the muster grounds removed a member from full fellowship with the church. The decision was severe but it must be understood that the church at that time was rather legalistic and involvement in war activities represented a serious problem for the Brethren.

The Annual Conference of 1822 asked that no brother "take the liberty to go on the muster-ground or take part in the festivities of Independence Day."[10] In 1835 the decision was made again that members were not allowed to go to muster and drill.[11] The following year it was interpreted that a brother would have no gospel right to take money "which he had acquired as a soldier of war."[12] The war with Mexico in 1845 brought from the Brethren another statement of their doctrine of nonresistance:

In regard to our being altogether defenseless, not to withstand the evil, but overcome evil with good,

Considered, that the nearer we follow the bright example of the Lamb of God, who willingly suffered the cross, and prayed for his enemies; who, though heir of all things, had on earth not where to lay his head—the more we shall fulfill our high calling and obtain grace to deny ourselves for Christ's and his gospel's sake, even to the loss of our property, our liberty and our lives.[13]

The Annual Conference of 1855 answered the difficult question, "Has a brother a right to defend himself with a deadly weapon at the appearance of being in danger?" This question dealt with the individual member's right to use weapons of war in self-defense. The decision was that

---

[9] *Ibid.*, pp. 40-41.
[10] *Revised Minutes of the Annual Meetings of the German Baptist Brethren,* p. 133.
[11] *Minutes of the Annual Meetings, 1778-1909,* p. 59.
[12] *Ibid.*, p. 62.
[13] *Ibid.*, p. 85.

"he hath not, inasmuch as the Savior says to Peter: 'put up thy sword into his place; for all they that take the sword shall perish with the sword!'"[14]

As the Civil War was approaching the problems became more severe for the church. A query was brought to the Annual Conference of 1859 which presented a very complex problem. Brethren were paying fines to be free from military drill and in some states the fines were high. In fact, there were places where the military musters were kept up largely through fines. Some Brethren wondered whether it would be preferable to muster a few times rather than pay the money which was keeping up the military system. It was the problem of whether it was more Christian to give limited participation in military drill than to pay extra taxes which perpetuated the military. The Brethren were strongly opposed to personal participation in the military but were not as definite in their opposition to taxes for the purpose of war. They seemed to feel that when fines and taxes were imposed upon them by the government, it was the nation's responsibility. Hence the Brethren answered the above problem by saying that it would not be better to muster a few times rather than pay fines because they said the "Savior teaches nonresistance in the Gospel, throughout. And when we go to musters we there learn the art of war, and the most appropriate method of shedding our fellow-creatures' blood."[15]

The Brethren during this period had no peace committee and no vigorous peace education program. There were no united efforts of the church to prevent the coming of war. War was wrong for them because Christ taught against it. But they had not clearly interpreted the rightness or wrongness of the government to wage war.

---

[14] *Ibid.*, p. 148.
[15] *Ibid.*, p. 187.

The Church of the Brethren and the State

Why the Brethren Did Not Vote

Following the experiences of the Revolutionary War there were seventy-five years in which the Brethren did little voting. This can be understood in terms of the persecutions inflicted upon them by the government and the fact that the Brethren interpreted voting as having a relationship to war. The decision of the Annual Conference of 1813 makes this clear:

Inasmuch as the appearance of the times into which we have come are grievous (it was the time of war with England), and inasmuch as party spirit has risen so high in the kingdoms of this world that men, and even the heads of government are among themselves at variance, therefore it has been viewed in union, that it would be much better if no votes were given in at elections for such officers (by the brethren); for so long as there is such division of parties, we make ourselves suspicious and unpropitious on the one side, on whatever side we may vote. Thereby every one that desires to be defenseless (or nonresistant) may readily see what might be best (for him to do). Moreover, is (not only) our land and (but also) almost all empires engaged in war (in Europe especially); hence it was considered to be best to give in no vote, else we might, perhaps, assist in electing such that would afterward oppress us with war. To pray diligently for our government we believe to be our duty, and to call upon the Lord we think will be most acceptable.[16]

In 1841 the Annual Conference asked the members of the church not to attend political meetings.[17]

About 1850 the church's point of view regarding voting and holding office began to change. The Annual Conference of 1850 did not directly refuse Brethren the opportunity to hold "worldly offices" but when called upon to do so they were to lay the matter before the church for counsel.[18] In 1852 the church declared that "if they (Brethren) give in their vote, they should do it in a quiet and peaceable

---

[16] *Ibid.*, p. 32.
[17] *Ibid.*, p. 73.
[18] *Ibid.*, p. 115.

manner, without taking part in electioneering, and return immediately from the ground; that Brethren should hold no office under the civil government that would cause them to betray their faith."[19]   While some Brethren voted prior to the Civil War, the members as a whole did not. The church practiced the doctrine of nonconformity to the world.

Brethren Held Civil Laws Not Always of God

The fact that the practices of the Church of the Brethren were based upon the New Testament, and that the church accepted the teachings of Jesus on peace, made it imperative for the Brethren to define clearly their attitude toward civil law. Several scriptural passages presented a great deal of difficulty and were the center of much discussion. The first verse of Romans 13 was often quoted:

> Let every soul be subject unto the higher powers. For there is no power but of God: the powers that be are ordained of God.

The 13th and 14th verses of the second chapter of 1 Peter were likewise often repeated:

> Submit yourselves to every ordinance of man for the Lord's sake: Whether it be to the king, as supreme; or unto governors, or unto them that are sent by him for the punishment of evildoers, and for the praise of them that do well.

Some Brethren were confused. They wanted to interpret the New Testament literally but how could civil laws be ordained of God when they frequently conflicted with the teachings of Jesus on peace? The church paper discussed this problem time and time again. In 1859, Elder James Quinter, one of the great thinkers and leaders of Brethren thought, gave an interpretation which was generally accepted. He held that the principle of civil government is ordained of God, but that not all civil laws are thus ordained. Because of its importance a section of his article is quoted:

---

[19] *Ibid.*, p. 129.

From such texts of scripture as the above, it is inferred by some that all civil authority is derived from God, and that all the laws of civil government are binding upon men. We cannot accept of this inference as a correct one. In what sense then, and how far, are the ordinances of civil authority, of God, and binding upon men? God is not only supreme in authority, but from him proceeded the first commandment given to mankind. He is said to be "not the author of confusion, but of peace." He governs the world by laws—laws physical and moral. And as the nature of men is such, and their relations to one another are such, that they cannot live in society without laws or rules and regulations; they therefore find it necessary to adopt some form of government and system of laws. These laws when adopted by a community to regulate their conduct, and to secure their civil rights, are called the municipal or civil laws. And in enacting such laws, men have a precedent in God's dealings with them, and an example in his manner of governing them. And not only so but as God delights in the happiness and prosperity of his creatures, and as wholesome laws and as wise and prudent regulations are conducive to human happiness and prosperity, it is God's will that men should adopt whatever rules will be most conducive to their welfare. Hence it may be said with propriety, that "the powers that be are ordained of God." That is, the principle of civil government is ordained of God, and is in harmony with his own manner of proceeding with his creatures.

But it does not therefore follow that all laws enacted by rulers and governors are right, and must be obeyed. If this should be admitted, we would have the kingdom of God divided against itself, and might then justly fear its stability. Ambitious and wicked men have abused their authority, and made laws and regulations subversive of human rights, and destructive of human happiness. And obeying such laws, in many cases, would have been obeying Satan rather than God; where this would be the case, it is our duty to disobey such laws.[20]

John Kline's Conception of Patriotism

Probably the most outstanding leader of the Church of the Brethren during the Civil War period was Elder John Kline of Virginia. In his diary of February 22, 1849, he

---

[20] *The Gospel Visitor* (Bound Volume), Dec. 1859, No. 12, IX, pp. 368-369.

gave his interpretation of patriotism, which represented the best of Brethren thought:

> Hear the distant report of cannon in commemoration of the birth of George Washington, which is said to have occurred on the twenty-second day of February, 1732. It is presumable that those who find pleasure in public demonstrations of this sort are moved by what they regard as patriotic feelings and principles. Let their motives and enjoyments spring from what they may, they have a lawful right to celebrate the anniversary of his birth in any civil way they may choose. But I have a somewhat higher conception of true patriotism than can be represented by the firing of guns which give forth nothing but meaningless sound. I am glad, however, that these guns report harmless sound, and nothing more. If some public speakers would do the same, it might be better for both them and their hearers. My highest conception of patriotism is found in the man who loves the Lord his God with all his heart and his neighbor as himself. Out of these affections spring the subordinate love for one's country; love truly virtuous for one's companion and children, relatives and friends; and in its most comprehensive sense takes in the whole human family. Were this love universal, the word patriotism, and its specific sense, meaning such a love for one's country as makes its possessors ready and willing to take up arms in its defense, might be appropriately expunged from every national vocabulary.[21]

Laws Affecting the Brethren

In considering the relation of the Church of the Brethren to the state in the period under review, it is important to notice whether there were any safeguards for nonresistant people represented in legislation. Since Pennsylvania remained the state with the most Brethren members, the laws enacted there are significant for this study. The Constitution of 1776, which passed the Pennsylvania Convention on the 28th of September, renewed the grant of religious freedom and guaranteed civil rights to all citizens who acknowledged "the Being of a God."[22] One may seri-

---

[21] Benjamin Funk, *Life of John Kline*, p. 246.
[22] *Pennsylvania Archives*, Series 1, XII, Section 2, Chap. 1, p. 53.

ously question whether the Oath Law was not out of harmony with the spirit and purpose of the constitution. The constitution of 1790 was about the same as that of 1776. It guaranteed freedom of worship, but made the significant pronouncement "that no person who acknowledges the being of a God and a future state of rewards and punishments, shall, on account of his religious sentiments, be disqualified to hold office or place of trust or profit under this Commonwealth."[23] According to this law a person's religious belief was not allowed to interfere with his right to hold office and to exercise leadership.

The Bill of Rights which became a part of the United States Constitution on December 15, 1791, was the greatest guarantee of freedom to nonresistant and nonconformist people. The Bill of Rights caused great rejoicing among the Brethren. They have regarded it through the years as a great protection to their religious rights. Because of its significance it is quoted as follows:

Congress shall make no law respecting an establishment of religion, or prohibiting the free exercise thereof; or abridging the freedom of speech, or of the press, or the right of the people peaceably to assemble, and to petition the government for a redress of grievances.[24]

But how far was the principle of religious freedom applied to those who opposed military training and war on religious grounds? The Pennsylvania Constitution of 1838 stated that "those who conscientiously scruple to bear arms, shall not be compelled to do so, but shall pay an equivalent for personal service."[25] The Pennsylvania Brethren faced the Civil War knowing that they would be exempted from military service but would have to pay an equivalent.

A canvass of state constitutions shows that equivalents

---

[23] *Pennsylvania Archives*, Series 1, XII, Article IX, Section 4, p. 22.
[24] *Bill of Rights*, First Amendment to the Constitution of the United States.
[25] *Pennsylvania Archives*, Series 4, VI, Article VI, Section 11, p. 511.

for personal service in the militia were often required by other states. The following states besides Pennsylvania provided through their constitutions for exemption from militia service upon the payment of some equivalent: Indiana, Iowa, Illinois, Kansas, Kentucky, Alabama, and Texas.[26] The provision in the Indiana constitution of 1851 is typical. Article XII, section 6, says,

No person conscientiously opposed to bearing arms shall be compelled to do militia duty; but such person shall pay an equivalent for exemption; the amount to be prescribed by law.[27]

The constitutions of Minnesota, New York, Ohio, Vermont, Mississippi, Tennessee, and Virginia placed the question of the militia in the hands of the legislature.[28] The Michigan state constitution of 1850 provided for exemption "upon such conditions as shall be prescribed by law."[29]

The constitutions of Arkansas, Florida, Georgia, Louisiana, North Carolina, South Carolina, and Wisconsin made no provision at all for those opposed to military service.[30] Maryland's constitution of 1864 allowed exceptions from military service on producing to the proper authorities satisfactory proof of conscientious objection to war but in earlier constitutions had only provided that

Quakers, Menonists, Tunkers, or Nicolites, or New Quakers, and who shall be conscientiously scrupulous of taking an oath on any occasion might make affirmation instead.[31]

Summary

The persecutions of the Revolutionary War caused the Brethren to move into many states and become a frontier people without educational advantages. A new enlighten-

---

[26] Francis Newton Thorpe, *The Federal and State Constitutions*, II, pp. 1089, 1132, 1004, 1190; III, p. 1307; I, p. 105; VI, p. 3559.
[27] *Ibid.*, II, p. 1089.
[28] *Ibid.*, IV, pp. 2017; V, pp. 2671, 2927; VI, p. 3768; IV, p. 2059; VI, p. 3437; VII, p. 3845.
[29] *Ibid.*, IV, p. 1966.
[30] *Ibid.*, I, p. 280; II, pp. 674, 791; III, p. 1421; V, p. 2791; VI, p. 3263; VII, pp. 4094-4095.
[31] *Ibid.*, III, pp. 1702, 1739-1740, 1773-1774.

ment came with the revival of printing in 1851 under
Henry Kurtz. With the printing press came a new interest in education and missions. The Brethren opposed
slavery on Biblical grounds and did not allow members
to own slaves. The Brethren during this period reaffirmed
their conviction that war was contrary to the teachings
of Jesus and refused to allow members to take part in muster practices. Whether it was right or wrong for Brethren
to pay taxes and fines which helped to support the military
system, was not clearly defined. The Brethren did not vote
very much before 1850 because they felt that voting would
be an indirect involvement in war. After 1850 the church
began to change its point of view regarding voting but
the members generally did not go to the polls until some
years later. The perplexing question regarding civil laws
being ordained of God was interpreted by James Quinter
in a satisfactory way. He said that the principle and necessity of civil government are ordained of God, but civil laws
may or may not represent God's will. John Kline interpreted patriotism in its higher aspects as love for God,
neighbor, family, friends and the whole human family.
The laws affecting the Brethren showed an increased recognition of the principle of religious freedom as represented
in the Bill of Rights, but did not clearly define what religious
freedom meant for minority groups that opposed war on
religious grounds. At least eight states granted exemption
from military service upon the payment of an equivalent.
An almost equal number placed the whole matter in the
hands of the legislature. Other constitutions were silent
on the matter. The Church of the Brethren as a religious
minority group, widely scattered over the United States,
ready to suffer rather than to fight, faced the approaching
Civil War with an uncertain status under the law.

Chapter V

THE POSITION OF THE CHURCH OF THE BRETHREN DURING THE CIVIL WAR

The Brethren as an antislavery people were located both in the North and in the South. While Pennsylvania contained more Brethren than any other state, there were many members in Virginia, some in Tennessee and the Carolinas, and still many others in the central and far western states. In spite of the scattered condition of the church, the "Gospel Visitor" as the church paper and the Annual Conferences kept the brotherhood united in ideals and fellowship. The three most outstanding men during the Civil War in representing the church in its relationships to the government were John Kline of Rockingham County, Virginia, B. F. Moomaw of near Roanoke, Virginia, and D. P. Sayler of Frederick County, Maryland.

The Brethren Opposed to Secession

It is clear that the Brethren were opposed to secession. John Kline in his diary of January 1, 1861, wrote:

The year opens with dark and lowering clouds on our national horizon. I feel a deep interest in the peace and prosperity of our country; but in my view both are sorely threatened now. Secession is the cry further south; and I greatly fear its poisonous breath is being wafted northward towards Virginia on the wings of fanatical discontent. A move is clearly on hand for holding a convention at Richmond, Virginia; and while its advocates publicly deny the charge, I, for one, feel sure that it signals the separation of our beloved old State from the family in which she has long lived and been happy. The perishable things of earth distress me not, only in so far as they affect the imperishable. Secession means war and war means tears and ashes and blood. It means bonds and imprisonments, and perhaps even death to many in our beloved Brotherhood, who, I have the confidence to believe, will die, rather than disobey God by taking up arms.[1]

On January 30, 1861, John Kline, representing the Church of the Brethren, wrote to Governor John Letcher, of Virginia, and opposed the breaking up of the Union. He said:

The General Government of the United States of America, constituted upon an inseparable union of the several states, has proved itself to be of incalculable worth to its citizens and the world, and therefore we, as a church and people, are heart and soul opposed to any move which looks toward its dismemberment.[2]

Then, again on February 1, 1861, John Kline wrote to John T. Harris, his representative in Congress, asking him to do all he could to avoid the threatening calamity "by pouring oil upon the troubled waters until the tempest of passion abates."[3]

The unrest and excitement of this period is described by John Kline in his notes of April 21, 1861.

Great excitement on account of secession and war movements. The volunteers are being called out to enter the field of war, and God only knows what the end will be. There is a great commotion everywhere in the realm of thought and sentiment, men's hearts failing them for fear, the sea and the waves of human passion roaring.[4]

THE POSITION OF THE CHURCH ON WAR

Secession came and war followed. How did the Brethren stand on the war problem?

John Kline Claimed the Brotherhood United Against Bearing Arms

There was no leader of the Brethren more universally respected and loved during the Civil War period than John Kline. No leader knew the point of view of the church better than this Dunker elder. This is established by the

---

[1] Funk, *The Life of John Kline.* p. 438,
[2] *Ibid.*, p. 439.
[3] *Ibid.*, p. 439.
[4] *Ibid.*, p. 440.

fact that he was elected as moderator of the Annual Conference four years in succession, 1861 to 1864. In his diary of December 20, 1862, John Kline expressed his convictions regarding the stand of the Brethren on the Civil War.

Write to John Hopkins, to John C. Woodson, and to Charles Lewis. I can but entreat these men to stand in defense of our Brethren, and try to devise some plan by which they can be exempted from the necessity of bearing arms. I feel sure that if we can be rightly understood as to our faith and life, there will be some way provided for their exemption. The Brotherhood is a unit, heart and hand against arms-bearing. These things I make known to these men; not, however, in any spirit of defiance, but in the spirit of meekness and obedience to what we in heart believe to be the will of the Lord. Many have already expressed to me their determination to flee from their homes rather than disobey God.[5]

The Church Disfellowshiped Members for Bearing Arms

The Brethren as in former years were united against bearing arms because of their loyalty to the teachings of Jesus. However, the discipline of the denomination had something to do with the unusual record of faithfulness of the members to this church principle. As early as 1848 Annual Conference outlined the procedure for receiving members into the church, which required each applicant to indicate his acceptance of the nonresistant principle, and there is evidence that this had been the general practice of, the Brethren many years before. The Church of the Brethren during the Civil War period was strict in requiring members to live according to the teachings of the church. Elder D. H. Zigler in "A History of the Brethren in Virginia" states, "But one brother is known to have yielded to the military spirit of the time."[6] Dr. Henry Geiger of Philadelphia, who desired to enter the medical division of the army, resigned both his ministry and membership before taking this step. His letter which follows, written

---

[5] *Ibid.,* p. 446.
[6] D. H. Zigler, *A History of the Brethren in Virginia,* p. 97.

to the elders of the First Church of Philadelphia, was accepted by the congregation after two separate readings and some serious discussion.

John Fox
Christian Custer
> Elders of German Baptist Church

Being about to engage in the service of our country and thus violate the rules of our church, I respectfully beg leave to offer my resignation as a member. Be so kind as to receive in behalf of yourselves and the members generally my grateful thanks for the past kindness and allow me to remain

> Very truly yours,
>
> H. Geiger

Philadelphia, June 27, 1863[7]

The Annual Conference of 1865 faced the serious question: "Can a brother be held as a member of the church who will, when put into the army, take up arms and aim to shed the blood of his fellowmen?" The Conference answered: "He cannot."[8] In 1864 the Annual Conference was asked whether soldiers should be baptized and received into the church while they were still bearing arms or whether a full discharge should be received first. The answer was:

We cannot encourage such proceedings: but in case of extreme sickness, and when there is a promise to shed no more blood, we will let the churches applied to, decide what shall be done; but let the principles of the church be acceded to by all candidates.[9]

Likewise, the Brethren took action in 1864 against the wearing of military clothing:

It is considered not advisable for any brother, whether a minister or a private member, to wear any military clothing, and if he is admonished, and still persists in being disobedient, he should be dealt with according to Matthew 18.[10]

---

[7] *Original Minute Book of the First Church of the Brethren,* Philadelphia (1861-1875), p. 46. The Minute Book is in the private library of Roland Howe, Philadelphia.
[8] *Minutes of the Annual Meetings, 1778-1909,* p. 237.
[9] *Ibid.,* p. 230.
[10] *Ibid.,* p. 237.

Stonewall Jackson's Testimony

In the early days of the war, before the status of Mennonites, Brethren and Friends was well established in the conscription laws, some of these people in Virginia were literally bound and hauled away to the army. The difficulty in handling them in .the army led General T. J. Jackson to make this statement:

There lives a people in the Valley of Virginia, that are not hard to bring to the army. While there they are obedient to their officers. Nor is it difficult to have them take aim, but it is impossible to get them to take correct aim. I, therefore, think it better to leave them at their homes that they may produce supplies for the army.[11]

Attitude of the Brethren Toward the Hiring of Substitutes and the Paying of War Taxes

It is known that some of the Brethren hired substitutes in the early days of the Civil War, but this was not officially endorsed by the church. The church preferred the payment of taxes in lieu of military service. A query came to the Annual Conference of 1865 asking this question:

How is it considered if a brother who is drafted hires a substitute to perform military service, and afterward removes to another district—shall the church grant him a certificate of membership?

The answer was:

Since the law has exempted brethren from military duty, by paying a tax in lieu of service, we consider that Brethren do wrong to resort to other means, unless they are ignorant of the provisions of the law.[12]

Probably the most significant church decision during the Civil War was made by the Annual Conference of 1864. It is quoted in full:

We exhort the Brethren to steadfastness in the faith, and believe that the times in which our lots are cast strongly demand of us a strict adherence to all our principles, and especially to our non-resistant principle, a principle dear to every subject of the Prince of

[11] Zigler, *A History of the Brethren in Virginia*, p. 98.
[12] *Minutes of the Annual Meetings, 1778-1909*, p. 237.

Peace, and a prominent doctrine of our fraternity, and to endure whatever sufferings and to make whatever sacrifice the maintaining of the principle may require, and not to encourage in any way the practice of war. And we think it more in accordance with our principles, that instead of paying bounty-money, and especially in taking an active part in raising bounty-money, to await the demands of the government, whether general, state, or local, and pay the fines and taxes required of us, as the gospel permits, and, indeed, requires. Matt. 22:21; Rom. 13:7. And lest the position we have taken upon political matters in general, the war matters in particular, should seem to make us, as a body, appear to be indifferent to our government, or in opposition thereto, in its efforts to suppress the rebellion, we hereby declare that it has our sympathies and our prayers, and that it shall have our aid in any way which does not conflict with the principles of the gospel of Christ. But since, in our Christian profession, we regard these gospel principles as superior or paramount to all others, consistency requires that we so regard them in our practices.[13]

Inconsistencies in the Brethren Peace Position

These Conference decisions reveal a basic inconsistency in the Brethren peace position at the time. The discouragement against the hiring of substitutes was mild and shows that the church had not thought through the implications of its peace position. There was no organized protest against the payment of war taxes but rather a submission to what the government demanded. The church advised its members not to give voluntary efforts for the raising of war money, but held that the gospel required the payment of fines and taxes. The peace position of the Brethren based upon the teachings of Jesus was applied more to the overt acts of war than to the economic and moral problems of the whole war system. The Brethren leaders then probably would not have said that all war is sin.

New light on the Brethren peace position may come through a further clarification of the church's concept of

---

[13] *Ibid.*, p. 231-232.

the civil government. Edward Frantz, long-time editor of the "Gospel Messenger," gives this illuminating interpretation about the point of view of the Church of the Brethren during the Civil War:

> The general attitude of the church was that war was anti-Christian, and a Christian should not participate in it. But the Church of the Brethren was one thing, the civil government another thing. The church could not use the sword, but the civil government could and must. There was a feeling in the church for a long time that the church should have no connection with the civil government. Any use of force for a churchman was wrong. However, the government might have to do it. The church thought that war was wrong for the Christian but not wrong for the government.
>
> This interpretation, of course, is open for serious question. If the civil government must do something which a Christian cannot, then it is some men's duty not to be Christian.[14]

J. E. Miller, extensive student of Brethren history, makes this interpretation of the Brethren position during the Civil War:

> The church held that there were two classes of persons: the Christian and the non-Christian. There was the civil government and God's government. The civil government could do what the church could not do. And the civil government was not bound by the same laws as the church. This allowed the civil government to carry on war. It was right for the civil government to do some things which it would be wrong for the church to do.[15]

The inconsistency of this position is easily seen. They felt that it was wrong for Brethren to fight but they did not apply this moral and Biblical principle to everybody.

A further inconsistency is revealed in the Annual Conference decision of 1864, which has been quoted earlier. In order to avoid appearing indifferent to the government "in its efforts to suppress the rebellion," the church declared that "it has our sympathies and our prayers."[16] How could the Brethren pray for the victory of the North without

---

[14] Personal interview with Edward Frantz, Elgin, Illinois, Dec. 30, 1942.
[15] Personal interview with J. E. Miller, Elgin, Illinois, Dec. 31, 1942.
[16] *Minutes of the Annual Meetings, 1778-1909*, p. 232.

taking part in the war? The Brethren were not neutral in their sympathies. They did not want the war to come, but after it came, as an antislavery people, they favored the Union cause. J. E. Miller says that "it was a matter of knowledge to the older Brethren that D. P. Sayler made regular visits to President Lincoln and assured him of the sympathy of the Brethren with the Union cause."[17] At the Annual Conference of 1865, held at Franklin Grove, Illinois, D. P. Sayler said: "I have often prayed God that what he cannot do otherwise, he will do at the mouth of the cannon."[18] This statement shows again that this Dunker elder placed the church and the civil government into two different classes.

John Kline in a letter to Governor John Letcher of Virginia, January 30, 1861, outlined the doctrine of the Brethren regarding obedience to the state:

We teach and are taught obedience to the "powers that be," believing as we do that "the powers that be are ordained of God," and under his divine sanction so far as such powers keep within God's bounds. By God's bounds we understand such laws and their administrations and enforcements as do not conflict with, oppose, or violate any precept or command contained in the Divine Word which he has given for the moral and spiritual government of his people. By government, to which we as a body acknowledge and teach our obligations of duty and obedience, we understand rightful human authority. And by this, again, we understand, as the Apostle Paul puts it, "the power that protects and blesses the good, and punishes the evildoer."[19]

This may explain why the Church of the Brethren was not a stronger protesting church. Obedience to civil government was taught except where civil laws conflicted with the Bible. The Brethren were not voting much during the Civil War. The Annual Conference of 1864 asked the mem-

---

[17] Personal interview with J. E. Miller, Elgin, Illinois, December 31, 1942.
[18] This story was told to J. E. Miller by his father, who attended this Annual Conference.
[19] Funk, *Life of John Kline,* p. 439.

bers "to have nothing at all to do with politics, and entirely to abstain from voting."[20]   The Annual Conference of 1863 had stated: "In the present crisis we recommend that Brethren abstain as much as possible from attending elections, according to John 18: 36; 2 Cor. 6: 14-17."[21]   The church became more pronounced in its opposition to voting as the war progressed.   The Brethren feared that voting would involve them in war.

How the Government Dealt With the Brethren As a Minority Group in the North

At the outbreak of the war conscription was carried on through state laws.   As has already been noted, the Pennsylvania Constitution of 1838 allowed exemption for those conscientiously opposed to bearing arms upon the payment of an equivalent for personal service.   The ranks of the army were at first filled through volunteers.

The Federal Militia Act

However, the passing of the Federal Militia Act of July 17, 1862, gave the President power to muster in the militia between the ages of 18 and 45.   The enrollment was to be under state control unless state laws were deficient, and in such cases the President was empowered to make the necessary rules and regulations.[22]   On August 4, 1862, President Lincoln issued a call for 300,000 men for nine months' service and on August 9 the Adjutant General issued General Order Number 99 regulating the enrollment and drafting of these men.[23]

Neither the Militia Act nor the General Order was specific in the matter of exemption.   The General Order provided for the exemption of "all persons exempted by the

---

[20] *Minutes of the Annual Meetings, 1778-1909*, p. 225.
[21] *Ibid.*, p. 221.
[22] *U. S. Statutes at Large* (37th Cong., Sess. II, Chap. 201), XII, pp. 597-600.
[23] *Official Records*, Series 3, II, pp. 333-335.

laws of the respective states from military duty, on sufficient evidence."[24] Naturally, the historic peace churches began to work with state governments.

The following letters are illustrative of how the matter was being worked out by the states. The governor of Indiana wrote to Honorable E. M. Stanton:

Indianapolis, Ind., Sept. 24, 1862

Hon. E. M. Stanton:

The constitution of the State of Indiana contains the following provision:

No person conscientiously opposed to bearing arms shall be compelled to do military duty, but such person shall pay an equivalent for exemption, the amount to be prescribed by law.

Our legislature has omitted to fix any equivalent for such exemption. This omission can be supplied by you under section 1 of the act of July 17, 1862. Will you please fix the amount and advise me of it as early as possible?

O. P. Morton[25]

To this the War Department replied:

War Department
Washington City, D. C.,
Sept. 26, 1862

His Excellency Governor Morton,
Indianapolis:

Please say what amount would in your opinion be a fair commutation to be paid by persons conscientiously opposed to bearing arms, and thus exempt under the constitution of Indiana.

By order of the Secretary of War:

C. P. Buckingham
Brigadier-General and Assistant Adjutant-General[26]

Governor Morton then gave his suggestion of what the payment for exemption should be:

[24] *Ibid.*, p. 334.
[25] *Ibid.*, p. 587.
[26] *Ibid.*, p. 588.

Indianapolis, Ind., Sept. 26, 1862

Brig. Gen. C. P. Buckingham:

In reply to your dispatch of this date, in my opinion a fair commutation to be paid by persons conscientiously opposed to bearing arms, and thus exempt under the constitution of Indiana, should not be less than $200 per man.

O. P. Morton
Governor of Indiana[27]

Following that answer the Secretary of War made his decision:

War Department
Washington City, D. C.,
Sept. 27, 1862

His Excellency Governor Morton,
Indianapolis:

The commutation to be paid by persons conscientiously opposed to bearing arms, and thus exempt under the constitution of Indiana, will be $200.

By order of the Secretary of War:

C. P. Buckingham
Brigadier-General and Assistant Adjutant-General[28]

The governor of Ohio wrote to the Secretary of War indicating how he was handling the problem:

Columbus, Ohio
October 5, 1862

Hon. E. M. Stanton:

Without any well defined authority, therefore, I have exempted all State and County officers, also members of religious denominations whose creed forbids taking up arms, upon payment of $200 each; all of which I ask you to approve. I purpose using the money thus obtained in hiring substitutes and in caring for the sick and wounded, through Quartermaster-General Wright.

David Tod,
Governor[29]

---

[27] *Ibid.*, p. 589.
[28] *Ibid.*, p. 590.
[29] *Ibid.*, p. 650.

Act of March 3, 1863

The Federal Act of March 3, 1863, entitled "An Act for enrolling and calling out the National Forces," did not exempt those conscientiously opposed to war, but provided for the hiring of substitutes or the payment of the sum of $300 for the purpose of employing substitutes. Section 13 reads:

And be it further enacted, that any person drafted and notified to appear as aforesaid, may, on or before the day fixed for his appearance, furnish an acceptable substitute to take his place in the draft; or he may pay to such person as the Secretary of War may authorize to receive it, such sum, not exceeding three hundred dollars, as the Secretary may determine, for the procuration of such substitute, etc.[30]

The law of December 23, 1863, was in reality an interpretation of the Act of March 3. It provided "that the money paid by drafted persons" was to be kept "as a special deposit" in the United States Treasury, applicable only to the expenses of draft and for the procuration of substitutes."[31]

The Acts of March 3 and December 23 in reality transferred the problem of handling religious objectors to war from the states to the national government. These laws did not represent any genuine recognition of conscience for members of the historic peace churches. This conviction is verified by the published opinions of Colonel Joseph Holt, Judge-Advocate General of the Army:

War Dept. Prov. General's Office
Washington, D. C., August 1, 1863

Circular
No. 61

The following opinions of Col. Joseph Holt, Judge-Advocate General of the Army, are published for the information and guidance of all officers of this bureau:

Persons having conscientious scruples in regard to bearing arms

---

[30] *United States Statutes at Large* (37th Cong., Sess. III, Chap. 75), XII, p. 733.
[31] *Ibid.,* 38th Congress, Session I, p. 400.

are not on that account exempt.   They are not found in the list of exempted classes, and the act expressly declares that no persons but those enumerated in that list shall be exempt.   The Society of Friends, and others entertaining similar sentiments, if drafted, may find relief from their scruples in the employment of substitutes, or in the payment of the $300.[32]

The Act of February 24, 1864

The Society of Friends was opposed to the tax and the substitutes.   The Friends, Mennonites and Brethren worked with the government to get a greater recognition of conscience.   Finally the Act of February 24, 1864, was enacted, of which section 17 is quoted here:

And be it further enacted, "that members of religious denominations who shall by oath or affirmation declare that they are conscientiously opposed to the bearing of arms, and who are prohibited from doing so by the rules and articles of faith and practice of said religious denominations, shall, when drafted into military service, be considered noncombatants, and shall be assigned by the Secretary of War to duty in the hospitals, or to the care of freedmen, or shall pay the sum of three hundred dollars to such person as the Secretary of War shall designate to receive it, to be applied to the benefit of the sick and wounded soldiers: Provided that no person shall be entitled to the benefit of the provisions of this section unless his declaration of conscientious scruples against bearing arms shall be supported by satisfactory evidence that his deportment has been uniformly consistent with such declaration.[33]

This Act was superior to the earlier laws because it recognized the conscientious convictions against war of members of the historic peace churches, and gave the alternative of being assigned "to duty in the hospitals, or to the care of freedmen" or to "pay the sum of three hundred dollars."   The money paid was to go to the benefit of "the sick and wounded soldiers" rather than for the hiring of substitutes.   While several other laws bearing on the war were passed by the United States government, the pro-

---

[32] *Official Records*, Series 3, III, p. 606.
[33] *United States Statutes at Large* (38th Cong., Sess. I, Chap. 13), XIII, p. 9.

visions of this act relating to conscientious objectors remained in force until the end of the war. The Brethren located in the North paid the $300 and remained on their farms. There was not nearly so much suffering among non-resistant people in the North as in the South.

How THE LAW WAS CARRIED OUT

The following letter of instructions to David Neport outlined the proper procedure for paying the tax and securing exemption:

Washington, D. C., Nov. 8th, 1864

Drafted persons who claim the benefit of section 17 of the Act approved Feb. 24th, 1864 and desire to avail themselves thereof must first satisfy the Board of Enrolment in their respective districts that they are non-combatants, within the meaning of the law.

The Provost Marshal will then give a Certificate to this effect to the drafted man and upon presentation of this certificate to the Receiver of Commutation money, he will receive the $300 (and the amount fixed by the Secretary of War), and issue his receipt therefor in triplicate—the duplicate thereof to be presented by the drafted person to the Board of Enrolment for their action.

James B. Fry
Provost Marshal General[34]

APPEALS FOR EXEMPTION

Not many records have been preserved regarding the Brethren appeals for exemption but the following is an illustration of the method used by the church in certifying individual members to the government:

Indian Creek, Montgomery Co., Pa.
October 20, 1862

To His Excellency, Andrew G. Curtain, Governor
of Pennsylvania, Greeting

We the undersigned, Bishop, and Elders, of the German Baptist, or

[34] Letter in the Cassel Library at Juniata College, Huntingdon, Pennsylvania, in the original handwriting of James B. Fry.

Dunkard Society, of Indian Creek, Montgomery Co., Pa., certify herewith that the following named persons to wit

Henry A. Price, David Gyson, Abraham Stauffer and the Bearer Abrm H. Cassel, are well established members of said church at Indian Creek, whose avowed principles are well known to be strictly non-resistant, and that for conscience sake we do not defend nor avenge ourselves in any wrongs or injuries that may befall us—believing it to be contrary to the teachings of our Divine Lord and Master, whose footsteps we endeavor to follow to the best of our knowledge and ability. Therefore it is utterly impossible for us to bear arms under any circumstance whatsoever. And, for that reason appeal to your Excellency and Clemency as the supreme Magistrate of our State, to exempt said persons from such service, consistent with the dignity of your office and the Constitution of our State, and we subscribe ourselves your most devoted and also most loyal subjects.

> Samuel Harley, Bishop
> Jacob Prise
> Yelles Cassel
> Jonas Harley[35]

A second appeal for exemption came from the same local church:

> Indian Creek, Montgomery Co., Pa.,
> March 23, 1865

We, the undersigned Elder, and Deacons of the German Baptist, or Dunker Church, at Indian Creek, certify herewith, that John Bechtel, of Upper Salford Township, is a member of our fraternity, and is well established in the Articles of our Faith, which are known to be strictly Nonresistant in Practice and Principle. He is therefore conscientiously opposed to the bearing of arms, and craves exemption from such service according to the provision of the law.[36]

The original form used by the members of the church to claim exemption is as follows:

I .... of ....
do hereby certify that I have been drafted as a soldier owing service to the United States and that I am not liable for the following reasons:

---

[35] The original document is in the Cassel Library at Juniata College.
[36] Another original document from the Cassel Library at Juniata College.

I am a member of the Religious Society called German Baptists or Dunkards, a cardinal principle of whose faith and practice is non-resistance, and that it is sinful and unchristian for man to bear arms in hostility to his fellow-man—That violation of the above rule of faith and practice is attended with censorship and disownment from the society—That I have been a member for .... years past and do most sincerely believe in the above doctrine and principle of said society and believe that my life hitherto has been in accordance with said principles, both outside of the church among my fellowmen as well as in it.

We ....do herewith certify that we are members of said Society, that we know said

..................................for many years and we believe his statement above made is correct and true both to the principles of faith and practice of said Society as well as of his life in accordance therewith.

Personally appeared before me the above named ....

....
and severally affirmed that the above certificates are true and correct to the best of their knowledge and belief.

Notary ....[37]

ATTITUDE OF LINCOLN TOWARD CONSCIENTIOUS OBJECTORS

J. E. Miller states that his father, who lived during Civil War days, told him that there were people who urged Lincoln to force the Friends, Mennonites and Brethren into the army. They held that it was not right to excuse them while others had to fight. To all this Lincoln replied:

No, I will not do that. These people do not believe in war. People who do not believe in war make poor soldiers. Besides, the attitude of these people has always been against slavery. If all our people had held the same views about slavery as these people hold there would be no war. These people are largely a rural people, sturdy and honest. They are excellent farmers. The country needs

---

[37] Still another original document from the Cassel Library at Juniata College.

good farmers fully as much as it needs good soldiers. We will leave them on their farms where they are at home and where they will make their contribution better than they would with a gun.[38]

D. P. SAYLER'S GOVERNMENT CONTACTS

Elder D. P. Sayler was frequently called before the War Department to explain the Brethren position. He was a strong personality and his statesmanship in working with the government was probably an influential factor in getting consideration for his church people. Sayler also made regular visits to the President, and Lincoln invited him to come and pray with him during the Civil War. Henry Ward Beecher and D. P. Sayler were the only ministers, seemingly, who had that invitation.[39]

It is related that on one occasion Sayler told Lincoln of the desire of his friends to have him accept some civil office, but that he felt called to be a minister of the gospel. The President assured him that he considered him capable of filling any office to which he might be called. Then the President said, "But, Brother Sayler, I ordain you a Dunker preacher forever."[40]

HOW THE GOVERNMENT DEALT WITH THE BRETHREN AS A MINORITY GROUP IN THE SOUTH

The Brethren had more trouble in the South. Their anti-slavery convictions brought them under criticism; the government was more unstable and more in need of men and money. It has been noted that the constitutions of Virginia and Tennessee left the matter of caring for conscientious objectors in the hands of the state legislatures. The constitutions of the Carolinas made no provision at all for those scrupulous against bearing arms. The first important

---

[38] J. E. Miller, *Stories from Brethren Life,* pp. 137-138.
[39] Personal letter from M. J. Weaver, Nappanee, Ind., Jan. 18, 1943, in which he stated that the above information came from D. P. Sayler through his friend, James Quinter.
[40] *Brethren Family Almanac,* 1908, p. 29.

military measure passed by the Provisional Congress was the Act of March 6, 1861. This law provided for the public defense and for the enlistment of volunteers, but it did not deal with those opposed to bearing arms.[41] The military measures of May 16 and August 8, 1861, allowed recruiting to be carried on by state agencies and under state laws.[42] Thus, the Brethren addressed their own state legislatures.

The Brethren Worked for Exemption

On January 30, 1861, John Kline wrote a letter to John Letcher, governor of Virginia, commending him for the stand he had taken regarding the Union and asking that Brethren be exempted from military services. To this letter the governor replied:

> Richmond, Virginia,
> February 1, 1861.

My Dear Sir:

I received your kind letter this evening, and am gratified to find that our views upon public questions are so nearly in accordance. I have never doubted, that I would in the main, be sustained by the reflecting and conservative men, in all sections of our State, and I am now receiving numerous evidences, of the correctness of that opinion.

We have many men in the North and South, who are anxious to see the Union destroyed. By far the larger number, are reckless adventurers, without property, who have nothing to lose; and no revolution in the country or its business can therefore injure them. They think they may in a war better their condition, and they are therefore disposed to take chances, and run all hazards.

I would be glad to see the arrangement in regard to military service, suggested in your letter adopted. I think it entirely reasonable, that those who have conscientious scruples, in regard to the performance of militia duty, should be relieved by the payment of a small pecuniary compensation. There are enough of others who take pleasure in the performance of such duties.

---

[41] *Confederate Statutes at Large* (Prov. Cong., Sess. I, Chap. 26), I, pp. 45-46.
[42] *Ibid.* (Prov. Cong., Sess. II, Chap. 20, and Sess. III, Chap. 20), pp. 114-116.

It is gratifying to hear that my old friends in the Tenth Legion sustain me now, as in other days. I appreciate a compliment from such people most highly.

I have great hopes that the controversy now unhappily existing between the North and the South will be eventually settled, to the satisfaction of the conservative men of all parties.

I am truly

Your friend,

John Letcher[43]

John Kline wrote many letters on behalf of his members. One of the most important letters is the one which was written to Colonel Lewis of the Confederate army. It shows how some of the Brethren were forced into armed service.

Bowman's Mill, Rockingham County, Va.

December 16, 1861.

My dear friend Col. Lewis:

I arrived home safe and have been looking to hear from you. . . .

I now desire to approach you to consider and use your influence with the generals and other officers in the army. The subject is this: We German Baptists (called Tunkers) do most solemnly believe that the bearing of carnal weapons in order to destroy life, is in direct opposition to the Gospel of Christ, which we accept as the rule of our faith and practice. To this we have most solemnly vowed to be true until death. Hence we stand pledged to our God to carry out that which we believe to be his commandment. . . .

ʼ We feel bound to pay our taxes, fines, and to do whatever is in our power which does not conflict with our obligation to God. Whenever God speaks we think we should obey Him rather than man. But in this unholy contest, both law and all former precedents of making drafts have been set aside. The privilege usually granted Christian people to pay a fine has been overruled and set aside, and they are compelled to take up weapons of carnal warfare to drill and if need be to shoot down their fellow man. This is not only revolting to them, but a positive violation to their solemn vow to their God. This is without precedent in a land of Christian liberty. Who the prosecutor of this outrage on our constitutional rights is I know

---

[43] Zigler, *A History of the Brethren in Virginia,* pp. 95-96.

not, but that it is so is clear. That it has been driven by some one is also clear. This state of things the much abused Abe Lincoln would have much deplored. For I am credibly informed that he issued a proclamation that no conscientious Christian should be forced to war or to take up arms.

Thus it should be in a land of Christian liberty. None but those who have a disposition or desire to rear up a hierarchy or despotic government could feel otherwise. None that have the spirit of Washington or Jefferson in their hearts would desire to compel their fellow countrymen to take up arms against their conscience, and to force them to kill their fellow man. Let any one look at and read the fifteenth section of the Constitution as before the convention: "Nor shall any man be enforced, restrained, molested, or burdened in his body or goods or otherwise suffer on account of his religious opinion or belief. This I understand is unchanged. Neither should it be. Therefore, a great breach of the constitution has been practiced on us for we have been enforced, restrained and molested because of our religious belief and opinion.

Please give this matter your earnest attention and tell it or read it to your fellow officers, and if expedient, to Gen. Jackson.

From your friend,

John Kline[44]

In the early days of the war some of the Brethren were dragged into the army. D. H. Zigler says that "a few were literally bound and hauled away from their homes."[45] Some secured substitutes, paying from $600 to $1,500 each. That this was an economic burden is revealed by a letter which John Kline wrote to the "Gospel Visitor," July 2, 1862. A part of it follows:

Times however, dear brethren, are truly pretty squally and things uncertain. What will at last be the final result no man on earth can tell. Our brethren truly have much to pay, so much so, it will be a considerable burden for them to bear. Those that are able have paid for substitutes before the law of fines was in existence to rid themselves from going to the army, from $600 to $1,500, and now to help those that have not to pay, to pay the $500 fine falls heavy,

---

[44] *Ibid.*, pp. 99-101.
[45] *Ibid.*, p. 98.

yet it may be the means to relieve the brethren from some of the worldly burden, and do us good, and wean our affections to the heavenly treasures.   So now brethren I recommend us all both North and South, East and West into the hands of God and his mercy.   May it and his grace be with us all, and may the Lord so overrule things, so that peace and amity might be restored.   Farewell brethren.   Pray for us when you approach a throne of grace. My hearty greetings to you all.   Amen.

John Kline [46]

State officials were seen in behalf of the Brethren. Samuel Cline, a lay member living near Staunton, Virginia, made a special trip to Richmond to appeal for the Brethren. Elders B. F. Moomaw, Peter Nininger and Jonas Graybill championed the cause of the Brethren in Botetourt and Roanoke counties.   A joint petition from the Brethren and the Mennonites in Virginia was presented to the law makers. The Brethren worked largely through Col. John B. Baldwin, who was well acquainted with the peace position, and was willing to represent their interests in the Virginia Congress and later in the legislative hall of the Confederate States.

The Virginia and North Carolina Laws

How much influence the resolutions and efforts of the Brethren had on the legislators cannot be determined.   However, the following Act was passed March 29, 1862, recognizing members of churches whose tenets forbade participation in war, and granting exemption for the payment of $500 and two percent of the assessed value of the applicant's taxable property.   A portion of the law is quoted:

"That whenever upon application for exemption to the board of exemption it shall appear to said board that the party applying for said exemption is bona fide prevented from bearing arms, by the tenets of the Church to which said applicant belongs, and did actually belong at the passage of this act, and further, that said applicant has paid to the sheriff of the county or collector of taxes for the city or town in which said applicant resides, the sum of five hundred

---

[46] *Gospel Visitor,* Oct. 1, 1862, No. 10, XII, p. 318.

dollars, and in addition thereto, the further sum of two per cent of the assessed value of said applicant's taxable property, then the said board, on the presentation of the receipt of said officers for said moneys, and after the said applicant shall have taken an oath or affirmation that he will sustain the confederate government, and will not in any way give aid and comfort to the enemy of the said confederate government, then the said board shall exempt the said applicant: provided, that whenever said party may be unable, or shall fail to pay the sum of five hundred dollars, and the tax of two per centum on their property, he shall be employed (when liable to military duty) in the capacity of teamster, or in such other character as the service may need, which does not require the actual bearing of arms; and provided further, that the persons so exempted do surrender to the board of exemption all arms which they may own to be held subject to the order of the governor, for the public use.[47]

The law of North Carolina, ratified September 20, 1861, was more liberal than that of Virginia. Section 5 reads:

Persons having scruples of conscience against bearing arms, who shall produce to the captains of their respective districts certificates, signed by the clerks of their respective churches, that they are regular members thereof, and shall make oath or affirmation, before a justice of the peace, that they are from religious scruples, averse to bearing arms, and shall also produce a certificate from such justice of the peace that such oath or affirmation has been duly made, shall not be compelled to muster or perform military duty except in cases of insurrection or invasion, or pay any tax for said exemption, but they shall be subject to taxation in time of insurrection, invasion or war, and also to furnish their quota of men or pay an equivalent.[48]

Unrest Among the Brethren

Before the Virginia law was passed there was much unrest among the Brethren. Some of them had been forced into the army against their will, and no adequate protection had come either from the state or the Confederate Congress. Consequently in March, 1862, two groups of about ninety Mennonites and Dunkers fled from their homes

---

[47] *Acts of the General Assembly of the State of Virginia* (Passed in 1861, Chap. 25), pp. 50-51.
[48] *Public Laws of the State of North Carolina* (Second Extra Session, 1861, Chap. 17), pp. 23-24.

in the Valley of Virginia and attempted to make their escape to the West. They were captured and returned, one group of eighteen to Harrisonburg, Virginia, and the other group of seventy to Richmond, Virginia. While in prison they were examined by Sidney S. Baxter of the War Department, who made the following reports:

> Richmond
> March 31, 1862

I have examined a number of persons, fugitives from Rockingham and Augusta Counties, who were arrested at Petersburg, in Hardy County. These men are all regular members in good standing in the Tunker (Dunker) and Mennonite Churches. One of the tenets of these churches is that the law of God forbids shedding human blood in battle and this doctrine is uniformly taught to all their people. As all of these persons are members in good standing in these churches and bear good characters as citizens and Christians I cannot doubt the sincerity of their declaration that they left home to avoid the draft of the militia and under the belief that by the draft they would be placed in a situation in which they would be compelled to violate their consciences. They all declared that they had no intention to go to the enemy or to remain with them. They all intended to return home as soon as the draft was over. Some of them had made exertions to procure substitutes. One man had sent the money to Richmond to hire a substitute. Others had done much to support the families of volunteers. Some had furnished horses to the cavalry. All of them are friendly to the South and they express a willingness to contribute all their property if necessary to establish their liberties. I am informed a law will probably pass exempting these persons from military duty on payment of a pecuniary compensation. These parties assure me all who are able will cheerfully pay this compensation. Those who are unable to make the payment will cheerfully go into service as teamsters or in any employment in which they are not required to shed blood. I recommend all the persons in the annexed list be discharged on taking the oath of allegiance and agreeing to submit to the laws of Virginia and the Confederate States in all things except taking arms in war.

In addition to these cases I report the case of Peter L. Goode, a broken-legged man, whom I believe to be incapable of military duty, and of John Sanger a youth of sixteen years. Both these persons were arrested. They seem to have partaken in the Tunker (Dunkard) panic and fled with the others. I believe that both of them are faithful and loyal to Virginia and the Confederate States. I recommend they also be discharged from prison here on taking the oath of allegiance and reporting themselves to the proper officer of the regiment of Virginia militia to have their claims to exemption acted on.

S. S. Baxter[49]

A few days later Mr. Baxter gave a supplementary report:

April 2, 1862

Since my last report I have seen the copy of the law passed by the legislature of Virginia on the 29th of March, 1862. It exempts from military duty persons prevented from bearing arms by the tenets of the church to which they belong on condition of paying $500 and 2 per cent on the assessed value of their taxable property, taking an oath to sustain the Confederate Government, with the proviso that if the person exempted is not able to pay the tax he shall be employed as a teamster or in some character which will not require the actual bearing of arms, and surrender any arms they possess for public use. I renew my recommendation that these persons be discharged on taking the oath of allegiance and an obligation to conform to the laws of Virginia.

S. S. Baxter[50]

The recommendations of the War Department were accepted and the Brethren were released from prison. But these were not the only prison experiences. John Kline because of his activities in getting members of the church released from army service was thrown into the guard house at Harrisonburg, Virginia, on April 5, 1862. The next day he preached to his fellow captives on "Righteousness, Temperance, and a Judgment to Come."[51] His diary states that two of the Brethren, John and Joseph Cline, were released from imprisonment on April 14.[52] The prison was damp and the Dunker elder suffered from cold. He was

---

[49] *Official Records of the Union and Confederate Armies,* Series 2, III, p. 835.
[50] *Ibid.,* p. 837.
[51] Funk, *op. cit.,* p. 448.
[52] *Ibid.,* 453.

released on April 18, and returned to his home to continue his fearless work.

REGULATION OF DRAFT REMOVED FROM STATE CONTROL

The draft laws of Virginia and North Carolina were short lived. On April 16, 1862, the Confederate Congress passed "an Act to further provide for the public defense." By this law substitutes were allowed under conditions to be prescribed by the Secretary of War, but no specific provision was made for religious objectors to war.[53] Thus the peace churches turned from petitioning state governments to the Confederate government. B. F. Moomaw and Jonas Graybill visited their representative in Congress, endeavoring to secure his assistance in obtaining recognition for the Brethren in appropriate legislation. John Kline wrote the following letter to Colonel John B. Baldwin of Virginia urging that the Virginia State Exemption Law be recognized by the Confederate Congress:

> Bowman's Mill, Rockingham County,
> Virginia. July 23, 1862.

Much esteemed friend Col. John Baldwin:

I seat myself in behalf of my Brotherhood, the German Baptists, so-called Tunkers, to drop a few lines in order to give you a correct view of our faith toward our God, and, in consequence of that, our unpleasant standing in and under our government which we now live.

As there is now a session of Congress of the Confederate States on hand of which you are a member and the special representative of our immediate district, I wish to enlist you to advocate our cause in that body. I wish to be short as possible. I will, therefore, at once inform you that we are a noncombatant people. We believe most conscientiously that it is the doctrine taught by our Lord in the New Testament which we feel bound to obey. Having made in our conversion a most solemn vow to be faithful to God in all his commandments, it is and should be regarded by us as the first in importance and above all made by man to man or to earthly govern-

[53] *Confederate Statutes at Large* (First Cong., Sess. I, Chap. 31), II, p. 29.

ment. Hence we feel rather to suffer persecution, bonds, and if need be death than break the vow made to our God.

Yet, as touching things and obligations, which in our view do not come in conflict with the law of God, in whatever way our government may demand of us we feel always ready and willing to do. Such as paying our dues and taxes imposed upon us and assisting in internal improvements, our profession binds us to do. Paying unto the government that which is due it, but that which is due to God we wish to give to him. Through his Son and the apostles, he says, "Recompense to no man evil for evil." To him we feel to render obedience and therefore are bound not to take up carnal weapons to destroy our fellow men whom he teaches us to love.

We have noticed that those who have been made prisoners and paroled their oath is regarded by the government. They are let alone and no one presses them into the army. This obligation is only made to man. Why then should not that solemn obligation be regarded by our government, which we have made to our God without any earthly interest whatever? Why not leave that class of men at their homes who can not, for conscience sake, make soldiers to kill others, that they may make provisions for the sustenance of life, which is as necessary to any government as soldiers?

It seems that the late conscript law made by the Confederate Congress, whether so intended or not, is made use of to overrule or nullify our state law. This law was made by our State Legislature to exempt us from military duty provided each one pays a tax of $500 and 2 per cent on all taxable property. This, though as oppressive as it is, we were willing to pay, hard as it went with some. Now as we are informed through the above cited conscript act of Congress, we are again to be troubled. Our rights given to us by our kind legislature, for which privilege we have paid so dearly, is to be made null and void.

Please use all your powers and influence in behalf of us, so that the conscript law or all other Confederate laws be so constructed that Christian conscience be so protected that the South shall not be polluted with bloody persecution.

Please give this, our request, a candid consideration. At least so much as to write to me your opinion. If we cannot get protection of our Christian liberty in the south, the home of our nativity, we will be compelled to seek shelter in some other place, or suffer bonds and persecutions as did many of our forefathers. For we cannot take up carnal weapons of warfare and fight our fellow man to kill him.

Yours with highest esteem,

John Kline[54]

Colonel Baldwin replied and suggested that a petition be prepared and presented to Congress. John Kline, in response, drew up the following resolution representing the Brethren and Mennonite churches:

To the Senate and House of Representatives of the Confederate States of America:

The undersigned members of the Tunker and Mennonite Churches in the State of Virginia, respectfully and humbly represent, That at the late Session of the State Legislature of Virginia, That body passed a law exempting from military duty, the members of our Churches, upon each member paying the sum of $500 and 2 per cent upon all his taxable Estate. This exemption was based upon the long established creed or faith of our Churches, against bearing arms. This doctrine is coequal with the foundation of our Churches, and is we think and feel, the Command of God. While we know there is a strong popular feeling against such doctrine, yet it is none the less dear and sacred to us who believe it. The question which we present to you is not one of persuasion in favor of our peculiar doctrine, but a prayer, that you may exercise that same charity and respect for our opinions, and faith, that we so freely accord to others. There are many forms of religious creeds, and various are the doctrines of Religious faith; but there is no Arbiter on earth. God alone is to judge. But there is a coincidence in civilized society in its universal respect for the conscientious convictions of all Christian Churches. With this feeling, and in this spirit, we appeal to you, to pass a law, ratifying the act of the Legislature of Virginia, on this subject.

It may not be amiss to state here, that under the excitement of the hour, indiscreet, and inconsiderate persons have preferred the charge of disloyalty against our Churches. This charge has not the semblance of truth, in fact, and has doubtless originated from our faith against bearing arms. We would further state, that those of our members embraced in said act of the General Assembly of Va. have already paid the penalty of $500 and 2 per cent to the officers

---

[54] Zigler, *op. cit.*, pp. 115-117.

of the State, and thus fulfilled our contract, and have complied with the law. We only ask Congress so far to respect our rights, our Consciences, and the Act of the State of Virginia, as to Ratify the same, and we will ever pray.

Signatures of Males	Signatures of Females	Signatures of Non-Members
		We, the undersigned of this column, n o t being members of the a b o v e Churches, yet pray Congress to hear the above petition, and respect the laws of the State of Virginia a n d State Rights.

These petitions were entrusted to the hands of Colonel Baldwin.[55]

In Botetourt, Roanoke, and Franklin counties, Virginia, the church was likewise active. B. F. Moomaw and Jonas Graybill secured more than one hundred signatures to a petition, presented it to Honorable B. F. Anderson of the Confederate Congress and pled with him to do all he could to have an exemption law passed. About this same time a pamphlet entitled "Non-Resistance," written by W. C. Thurman, was circulated among the members of Congress, at Richmond, Virginia. It appears to have been widely used and may have had some influence on legislation. It is known that Colonel Baldwin wrote to Samuel Cline to send him the best work he had on nonresistance and Thurman's pamphlet was sent. Afterward Baldwin notified Cline that the pamphlet was a decided help. A short portion of it is quoted:

In war there is a continual retaliation, returning of evil for evil.

[55] *Ibid.*, pp. 119-120. The names of those who signed the petition are not given.

But the Christian can "recompense to no man evil for evil," (Rom. XII: 17). Hence cannot go to war. In war men avenge the evils imposed by other nations, which the Christian is forbidden to do. "Avenge not yourselves, but rather give place unto wrath."

In war men overcome their enemies, by pouring on them more evil than they are enabled to return or withstand.

But the little flock of Christ must take a path, leading just in the opposite direction: they must "overcome evil with good." (Rom. XII: 21)[56]

The presentation of resolutions from the historic peace churches is recorded in the "Journal of the Confederate States of America." The journal of September 1, 1862, states: "Mr. Baldwin introduced 'memorial from two religious societies asking the benefit of a certain Act of the Virginia Legislature in relation to exemptions."[57] The journal of September 13, 1862, says: "Mr. Baldwin, by consent, presented two memorials from members of the Quaker and Dunkard religious denominations, asking for exemption from military duty."[58] Both petitions were referred to the Committee on Military Affairs without being read.

The Confederate Law of October 11, 1862

The petitions, conferences with Congressmen, and pamphlet on nonresistance must have had some effect. On October 11, 1862, the Confederate Congress passed the following law:

> . . . . all persons who have been and are now members of the Society of Friends, and the association of Dunkards, Nazarenes, and Mennonists, in regular membership of their respective denominations: provided, Members of the society of Friends, Nazarenes, Mennonists, and Dunkards shall furnish substitutes or pay a tax of five hundred dollars each into the public treasury.[59]

Several days after the passage of the Exemption Act a

---

[56] W. C. Thurman, *Non-Resistance* or *The Spirit of Christianity*, pp. 21-22. Thurman was not a member of the Church of the Brethren when this pamphlet was written. Later he united with this denomination.
[57] *Journal of the Confederate States of America*, V, p. 336.
[58] *Ibid.*, p. 379.
[59] *Confederate Statutes at Large* (First Cong., Sess. II, Chap. 45), II, p. 105.

special officer was chosen to collect the money as the following letter indicates:

Richmond, October 15, 1862

Col. A. C. Myers

Quartermaster-General, Richmond:

Sir: The Secretary of War directs that you select some suitable officer of your department in this city to receive the sums paid in by members of the Dunkard Society to secure exemption from military service. This officer will perform this duty until further orders. This order will include also the members of the societies of Friends, Mennonites, and Nazarenes.

Very respectfully,

S. Cooper

Adjutant and Inspector General[60]

On November 3, 1862, a general order was issued likewise from the Adjutant and Inspector General giving in detail the procedure to be followed by the members of the denominations claiming exemption. The order stated:

Friends, Dunkards, Nazarenes, Mennonites.

All persons of the above denominations in regular membership therein on the 11th day of October, 1862, shall be exempt from enrollment on furnishing a substitute, or on presenting to the enrolling officer a receipt from a bonded Quartermaster for the tax of $500.00 imposed by Act of Congress and an affidavit by the bishop, presiding elder, or other officer, whose duty it is to preserve the records of membership in the denomination to which the party belongs, setting forth distinctly . . . etc.[61]

The terms of the exemption worked quite a hardship on some of the Brethren who were not able to pay. The wealthier Brethren helped the poorer members. The churches took this as an obligation for all members. Some Brethren had made payment to the state and when the Confederate law was passed, there were officers who tried to collect a second payment. The church had no little trouble in getting this matter straightened out. It is re-

[60] *Official Records*, Series 4, II, p. 122.
[61] *Ibid.*, p. 166.

corded that on December 30, 1862, John Kline paid Mr. Woodward, the Receiver of Fines, $9,000 for the exemption of Brethren.[62]

The exemption through the payment of $500 was not always honored by local authorities. The Brethren in Tennessee also suffered much. These sufferings are related by Elder P. R. Wrightsman in his description of his adventure with the Confederate Congress:

In framing an Act for the relief of nonresistants, the Confederate Government, upon the payment of a tax of $500 each into the public treasury, relieved our Brethren for the time; but in the latter part of the war when the South needed all her men in her borders, the local authorities arrested many of our Brethren and shut them up in prison and in the stockades in various places, even after they had paid the $500 penalty. This very much tried our Brethren in East Tennessee. So a council meeting was called at Limestone Church, and a petition was drawn up to send to the Confederate Congress, asking that our brethren be released from military service, as we were and always had been opposed to bearing arms. Nearly all the members of our church signed the petition. It then became a matter of anxious concern who would carry this petition to Congress and represent our claims. All our older brethren shrank from going to Richmond where Congress was in session. I was away at school; yet it was decided to send me though a youth as I was. The deacon brethren came to see me and to report their mission. I regretted to leave school and pleaded with them that older brethren should go, but they replied that it was the act of the church. I replied that I was willing to do anything in my power for my brethren in prison. 'If you and the church will aid me in your prayers, I will go.'

At the proper time I went to the House of the Confederate Congress, presented my petition and made my plea, stating among other things that our people were always a peace people; it is no use to take them to the army, for they will not fight. They would be just in your way. They are the best subjects in your government, for they stay at home and mind their own business. They are mostly farmers, raise grain and your men come and take it. In this way we feed the hungry. Our people never molest your men, but are loyal

---

[62] Zigler, *op. cit.*, p. 125.

and law-abiding citizens to the powers that are over us. We humbly plead for your acceptance of our petition.

Alexander H. Stevens was then consulted; and finally my petition was accepted, and officially endorsed with the word 'GRANTED.'

With a heart overflowing with gratitude to our dear heavenly Father, I came to my home at Limestone, Tenn. Brother M. M. Bashor met me at the depot and urged me to continue on to Knoxville on the same train, as some of our brethren had been taken off while I was at Richmond. So I continued my journey eighty-four miles further to Knoxville. I went to see Col. E. D. Blake, commander of conscripts and prisoners and showed him my papers. With an uncouth remark he told me to go to the stockade and get my men. I went, entered the stockade, and got my brethren out of prison. We all went home like happy children. This was in the summer of 1863.[63]

The Brethren were deeply grateful for the Exemption Law which gave them a means of avoiding direct participation in war. January 1, 1863, was appointed as a day of thanksgiving.[64] Throughout Virginia the Dunkers met in their churches and thanked God for deliverance.

The anxieties of these people were not over. They lived in the constant danger of the laws' repeal. There were also irregularities in the enforcement of the laws' exemption provisions. B. F. Moomaw wrote to John Kline, December 16, 1862, and said:

I will here inform you that our military authorities are so construing the exemption bill as to deprive those few brethren that are in the army under the conscription act, from its benefit. I have just written to the Secretary of War upon the subject. If his answer is unfavorable, I will petition Congress for an amendment, as soon as it convenes. . . .[65]

No Change in Exemption Status During 1863

There were constant rumors that the exemption law would be changed, but the political status of conscientious objectors remained the same during 1863. The Act of May,

---

[63] Sanger and Hays, *The Olive Branch*, pp. 89-92.
[64] Zigler, *op. cit.*, p. 123.
[65] Zigler, *op. cit.*, pp. 123-124.

1863, repealed certain clauses of the October law but no mention was made of the peace churches. The Bureau of Conscription had been organized December 30, 1862, and functioned in an administrative capacity. During the year 1863 the Brethren kept in constant contact with the government. There was much criticism of those who refused to fight. There were constant annoyances by petty officials and many individual cases had to be taken up with the Richmond officials. On July 18, 1863, the Confederate Congress passed a second conscript law, levying a draft on all males between the ages of eighteen and forty-five. This act, however, did not abolish the exemption provision and the Brethren continued to contend strongly for their rights. B. F. Moomaw in writing to John Kline, August 31, 1863, gives an illuminating experience which he had in Salem, Virginia, with a quartermaster:

> The Brethren in Roanoke have been until lately much annoyed by the quartermaster in that county, refusing to allow them the benefit of the exemption. At length, however, I reported him to President Davis. He ordered him (the quartermaster) to report to Richmond and give an account of his conduct. I afterward met him in Salem, when he made a furious assault on me, cursing and threatening violently. I calmly told him I disregarded him; despised his threats; that he must understand that he could not intimidate me and when he interferes with our rights I will attend to him. Since that time the Brethren have been unmolested.[66]

President Davis Proposed Drastic Changes in the Conscription Laws

When the Confederate Congress met in its fourth session on December 7, 1863, President Davis made a startling speech and proposed drastic changes in the law. He said:

> In view of the large conscription recently ordered by the enemy and their subsequent call for volunteers, to be followed if effectual by a still further draft, we are admonished that no effort must be spared to add largely to our effective force as promptly as possible.

---

[66] Zigler, *op. cit.*, pp. 131-132.

The sources of supply are to be found by restoring to the Army all who are improperly absent, putting an end to substitution, modifying the exemption law, restricting details, and placing in the ranks such of the able-bodied men now employed as wagoners, nurses, cooks, and other employees as are doing service for which negroes may be found competent.[67]

The Struggle for Exemption During 1864

Naturally this speech caused great concern among the Brethren. Elder John Kline wrote to various members of Congress about the threatening danger. A reply from Colonel Baldwin on January 28, 1864, stated that the sentiment of Congress at that time was against repeal.[68] A little later Judge John T. Harris wrote that "the exemption on religious grounds stands firm in Congress."[69] However, the year 1864 was one of hardship for those who refused to fight. The government needed men and money. Those with scruples against war never knew whether their consciences would be respected by the local authorities. On February 17, 1864, the Confederate government passed another military measure, entitled "An Act to organize forces to serve during the War." Section four provided "That no person heretofore exempted on account of religious opinions, and who has paid the tax levied to relieve him from service, shall be required to render military service under this Act."[70] This was a protection for those scrupulous against bearing arms. But since the act extended the limits of the draft to all those between the ages of 17 and 50, it was not clear whether the exemption provision of section 4 included the noncombatants between the ages of 17 and 18 and 45 and 50. The peace churches went again to the government. This resulted in the following order of the Bureau of Conscription, March 22, 1864:

[67] James D. Richardson, *A Compilation of the Messages and Papers of the Confederacy*, I, p. 370.
[68] Zigler, *op. cit.*, p. 141.
[69] *Ibid.*, p. 141.
[70] *Confederate Statutes at Large*, II, p. 211.

Bureau of Conscription
Richmond, March 22, 1864

Circular No. 11

Section II. Upon general principles of justice, equity, and necessity the Government is disposed to relieve persons between seventeen and eighteen and forty-five and fifty, members of the Society of Friends, Dunkards, &c. When they are in a condition to be detailed for agricultural pursuits, it may be done under the conditions imposed upon other classes of producers. When there are clerical employments or artisan or mechanical labors that they can perform they may be selected for these objects. Every case, however, should be referred to this Bureau for its action, allowing the parties to remain at their employments until action is taken.

By command of Col. John S. Preston, superintendent:

Thos. Goldwaite
Acting Assistant Adjutant-General.[71]

As an aid in clarifying the procedure for exempting members of churches opposed to war, a bill was passed and became law June 7th, 1864, known as "An Act to amend so much of an Act entitled, 'An Act to organize forces to serve during the war' approved February seventeenth, eighteen hundred and sixty-four, as relates to the exemption of certain religious denominations." It provided:

That the Secretary of War shall be authorized to grant exemptions to the members of the various denominations mentioned in the exemption act of the eleventh of October, eighteen hundred and sixty-two, who, at that time, belonged to the same, and who were in regular association therewith, upon the terms and conditions specified in that act, or upon such other terms and conditions specified in that act, or upon such other terms and conditions as he is authorized to allow exemptions or grant details under any of the clauses of the act approved February seventeenth, eighteen hundred and sixty-four, to which this is an amendment.[72]

This amendment referred only to persons who were members of the churches on October 11, 1862. Judge Campbell, Assistant Secretary of War, claimed that the membership of

---

[71] *Official Records,* Series 4, III, p. 240.
[72] *Ibid.,* pp. 494-495.

these denominations had been substantially increased since the war and that this had been "a cause for distrust."[73] Circular Number 24, which follows, shows that the War Department was becoming stricter in its insistence upon sincerity on the part of conscientious objectors:

Confederate States of America
War Dept., Bureau of Conscription
Richmond, Va., June 27, 1864

Circular Number 24.

The attention of the Bureau is called to the Act of Congress, approved, June 7, 1864, and entitled an act to amend so much of an act to organize forces to serve during the War, approved February 17, 1864, as relates to the exemption of certain religious denominations. This act is published in Orders, No. 53 (No. 13).

. . . .

. . . It is understood that a large addition has been made to these denominations since the enactment of October, 1862, from families not previously connected with them. This has been a cause for distrust and probably led to the adoption of the precise language of the act.

The department has exercised a liberal indulgence in favor of those who held or were supposed to hold conscientious scruples upon the subject of bearing arms, but there is no reason for affording any countenance to efforts to avoid the performance of public duty by hypocritical pretenses of a religious belief, which has no root in the conscience or influence upon the conduct.

By order:

J. A. Campbell
Assistant Secretary of War[74]

The situation became extremely critical for those who sought exemption on religious grounds by the use of General Orders No. 77 from the Adjutant and Inspector General's Office at Richmond, October 8, 1864. It follows.

---

[73] *Ibid.*, p. 515.
[74] *Ibid.*, p. 515.

Adj. and Insp. General's Office
Richmond, October 8, 1864

General Orders
No. 77

1. All details granted under the authority of the War Department to persons between the ages of eighteen and forty-five years are hereby revoked; and all such detailed men, together with those within the said ages who hold furloughs or temporary exemptions by reasons of pending applications for detail, will be promptly assembled at the camps of instruction and appropriately assigned among the armies for service; except that men detailed and now actually employed as artisans, mechanics or persons of scientific skill (and those detailed and now engaged in the manufacture, collection and forwarding of indispensable supplies for the Army and Navy) will be continued in their present employments until their respective details be revised.

S. Cooper
Adjutant and Inspector General[75]

This was a hard blow for the Brethren but they worked constantly with the government on behalf of the sincere members who united with the church after October 11, 1862. B. F. Moomaw considered at one time petitioning the government to allow the Brethren to leave the state. The year 1864 was one of increasing hardships and anxieties for the historic peace churches.

The Brethren During 1865

On March 7, 1865, the Bureau of Conscription was abolished and the Generals of Reserves in the several states took over the task of enforcing conscription and granting exemptions.[76] This threw the Brethren again upon the mercy of state officers. While the church still worked with the government, the situation was so serious for the Brethren that many of them of draft age tried to escape across the lines to Northern territory. For the third time—in Germany, in colonial America, and in Virginia during the Civil

---

[75] *Ibid.*, p. 715.
[76] *Ibid.*, p. 1176.

War—the Brethren answered the severest tests of the war through emigration.

President Davis addressed the Senate and House of the Confederate States on March 13, 1865, in the following way:

The desire of the Executive and the Secretary of War to obtain for the Army the services of every man available for the public defense can hardly be doubted, and Congress may be assured that nothing but imperative public necessity could induce the exercise of any discretion vested in them to retain men out of the Army. But no government can be administered without vesting some discretion in Executive officers in the application of general rules to classes of the population. Individual exceptions exist to all such rules, in the very nature of things, and these exceptions cannot be provided for by legislation in advance.[77]

The pressure of the President had its effect. Bills were introduced in both houses of Congress entitled "An Act to diminish the number of exemptions and details." President Davis asked for a few changes in the proposed legislation. On March 18, 1865, the last day Congress met, the Senate approved a bill of the House supplemental to an act entitled "An Act to diminish the number of exemptions and details."[78] This bill canceled all exemptions on religious grounds and was a further stimulus for the Brethren to move westward. However, General Lee surrendered at Appomattox Courthouse, April 9, 1865, and the cessation of hostilities made the bill inoperative.

SUFFERINGS OF THE BRETHREN DURING THE CIVIL WAR

There was more suffering among the Brethren in the South than in the North. The reason can be readily seen. In the North there was more of a stable government and fewer changes were made in the draft law. In the South the Brethren were an antislavery people, were classed as Unionists, and thus were often misunderstood.

At the beginning of the war some Brethren in Virginia

---

[77] *Ibid.*, p. 1129.
[78] *Journal of Confederate Congress*, VII, p. 796.

were dragged into the army. Others paid large sums for substitutes. Later those who were drafted paid $500 each for exemption. The raising of this money was a hardship on the church. The Southern Brethren lived under the constant threat that the law would be changed. There were frequent imprisonments and local officials did not always honor the exemption law. Some of the leading Brethren like John Kline and P. R. Wrightsman were imprisoned.

Church of the Brethren members suffered greatly from Sheridan's destructive march through the Valley of Virginia. General Grant became aware that this section of Virginia was a great storehouse of supplies for the Southern Confederacy. He ordered Sheridan to spare nothing of any worth to his opponents. With flaming torches his army spread destruction between the Blue Ridge and the Alleghany Mountains. Sheridan said in his own report:

> I have destroyed a thousand barns filled with wheat, have driven in front of the army over 4,000 head of stock and have killed not less than 3,000 sheep. So entire has been the destruction that a crow flying across the Valley must carry its own rations.[79]

The writer's grandfather, Daniel Bowman, suffered the loss of his mill through fire. Many Brethren were farmers in the path of this army and they experienced great financial losses.

Brethren Martyrs

In Tennessee, John P. Bowman, a minister of unusual power, was killed by soldiers when he implored them not to take his horse, which he needed so greatly. His death brought grief to the church.

The greatest sorrow, however, that befell the Church of the Brethren during the Civil War was the death of Elder John Kline. He was undoubtedly the most loved man of the denomination. His activity in behalf of the Brethren,

---

[79] Zigler, *op. cit.*, p. 145.

.his fearlessness in crossing military lines, his courage in contacting military officials, and his straightforward preaching of the doctrine of peace brought him under severe criticism. His life was threatened a number of times and he was conscious of it. But his cause was more precious to him than his life. He was moderator of the Annual Conference held at Hagerstown, Indiana, in May, 1864. He closed that Conference with the following significant words which showed that he recognized what might befall him:

> Now, Brethren and friends, I have only touched some of the chords in the beautiful anthem of my theme. I now leave it with you, hoping that you may learn every note in it; and by the sweet music of a good life delight the ears and warm the hearts of all who hear its rich harmonies. Possibly you may never see my face or hear my voice again. I am now on my way back to Virginia, not knowing the things that shall befall me there. It may be that bonds and afflictions abide me. But I feel that I have done nothing worthy of bonds or of death; and none of these things move me; neither count I my life dear unto myself, so that I may finish my course with joy, and the ministry which I have received of the Lord Jesus, to testify the Gospel of the grace of God.[80]

After returning from this meeting, he resumed his active duties. On June 15, 1864, he went to a blacksmith shop a few miles from his home to get his horse shod. Upon his return from the shop and on his way to visit a sick neighbor he was shot by masked men and killed. His body when found had been pierced by several bullets. His passing was mourned throughout the Church of the Brethren. The denomination had lost one of its greatest leaders.

SUMMARY

The Brethren were located on both sides of the war between the states. They opposed secession and did not want war. The church faced the conflict well united against participation in war. The discipline of the denomination

---

[80] Funk, *op. cit.*, p. 477.

was strict. Members who joined the church had to promise not to take part in war. The Annual Conference decided not to keep members in the fellowship of the church
who went into the army and shed blood. Members were
advised not to wear any military clothing.

In the early days of the war, some of the Brethren hired
substitutes. The church members preferred to pay taxes
instead of using the system of substitutes. But the records do not indicate that the Brethren clearly recognized
the inconsistency with their peace position of employing
substitutes or paying heavy war taxes to keep free from
participation in armed conflicts. The Society of Friends
protested continually against war taxes. The Brethren and
the Mennonites took the position that they should pay what
the government required. The Brethren felt that the gospel required the payment of fines and taxes. They based
their opposition to war upon the teachings of Jesus but
related their opposition more to the overt acts of war
than to the whole war system. They felt that the Church
of the Brethren, for Biblical reasons, could not use the
sword, but that the civil government, likewise because of
Biblical reasons—"for the punishment of evildoers" (1
Peter 2: 14)—might have to use material force. There was
a dualism in the Brethren point of view. They felt that
the Christians who obeyed the New Testament were "not
of the world," and that the laws which governed such
Christians and the laws which governed the state were of
a different kind. They did not vote during this period because voting would have involved them in the war. They
wanted to be separate from the world.

The Brethren were not neutral in their sympathies. They
were classed in both North and South as Unionists. As
has been related, the Annual Conference of 1864 declared
that the government had the sympathy and prayers of the

Brethren in its "efforts to suppress the rebellion." This resolution was entirely out of harmony with the church's opposition to war.

In the North the Brethren fared much better than in the South. There was a more stable government in the North. President Lincoln was more sympathetic than President Davis toward religious objectors to war. But even in the North much work was necessary on the part of the peace churches before the law of February 24, 1864, was enacted. D. P. Sayler was very helpful in his government contacts. The Brethren men who were drafted paid the tax of $300 and remained on their farms.

The unstable government in the South, the need of men and money, and the growing hostility toward those who would not fight, caused much anxiety and suffering for members of the historic peace churches. It was necessary to make many government contacts and to work with government officials. The Brethren were very active in presenting the claims of the church to Congressmen and army officers. The Mennonites and Brethren, and the Quakers and Brethren offered joint petitions to the Confederate Congress. There is no record that the three churches ever offered a united petition. Most of the government contacts, however, made by these churches were carried on independently.

The Brethren in the South experienced frequent changes in the draft laws. They lived under the constant threat of these changes. There were many prison experiences. Some members escaped to neutral territory. The fines, war taxes, and losses suffered in Sheridan's raid worked a great hardship on the Brethren people. The death of Elder John Kline was a great blow to the entire church. Persecution again stimulated some Brethren to move westward.

In brief, in both North and South, recognition of religious objectors to war came after the most serious efforts on the part of the historic peace churches. On neither side was there exemption from responsibility for helping the war. The payment of a tax in lieu of personal service was only exemption from overt participation.

CHAPTER VI

PEACE WORK IN THE CHURCH OF THE BRETHREN BETWEEN THE CIVIL WAR AND WORLD WAR I

ANNUAL CONFERENCE DECISIONS

The Problem of Pensions

Almost immediately following the Civil War the problem of Brethren receiving pensions for army service arose. A number of members were received into the church after the war who had participated in armed service. While they were required to covenant to live according to the peace principles of the church, whether it was right for them to take pension money from the government for past war activities was not settled. The following query came to the Conference of 1870:

Is it considered right for a brother to take or receive a pension, back pay, or bounty, for service rendered to the government before he became a member of the church?

The answer was: "We think he may be allowed to do so."[1]

The Annual Conference of 1878 was asked the question: "A son of a sister, whose husband is living, perished in the army; is it right, under any circumstances for the sister to draw a pension from the government?" The Conference answered: "It is."[2] Thus, members were allowed to receive pensions from the government. Nowhere in the records are the reasons given for the above actions of the church. It should be understood, however, that the Brethren up to this time had not related the economic problem very definitely to their peace position. Since they felt that the gospel required them to pay their taxes, it may be assumed that they believed the receiving of pensions from the government did not involve them in war, especially

---

[1] *Annual Meeting Minutes, 1778-1909*, p. 284.
[2] *Ibid.*, p. 358.

when pensions came for service rendered before the members concerned united with the church.

No General Co-operation With Peace Associations

As early as 1875 the Annual Conference was asked "to adopt suitable measures to enable the church to co-operate actively with the Peace Association of America." The answer was:

Our church itself being a peace association, we need not, as a body, co-operate with others, but we may as individuals give our influence in favor of peace.[3]

The Annual Conference of 1884 turned down a petition to send delegates to the Annual National Peace Convention and re-emphasized the decision of 1875.[4]

Although these decisions show that the Church of the Brethren was not ready to work with peace organizations in an active peace program, they also reveal that there were individuals in the church much interested in seeing the denomination awakened to its possibilities as a peacemaker.

The Question of Police Protection at Communion Services

The old-time Brethren communion service lasted a whole day. There were sermons in the morning and afternoon with the communion service proper in the evening. Large crowds would often come and disturbances from people on the outside of the church were not uncommon. The Annual Conference of 1879 was asked to interpret the question of whether it was "according to the teaching of the gospel and the long established order of the Brethren, for any branch of the church to employ a police force to keep order at the communion meeting or other meetings." Conference answered: "Only in extreme cases."[5] The answer, though brief, is a summary of Brethren practice. These people asked

---

[3] *Ibid.*, p. 325.
[4] *Ibid.*, p. 432.
[5] *Ibid.*, p. 367.

for police protection for their meetings very rarely and depended upon goodwill and persuasion to handle disorders.

Members Not to Attach Themselves to the Grand Army of the Republic

Since former soldiers had come into the church, it was natural for some of them to keep connections with their war comrades. The Annual Conference of 1888 took action against any brother attaching himself to the "Association of the Grand Army of the Republic."[6] The minutes of the Annual Conference of 1890 show that there was a growing tendency for Brethren "who were soldiers in the late rebellion to attend soldiers' reunions, to march with and participate in their exercises," and the Conference decided that it was wrong for members of the church to attend such places.[7]

During the first twenty-five years after the Civil War the church was dealing with problems as they arose. There was no constructive peace program.

PEACE TRACTS PUBLISHED

In 1900 a book was printed entitled "The Brethren's Tracts and Pamphlets," which was a compilation of articles from various authors and aimed to present a complete statement of Brethren doctrine. Two of the writers dealt with the subject of peace and made a contribution to the Brethren philosophy of nonresistance. Daniel Hays wrote as follows:

The doctrine of non-resistance is a fundamental doctrine of the Christian religion. . . . In support of the principles of non-resistance we produce the following Scriptural facts:

1. Christ is the "Prince of Peace." Isa. 9: 6.
2. His "kingdom is not of this world." John 18: 36.
3. His "servants do not fight." John 18: 36.

---

[6] *Ibid.*, p. 481.
[7] *Ibid.*, p. 521.

4. "The weapons of our warfare are not carnal." 2 Cor. 10: 4.

5. We are to "love our enemies." Matt. 5: 43.

6. We are to "overcome evil with good." Rom. 12: 21.

7. We are to "pray for them which despitefully use us and persecute us." Matt. 5: 44.[8]

D. Vaniman wrote about "Christ and War":

Christ, its Author, says, "Love your enemies." War says, "Hate them."

Christ says, "Do them good." War says, "Do them harm."

Christ says, "Pray for them." War says, "Slay them."

Christ says, "Bless them." War says, "Curse them."

Christ says, "I come not to destroy men's lives; but to save them. War says, "I come to destroy men's lives; and for this purpose I want the most effectual weapons that can be invented."

Christ says, "Overcome evil with good." War says, "Render evil for evil, and more of it."

Paul says, "If thine enemy hunger, feed him." War says, "Starve him."

Paul says, "If he thirst, give him drink." War says, "Destroy his wells, cut off his supplies of every kind."

Paul says, "The weapons of our warfare are not carnal." War says, "Ours are carnal; bring on the sword and spear, the musket and cannon, with plenty of powder, shot, and shell."

Paul says, "We wrestle not against flesh and blood." War says, "We do wrestle against flesh and blood. Crowd them to the wall, and into the last ditch; utterly destroy them if they don't submit."

War unbridles the lusts and passions of man's depraved nature, destroys morals, imposes heavy burdens upon productive industries, makes widows and orphans, wastes money, begets envy, hatred, variance, wrath, strife, sedition, murders, drunkenness, revelings, and such like, of which Paul says: "I tell you before, as I have also told you in time past, that they which do such things shall not inherit the kingdom of God." Gal. 5: 21.[9]

These articles were possibly the clearest expression of the Church of the Brethren's Biblical position on peace which had been made up to this time.

---

[8] *The Brethren's Tracts and Pamphlets,* pp. 26-27.
[9] *Ibid.,* p. 1.

TWENTY YEARS BETWEEN PEACE DECLARATIONS

From 1890 to 1911 there was no Annual Conference declaration on peace. The only exception was the Annual Conference of 1902, which petitioned the king of Denmark against exile and imprisonment for those conscientiously opposed to war.[10] The Spanish-American War of 1898 passed by unnoticed as far as the church records show. The Brethren were occupied with the development of Sunday schools, colleges and missions. Peace work was not an outstanding feature of the church program.

A PEACE COMMITTEE FORMED

In 1910 the Annual Conference resolutions encouraged "the entire membership to activity in the cause of peace."[11] In 1911 the Brethren appointed a Peace Committee with the following duties:

First: to propagate and aid in the distribution of such literature as may be helpful to the better understanding as to the sinfulness and folly of resorting to arms in the settlement of differences;

Second: to use every lawful gospel means in bringing about peaceful settlements of difficulties when such may arise between governments or societies;

Third: to keep the Brotherhood informed, from time to time, through our publications, as to the true status of the peace movement.[12]

The Conference of 1911 was also petitioned to appoint a representative to the next Universal Peace Conference, but this was turned down. The duties of the Peace Committee, however, indicated the beginning of a change in the church's thinking. The Brethren were beginning to sense the need of a peace educational program within the church and the necessity for the church to become an active force for peace among the nations.

[10] *Minutes of the Annual Meetings, 1778-1909*, pp. 767-768.
[11] *Annual Conference Minutes*, 1910, p. 15.
[12] *Ibid.*, 1911, p. 7.

Peace Committee Without Funds

The Peace Committee reported to the Annual Conference of 1914 and stated that thus far it had received no funds for its work. The report showed that some peace programs had been given, articles had been furnished for the church periodicals, a peace pamphlet had been printed, and letters had been written to President Woodrow Wilson commending him for his peaceful methods.[13]

Peace Resolutions of 1915

The Peace Committee brought to the Annual Conference of 1915 a resolution which was unanimously accepted. This resolution expressed the Church of the Brethren's abhorrence of war, her opposition to increased armaments, her earnest prayer for the President and the cabinet to keep this country out of war, and her profound sorrow for the terrible conflict in the world.[14] The general resolutions of the 1915 Conference stated:

That the church renews its allegiance to its time-honored stand for peace and the brotherhood of man, and urges the judicial arbitration of all international differences; that it pledges itself to a greater zeal in spreading the peace gospel of Jesus Christ and urges frequent sermons by its ministers, discussions by its members in all their assemblies and through the Gospel Messenger, to the end that it may be an increasingly effective power in the hands of the Master for the maintenance of peace and good will among men and among the nations of the world.[15]

It is evident that the church recognized the increased war spirit in the nation and significant that the Brethren reaffirmed their faith in the absolute teachings of Jesus and "in the gospel of love and good will to men." The official position of the Church of the Brethren on the peace principle was clear.

The Peace Committee in 1916 made a report indicating

[13] *Ibid.*, 1914, pp. 16-17.
[14] *Ibid.*, 1915, pp. 25-26.
[15] *Ibid.*, 1915, p. 30.

again that it had received no financial aid. It called upon the church to express its opposition to military preparedness, recommended that all "congregations and colleges at once organize local peace committees and become active in distributing peace literature," and requested the Conference to petition the President and Congress to appropriate funds for "the relief of suffering humanity throughout the war zones, without respect to race, religion or nationality."[16]

The United States declared war against Germany, April 6, 1917, and the next General Conference was held in June of that year after the outbreak of hostilities.

THE CHURCH OF THE BRETHREN NOT PREPARED FOR WORLD WAR I

It is evident that the Church of the Brethren entered the first World War without having carried on an adequate peace educational program among the church members. The church had a strong general peace position based upon the teachings of Jesus but the leaders of the denomination had not thought this position through in relation to the complex involvements of war. Peace resolutions had been passed, pacifist articles written and without doubt the Brethren as a whole were acquainted with the traditional point of view. But since the Civil War something had happened to the church. The chief attention of the denomination had been focused upon the mission program and the development of colleges and Sunday schools. The peace position of the church was taken for granted. For twenty years there was no Conference declaration on this subject. While a peace committee was formed in 1911 no funds were provided for its work, and no far-reaching program was possible. The old exclusiveness which characterized the Brethren between the Revolutionary War and the Civil War was

---

[16] *Ibid.*, 1916, pp. 31-32.

gradually passing. The church was becoming less legalistic and more tolerant. More respect was being given to the consciences of the individual members whose views were different from the established position of the church. Brethren young people were going to public schools and colleges. They were becoming vital factors in community life. It was harder to break with their community associates on the peace question than in the days when the church maintained an exclusive church fellowship. The Brethren young people of draft age had not been placed in an educational setting where through stimulating discussions they were led to think through the problems of war and what attitude they should take regarding it. The Church of the Brethren faced World War I with her young people unprepared for the struggle.

THE CHURCH OF THE BRETHREN AND THE STATE

The changed condition of the church is evidenced again by the fact that the members were rather generally voting by World War I. The temperance movement in its development during the years prior to the war was a great influence in starting Brethren to vote. As early as 1866 the Annual Conference decided not to make voting a test of fellowship in the church.[17] The Annual Conference of 1912 advised "that Brethren neither vote nor accept office of any kind unless they are convinced that by so doing they can more completely fill their mission in the world relative to themselves, to their fellow-men and to God."[18] The church constantly advised members not to accept offices which required them to use physical force or to compromise the peace principles of the gospel of Christ. But the Brethren as a whole were voting and a few were holding office in the government when the World War came.

---

[17] *Minutes of the Annual Meetings, 1778-1909*, p. 249.
[18] *Annual Conference Minutes*, 1912, p. 3.

Many Brethren Supported Wilson

The political campaign of 1915 found church members, who normally voted the Republican ticket, on the side of Woodrow Wilson. They thought he would keep the country out of war. The slogan, "He kept us out of war," caught the ear of these peace-loving people. While no actual statistics are available, it is generally recognized in the Church of the Brethren that the members for the most part supported Wilson.

A New Interpretation of Citizenship

The Annual Conference of 1917, which met two months after the war started, made the following significant pronouncement:

Confronted as we are with an actual state of war, it behooves us to look within as well as without, to take heed to ourselves, and to keep steadily in mind the doctrine of peace we and our forefathers have held.

As a gratifying tribute to the consistency of our forefathers, and as a gracious concession to our own appeals, the President and the law-making bodies of our country have granted us exemption from militant, combative service. We desire hereby to make public and grateful recognition of this significant bestowment the honorable authorities of our Government have thus granted to us.

Averring our loyalty to the civil authorities, and desiring to serve our country in the peaceable arts and productive industries, we commit ourselves to a constructive patriotism and loyal citizenship of real service.

Therefore, we resolve, with one heart and soul, to be patriotic and loyal in the highest sense to our beloved country to which our forefathers fled for religious liberty. We resolve to invest our lives and all our energies for the conservation and promotion of all that is true, good and noble in our institutions of home and school, church and state, and in the high ideals of liberty and humanity which we covet for the whole world. We adopt the keynote of the Religious Educational Association of America, "to get away from pagan nationalism, to Christian internationalism."

We believe in constructive patriotism, therefore, we dedicate ourselves anew, and more earnestly than before, to the promotion of the great and fundamental interests of the church and state, namely, the cause of the Sunday School, missions, and Christian education. We would lay upon the conscience of every member of the church the solemn obligation of making sacrifices commensurate with the sacrifices made by those who are not exempted from military service.

We call upon all our ministers to make the spirit of these resolutions operative in the lives of all the ministers of our Brotherhood.[19]

This resolution is very important because it gives a constructive interpretation of citizenship. The old dualism was gone which held that the church and the civil government operate under different laws. The church, holding to convictions against war, recognized the responsibility of its members to promote "all that is true, good and noble," in home, church, school and state. The old rigidness in the church's traditional doctrine of separateness from the world had relaxed. A social gospel consciousness had developed in the church.

CHURCH DIVISIONS

Between the Civil War and the World War the Church of the Brethren experienced two church divisions. In 1881 about four thousand people left the main body and called themselves the Old German Baptist Brethren. This group could not reconcile themselves to Sunday schools, academies, evangelistic meetings, and salaried ministers. It did not seem possible at that time to harmonize the more forward-looking program of the main church body and the equally sincere but more conservative thinking of these members. In 1882 a second division occurred and the denomination known as the Brethren Church was formed. This division is now recognized by both the Church of the Brethren and the Brethren Church as having been unfortunate. Both denominations at the present time have com-

---
[19] *Ibid.*, 1917, p. 16.

mittees on fraternal relations working to unite them. When the Brethren Church was organized it numbered about ten thousand members. While it is true that some leaders of the Brethren Church wanted to take more forward-looking steps in the church program than the main church body would endorse, any careful study of the church proceedings during the division shows that the disruption came because of radical leadership, an impatient spirit, and a lack of self-control on both sides.[20] Some bitter words were spoken. This action was inconsistent with the church's peace position.

When the Peace Committee of the Church of the Brethren was visiting General Crowder during the first World War, he asked of Elder W. J. Swigart: "How many divisions are there to your denomination?" After receiving the reply he commented: "You are pretty good scrappers for a peace people after all."[21]

SUMMARY

The period under review was one of profound changes in the Church of the Brethren. The church gradually relaxed the severe discipline of its members and became less legalistic and more tolerant. The church exclusiveness gradually passed, Brethren people went to public schools and colleges and became vital factors in community life. Brethren homes, which through the years had been centers for the transmission of Brethren culture and ideals, were invaded by community influences. Brethren young people found it hard to break with their comrades in public schools on the peace question. The church's peace doctrine had not been an outstanding factor in Brethren thought during this period. No adequate peace educational program had been carried on for Brethren youth. The church divisions

---

[20] John S. Flory, *Flashlights from History*, p. 86.
[21] J. E. Miller, *Stories from Brethren Life*, p. 137.

were not consistent with peace principles, but the main body of the church was well united by the World War period. A more constructive view of citizenship was taken and the church members were recognizing their responsibility to vote and help influence legislation. A church which had changed in character since Civil War days faced the World War unprepared for the struggle.

CHAPTER VII

THE POSITION OF THE CHURCH OF THE BRETHREN DURING WORLD WAR I

THE BRETHREN OPPOSED THE ENTRANCE OF THE UNITED STATES INTO THE WORLD WAR

As lovers of peace, the members of the Church of the Brethren did not want the World War to come. Many of them felt that Woodrow Wilson would keep this country out of war. Daniel Hays wrote in the "Gospel Messenger" of February 19, 1916, asking ministers to preach on peace from their pulpits, the members of the church to send petitions to the President and to write to their representatives in Congress opposing the increased militarism. He said further: "War is the greatest calamity that ever befell the human race. It is sin run mad. Peace is the greatest blessing that can come upon a people."[1] After President Wilson's tour of the Middle West in which he advocated that the American navy should be the greatest navy in the world, H. C. Early wrote:

What if the United States sets out to build up a military equipment as great as that of any other nation, or, as the President sanguinely states, "incomparably greater?" What will happen? Will the other nations lie still, looking on, seeing the United States providing equipment "incomparably greater" than that of any other nation in the world? Hardly. Competition will arise,—the sharpest in the world. Nothing else. War right on the spot, nation warring with nation in the scramble for the biggest and best armies and navies, each nation going to the limit of its resources. Who wants such a war? . . .
. . . .

Instead of military preparation, our nation ought to use her great influence in favor of ultimate, universal peace. Instead of multiplying her arms and arsenals, she ought to stand, firm and fast, for disarmament, based on the sanity of peace, and insist that the wealth

---

[1] Daniel Hays, article in *Gospel Messenger*, Feb. 19, 1916, pp. 114-115.

and lifeblood of the nations be turned to the building of the home, the school, the church,—the bulwark of national security. Instead of preparing for war,—though it may be for defense,— let her give herself to making strong the tie of international peace and brotherhood, working, with a fixed hand, for the conditions that will make future wars impossible, for her opportunities to do such things will be unprecedented at the close of the European War.[2]

Early and Hays were two of the great leaders and thinkers of the church. Following their expressions of concern, the Annual Conference of June 8-15, 1916, drew up the following resolution in opposition to war, passed it unanimously, and appointed a committee of three members to present it in person to the President. It is quoted in part:

The church reaffirms its position in favor of peace even at the cost of suffering wrongfully, if need be, and its unalterable opposition to war and bloodshed under any conditions of provocation, and all preparation for war as one of its primal teachings, maintaining that all disputes, national and international, not settled by those involved, should be submitted to a Commission on Arbitration as the highest and final appeal of nations. And since the government of the United States in its just dealings with its citizens has graciously provided for the free exercise of conscience in these matters, by authority of this Conference copies of this resolution shall, if needed, be furnished to all members applying therefor which may be used in connection with a certificate of membership from the local church in which one may reside, all of which may, if occasion arise, be presented to the authorities of our Government in seeking exemption from military service in accordance with any provision of the United States laws. . . .[3]

Committee: I. W. Taylor, H. C. Early, W. J. Swigart.

The resolution was presented to President Wilson by the committee at 12:45 P.M., July 13, 1916. The delegates reported in the "Gospel Messenger" of August 5, 1916, that the President received them with courtesy. The resolution was very clear in reaffirming the Biblical basis of the church's peace position. It informed the government be-

---

[2] H. C. Early, *Ibid.*, April 1, 1916, p. 218.
[3] *Minutes of the Annual Meeting*, 1916, p. 12.

fore hostilities began concerning the peace doctrine of the Brethren. It expressed the Church of the Brethren's unalterable opposition to increased militarism. It even stated that copies of this resolution would be furnished to church members to be used with government authorities in case of war. But the resolution had one outstanding weakness. It was not specific enough in applying the general position of the church to war situations.

THE ATTITUDE OF THE BRETHREN TOWARD WAR DURING WORLD WAR I

The Annual Conference of 1916 reaffirmed the church's historic peace position, and the Conference of 1917, meeting shortly after the United States entered the war, held that Brethren had a responsibility for making a constructive contribution to their country, but both Conferences dealt with the war problem in general terms.

Confusion Regarding Noncombatant Service

The church had passed peace resolutions but had not instructed her young people. The draft law of May 18, 1917, exempted Brethren from only combatant service. Section 1644 is quoted:

And nothing in this act contained shall be construed to require or compel any person to serve in any of the forces herewith provided for who is found to be a member of any well recognized religious sect or organization at present organized and existing and whose existing creed or principles forbid its members to participate in war in any form and whose religious convictions are against war or participation therein in accordance with the creed or principles of said religious organization; but no person so exempted shall be exempted from service in any capacity that the President shall declare to be noncombatant.[4]

The young men of the Church of the Brethren were called to camp unprepared to meet the problems which faced

---

[4] Walter G. Kellogg, *The Conscientious Objector*, p. 17.

them. Should they wear the uniform or should they not?
Should they submit to military drill or should they not?
Should they go inside the army and accept noncombatant
service, or should they refuse all army service? On these
problems the church had taken no clear-cut position. The
boys wrote many frantic appeals to the home ministers
for guidance. And.they received different kinds of advice
from the ministers.

The leaders of the church were confused as to the posi-
tion the young people should be advised to take. J. M.
Henry, who served as a member of the Central Service
Committee during the war, says:

> As might be expected there arose two groups of peace advisers.
> One group advised the drafted young men to have absolutely noth-
> ing to do with the military machine, and refuse to do any kind of
> service. They argued—with some degree of consistent validity—
> that there could be no such thing as non-military service as long as
> the government, through its military arm, the War Department,
> regimented life and directed all physical force, including the lives
> of people, to prosecute war to the end of killing and defeating the
> enemy. The other group advised the young men to be loyal citizens
> of the government and accept noncombatant service, as long as it
> did not violate the individual conscience.[5]

Charles D. Bonsack, another member of the Central
Service Committee, says:

> The First World War brought new issues that confused our church
> people. Prior to this our government had depended for the most
> part on volunteers for the army. World War No. I laid hands on
> all men over twenty-one. The church had strong decisions about
> peace and war; but its members were also careful citizens of the
> state, paying taxes, conforming to its laws and upholding its institu-
> tions. Between these two conflicting attitudes in the time of war,
> the church became confused and somewhat uncertain about the di-
> rection it should take. To train for war and engage therein seemed
> impossible to our people. On the other hand, to lie in a detention
> camp and do nothing seemed contrary to our loyal citizen idea

---

[5] J. M. Henry, *History of the Church of the Brethren in Maryland*, p. 526.

through the years. The government was also confused and was a long time designating what noncombatant service in the army implied. Meanwhile mistakes were made by all parties involved. But the result of it was that some accepted service in the regular armed forces; most of the young men found service in the noncombatant service of the army and some remained in the detention camps, until the government planned to furlough them on farms, for which soldiers' compensation was paid by the government.[6]

The moderator of the 1917 Conference, H. C. Early, in a letter written to the chairman of the Peace Committee, stated his opinion regarding noncombatant service. He wrote thus: "Like yourself, I have not come to the point where I can recommend to our young men to refuse noncombatant service and take the consequences. My judgment is that they should obey the government as far as it can be done without violation to their conscience."[7]

J. E. Miller says: "When the World War came we were not prepared for it. The church was uncertain as to the position it should take."[8]

J. A. Robinson, a visiting minister in camps during World War I, says: "The church was not organized and was confused as to what was best to do and the boys had little or no help upon which they could depend. The government was not clear in what attitude it should take, and this was much more true among the many officers in the camps."[9]

W. J. Swigart, chairman of the Peace Committee, wrote to the "Gospel Messenger" of July 7, 1917, stating that "the Conscription Law, passed by both Houses of Congress, and approved by President Wilson, and now in force, makes probably the most liberal provision for exemption on conscientious grounds that has ever been enacted by any gov-

---

[6] Personal interview with Charles D. Bonsack, Elgin, Ill., Dec. 30, 1942.
[7] Henry, *op. cit.*, p. 527.
[8] Personal interview with J. E. Miller, Elgin, Ill., Dec. 31, 1942.
[9] Personal letter from J. A. Robinson, Johnstown, Pa., Feb. 16, 1943.

ernment. . . . The law definitely provides exemption from militant service for our people."[10]

D. L. Miller, one of the older and most respected leaders among the Brethren, wrote in the church paper September 22, 1917, and gave his influence toward the young men accepting noncombatant service. He said:

The question of refusing service that would violate our non-resistant principles and imprisonment for refusal, was brought before the Provost Marshal General by the brethren. His reply, given incidentally, was that he did not want to see, as in some foreign countries, our land occupied with prisons filled with noncombatant people.

How far one may go in serving the Government, at this time, without violating the Gospel doctrine of peace, is one of the important problems to be solved. After writing this it was learned that President Wilson has placed hospital work and caring for the suffering wounded as noncombatant service. As to whether we can engage in this service, may result in a difference of opinion. If it is simply caring for the sick and wounded, feeding the hungry and clothing the naked, it is fully in accord with the teachings of Jesus. It is always right, and not only right but our duty, to help suffering, no matter how the suffering has been brought about. When Jesus commended the good Samaritan because he cared for the naked, wounded man by the wayside, he did not favor the robber. The care for the suffering, caused by the war, is not favoring war. So it seems to the writer.[11]

The church paper, which kept informed regarding the problems of the brotherhood, presented a stirring editorial in the September 15, 1917, issue, calling upon the church to define its attitude toward "noncombatant service." The editor indicated that the number of inquiries from members on this question had been embarrassing. He wrote:

And yet, when we looked for an answer to this question, what is the position of the church on the points involved? We looked in vain. Not, of course, as to the church's attitude toward war in general,—war in the abstract,—war a long way off. The answer to that

[10] W. J. Swigart, *Gospel Messenger* article, July 7, 1917, p. 419.
[11] D. L. Miller, *Gospel Messenger* article, Sept. 22, 1917, p. 594.

is easy. But as to the church's position in this war,—the war that is actually upon us, the war in which our brethren are being drafted for whatsoever service the authorities may choose to call non-combatant,—to this we found no answer.[12]

H. C. Early wrote an article in the "Gospel Messenger" of November 10, 1917, entitled "Why Does Not the Church Declare Her Position?" The article reveals that the leaders of the denomination were under a great deal of pressure to define the attitude of the church toward noncombatant service. Early answered the situation by saying that "the government shall first state what it demands of us, and then it is our duty to say whether or not we will accept it. It is hardly to be expected of the church to say what she will and will not do, previous to a statement of what the government defines as noncombatant duties. This is the reason, as I see it, why the church has not, up to this time, declared herself."[13] As moderator of the Annual Conference, Early spoke in a general way for the denomination. In fact, the church did not declare itself until January, 1918, when America's participation in the war was about half over.

Leaders of the denomination during World War I are not the only source of information regarding the church's attitude toward noncombatant service. There are outstanding Brethren today who had army experiences and whose testimonies are valuable. Professor C. Ray Keim of Manchester College, North Manchester, Indiana, says, "Our church did not have a policy worked out beforehand. . . . The government did not define its position soon enough."[14]

Dan West, Director of Peace Education, Church of the Brethren, says, "The church was confused. It dealt in gen-

---

[12] Editorial in *Gospel Messenger*, Sept. 15, 1917, pp. 577-578.
[13] H. C. Early, *Gospel Messenger* article, Nov. 10, 1917, pp. 705-706.
[14] Personal letter from C. Ray Keim, North Manchester, Ind., Feb. 1, 1943.

eral principles but not in spècifics. . . . It had failed to
think through its relationship to the state."[15]

L. C. Blickenstaff, public school teacher, says:

Although I had tried very hard I could get little advice from our
church leaders either before going to camp or during my stay there.
Only one advised me and he suggested that I take noncombatant
service. I think that most of our people thought that noncombatant
service would not be participating in the war.

To me the fact that we had no alternative type of service to offer
was the greatest weakness of the church at that time. I saw young
men sacrificing everything in the army and I wanted to do something, too, but there was nothing to do but take a negative position.[16]

G. W. Phillips, pastor of the Church of the Brethren at
Elkhart, Indiana, speaking of the situation at Camp Taylor,
says:

After March 1918, contingents of boys came every month. In each
succeeding group the percentage of boys going into noncombatant
service became greater. The church at home was failing. You
asked if our church was confused in its program. I would definitely
say, yes. There was far greater peace loyalty among the boys who
went to camp—particularly the first ones—than there was in the
church at home. In fact, we were disgusted with some of the church
leaders who came to visit the boys in camp![17]

In the early part of the war the advice of the Brethren
who visited the boys in military camps was not very definite
and the young men took various positions. I. W. Taylor in
the "Gospel Messenger" of October 13, 1917, reported his
visit to Camp Meade, Admiral, Maryland, with H. K. Ober
and C. H. Hostetler. Taylor summarized H. K. Ober's talk
to the Brethren boys by saying: "The thought of Brother
Ober was that, as nonresistant Christians, they would abide
by what President Wilson might ask of them."[18]   But

---

[15] Personal interview with Dan West, Chicago, Ill., Dec. 28, 1942.
[16] Personal letter from L. C. Blickenstaff, Gary, Ind., Jan. 25, 1943.
[17] Personal letter from G. W. Phillips, Elkhart, Ind., Feb. 5, 1943.
[18] I. W. Taylor, *Gospel Messenger* article, Oct. 13, 1917, p. 645.

President Wilson had not defined noncombatant service and this was no help to boys under the daily pressure from camp officials.

D. H. Zigler wrote in the "Gospel Messenger" of November 3, 1917, about his visit with J. A. Dove and B. B. Garber to Camp Lee, Virginia. His statement which follows shows how hard is was for young men even to get consideration for noncombatant service:

Evidence showed that a few of the Brethren were in training for the trenches. A few others had yielded in part, because of threats. Some had endured the sorest persecution, because they refused, to the last, to take up arms and be trained for the army. Almost every indignity conceivable was heaped upon them. They were cursed, called the vilest of names, threatened, and stood up as gazing stock for the soldiers, but they stood true as steel, and won a great victory. However, they were afterward placed in a servitude almost equal to imprisonment.

The next day we called at the office of the commanding officer, Gen. Krinkite. At once we were most kindly received, but on being more fully informed, as to the import of our mission, his mien was somewhat changed. It seemed as if he would have turned us from our purpose, but being convinced of the earnestness of our plea, he summoned a number of his officers and men,—the greater part of whom were our Brethren. As a result of a proceeding, akin to a court trial, our Brethren were released from the army. All of them present were transferred to the Remount Station, and promises given that all Brethren in the camp, and others to be received later, would be transferred to the Remount Station, or to the Base Hospital. . . .[19]

M. Clyde Horst wrote in the "Gospel Messenger" of December 1, 1917, about his visits to army camps with H. S. Replogle. He reported further about the Camp Lee situation, analyzed the various types of conscientious objectors and gave his observations about the lack of advice to young men. He wrote thus:

One reason, perhaps, for this hostile attitude, is the fact that our

---

[19] D. H. Zigler, *Ibid.*, Nov. 3, 1917, p. 692.

brethren are not standing together. Even those who ask for exemption for conscience' sake, fall into three classes: (1) those who accept noncombatant service and wear the uniform; (2) those who accept noncombatant service and do not wear the uniform; (3) those who not only refuse to wear the uniform, but who will not accept any task whatever. The latter are in the guard-house, not only because of their disobedience to orders, but also for their protection against certain rough men of the camp who are bitter against them, because they will not work, and yet are fed just as they are. Members of various nonresistant sects, moreover,—at Camp Meade, as well as at Camp Lee,—take extreme positions, which cause needless persecutions to be visited upon all noncombatants.

A number of these brethren do not have Certificate No. 174 in their possession, and never did have. It seemed clear, from our conversation with several of them, that they did not have the help and counsel from their elders and pastors that they should have had. Some seem to have come to the camp like sheep without a shepherd. A few brethren who enlisted did so because their spiritual advisers told them that it is better to enlist and choose the line of service than to take the chances of a drafted noncombatant. Some have been under the influence of teaching that war is right under the circumstances. Others come from churches where the teaching has been sound but they have yielded to the pressure of the spirit of the age.[20]

Joseph Bowman reported his visit to Camp Lee in the church paper of January 5, 1918, in which he said that the brethren in the detention camp "are very earnest in saying with General Kuhn, commander-in-charge of Camp Meade, that there is no such a thing as absolute noncombatant service under military control, and they certainly do not believe in militarism."[21] This statement of General Kuhn caused leaders of the church to do serious thinking. It influenced the church to become more critical toward noncombatant service.

Most Brethren Took Noncombatant Service

Since the Church of the Brethren in the early part of the

---

[20] M. Clyde Horst, *Ibid.*, Dec. 1, 1917, p. 765.
[21] Joseph Bowman, *Ibid.*, Jan. 5, 1918, p. 12.

war was not clear in its attitude toward noncombatant service and did not advise against it, most brethren who were drafted accepted this service. These brethren were generally recognized as having respected the peace position of the church. The second largest group was composed of those who refused all military service and were kept in detention camps, and later furloughed to farms or sent to prison. There were some also who took combatant service and a few personally known to the writer became officers in the army.

No statistics are available regarding the number of brethren who belonged to each group. The evidence is clear, however, that the noncombatant group was largest. Two members of the Central Service Committee during the World War testify to this fact. Charles D. Bonsack says: "The problem of whether or not to take noncombatant service was a great one for many boys. This was also a problem for the church. The position of the Church of the Brethren was none too clear regarding it. Most of the Brethren boys, however, took noncombatant service."[22] J. Maurice Henry gives the same information: "The Church of the Brethren had a great number of men then who wouldn't fight but put on the uniform. This was our greatest number."[23]

There were, however, quite a number of Brethren men who refused noncombatant service from the start. It is unfortunate that no accurate figures are available. P. J. Blough reported on March 30, 1918, that he found fifty-five Brethren in the detention camp at Camp Lee.[24] Harry C. Spielman wrote in the church paper of April 6, 1918, that he visited forty-three Brethren boys in the detention camp

[22] Personal interview with Charles D. Bonsack, Dec. 29, 1942.
[23] Personal interview with J. M. Henry, Bridgewater, Va., March 4, 1943.
[24] P. J. Blough, article in *Gospel Messenger*, March 30, 1918, p. 199.

at Camp Meade, Maryland.[25]   When one thinks of the number of army camps to which Brethren went, the number of objectors to noncombatant service could easily have reached several hundred.   George W. Phillips says, "Some of the boys voluntarily took noncombatant service, some did under pressure, but many refused.   Some accepted after refusing for a time.   From the government's standpoint its mistake was in waiting so long to present the issue.   A winter together did something to the boys."[26]

The Goshen Annual Conference

   The trying experiences which young men were having in camps, the absence of any clear-cut position on the part of the church, the many appeals from members and districts for the church to define its position, the criticism on the part of young men that the advice of the church was not definite, the statement from General Kuhn that there was no such a thing as noncombatant service under military control, and the growing uneasiness in the minds of Brethren leaders regarding the consistency of noncombatant service with the church's peace principle, led to the calling of a special Conference at Goshen, Indiana, January 9, 1918.   The Northeastern District of Kansas had passed a resolution calling for a special Conference.   Moderator H. C. Early called the meeting after the majority of the members of Standing Committee had voted favorably.   Some, including J. M. Henry, opposed the calling of this Conference and took the position that the Peace Committee had sufficient authority to organize and set up an adequate program to meet the situation, that the calling of this special Conference was unwise in wartime, and that what was needed was for the Peace Committee to put the church's peace convictions into action.   However, the majority fa-

---

[25] Harry C. Spielman, article in *Gospel Messenger*, April 6, 1918, p. 213.
[26] Personal letter from G. W. Phillips, Feb. 5, 1943.

vored having the Conference. Delegates were sent from districts and some from local churches.

The first action of this Conference was the adoption of a resolution which was sent to President Wilson, Newton D. Baker and Provost Marshal General Crowder. The resolution reviewed the historic peace position of the church, discerned the unsatisfactory character of the detention camps, raised serious questions about the consistency of noncombatant service with Brethren convictions, and asked that the President assign the drafted members of the church to noncombatant activities in agriculture and peaceful industries.[27]

The second action of the Goshen Conference was the adoption of a special statement of the Brethren position on war. The resolution outlined in detail the Biblical foundation of the church's convictions regarding peace, and said that "the final authority and determining arbiter for us must be found, not in our feeling or popular acclaim, or persuasions of men, or in our own reasoning, but in the New Testament, which we claim as our creed,—a revelation of God's will, a standard of human conduct both as to morals and religion."[28] Then the Conference declared the church position to be taken during World War I:

I. We believe that war or any participation in war is wrong and entirely incompatible with the spirit, example, and teachings of Jesus Christ.

II. That we cannot conscientiously engage in any activity or perform any function contributing to the destruction of human life.

. . . . . .

We commend the loyalty of the brethren in camps for their firm stand in not participating in the acts of war. We do not wish to oppose the consciences of those brethren who, in some camps, found work which they felt they could conscientiously do, but we urge

[27] *Minutes of the Special General Conference,* pp. 2-3.
[28] *Ibid.,* p. 3.

them to do only such work as will not involve them in the arts of
destruction.

. . . .

We further urge our brethren not to enlist in any service which
would, in any way, compromise our time-honored position in relation to war; also that they refrain from wearing the military uniform. The tenets of the·church forbid military drilling, or learning
the art or arts of war, or doing anything which contributes to the
destruction of human life or property.

. . . . . .

We are petitioning the government to give our drafted brethren
such industrial noncombatant service as will contribute construc-
tively to the necessity, health and comfort of hungering, suffering
humanity, either here or elsewhere."[29]

These decisions were more definite and specific than any
earlier actions. The denomination declared itself as opposed to any participation in war. Drafted Brethren were
advised neither to drill nor to wear the military uniform.
The position of the church really became that of opposition
to noncombatant service under the military system. The
young men, however, who had accepted and were accepting noncombatant service in the army had the respect of
the church. This stricter position and change of attitude
toward noncombatant service probably came through two
things: first, many officers in the army used severe pressure
to get Brethren to take combatant service and even some
forms of noncombatant activity required men to be armed;
second, the growing feeling among many Brethren that noncombatant service under military control was a compromise of the church's peace principles.

There were two other important actions of the Goshen
Conference. A Central Service Committee, already mentioned in the discussion, and a War Relief and Reconstruction Committee were appointed. These committees rendered valuable service throughout the war. The Central

---

[29] *Ibid.,* pp. 2-6.

Service Committee represented the Brethren in all matters pertaining to the draft.

In June, 1918, J. M. Henry, pastor of the Washington City Church of the Brethren, became a member of the committee, replacing Charles D. Bonsack, who resigned because of other heavy duties.

The Goshen Memorial Before the Government

The Central Service Committee on January 23, 1918, carried the Special Goshen Resolution to the secretaries of Woodrow Wilson and Newton D. Baker, who assured them that the paper would get before the head officials. Secretary Baker responded in a personal letter to W. J. Swigart stating:

We are glad to have this expression of confidence on the part of the authoritative members of this church and to say that its recommendations will have the careful consideration of my military associates and myself, in the determination of a permanent solution of the problem presented by the fact that the tenets of such a religious body are in opposition to warfare."[30]

Woodrow Wilson likewise responded by a letter to H. C. Early:

My dear Sir:

I have received the memorial of the Church of the Brethren, with regard to the assignment of members of that church, now in the military service, to noncombatant occupations, in agriculture and other constructive pursuits. The Secretary of War has presented to the Congress for its approval, a bill which will authorize the War Department to furlough, without pay, men in the military service. Should the Congress enact this legislation, it will then be possible, under its provisions, to assign, by conditional furlough, men whose conscientious scruples can not otherwise be met, to civilian occupations of the general sort which you indicate. At the same time, the Secretary of War is endeavoring to broaden the list of noncombatant occupations directly associated with the activities of the

---

[30] Swigart, "The Goshen Memorial," *Gospel Messenger*, Feb. 2, 1918, p. 68.

Army, and tells me that he hopes soon to have prepared, for presentation to me, such a list. When this is done, it may well be that the members of your church will find services which they can render without invasion of their beliefs, and I trust that every effort will be made by your members, so that this difficult question can finally be settled in a way consistent at once with the sentiments of those involved and the best interests of the Government.

Cordially yours,

Woodrow Wilson.[31]

The Goshen Statement Under Ban

The Goshen Statement concerning the recommendations for the drafted brethren not to drill and wear the uniform was printed, broadcast to the churches, and given to camp visitors to carry to the boys in camps. It was not long before a young man defended his refusal to perform military service on the ground of this printed statement from his church. The officer asked to see the paper and upon receiving it, sent the Goshen Statement to Secretary of War Baker, asking for an opinion from the Advocate Generals of the army. On July 8, 1918, the Central Service Committee was called to Washington for an emergency meeting. What happened can best be described by J. M. Henry:

Dr. Frederick P. Keppel, Third Assistant of War, who had been selected by President Woodrow Wilson to look after the questions arising concerning conscientious objectors, called one evening by telephone and asked that I come to his office at once. I had already had many conferences with Dr. Keppel on the problems arising in the camps, and had learned to admire his earnestness and fairmindedness. He received me very courteously, took me to his private desk and picked up a document bearing the seal of the War Department from the office of the Advocate Generals.

I listened to the reading of the document with its charges which still ring sometimes like a nightmare in my ears. After reciting the law, the document charged the officers of the Goshen Conference, and authors of the Goshen Statement as guilty of treasonable intent of obstructing the operation of the Selective Draft Law. Dr. Keppel

---

[31] "A Letter From President Wilson," *Gospel Messenger*, March 2, 1918, p. 136.

turned to me and said, "What have you to say about this matter?" I studied a moment and quietly explained the facts about the Goshen Conference, and then asked, "Will you have the case stayed forty-eight hours and give us time to prepare an answer?" The request was granted and the two other members of the Central Service Committee were called to Washington by telegram.

We met in the parlor at the parsonage on North Carolina Avenue. The Central Service Committee was facing a tragic situation. We stood between our dear brethren and the federal prisons. The honor and sacred name of our beloved fraternity were at stake. We needed wisdom and guidance, not born of flesh and blood, nor of the will of man, but from the Giver of all wisdom. To him we went on our knees in the parlor on that crucial morning. After a long season of prayer and meditation each member of the Committee was asked to write down his plea and answer. The secretary was given the task of putting into final written form the document. In abbreviated form, but not in change of words, it reads:

The Goshen Pronouncement of the Special Conference of the Church of the Brethren was issued at a called meeting of the General National Conference held January 9, 1918. That Conference was called to provide for the conditions relative to the draft, prior to the President's pronouncements on noncombatant service.

At a meeting of the Brethren and representatives of other non-resistant churches with the War Department, officials there asked for a copy of the written creeds of the peace churches on the question and subject of war. The Mennonites left a copy of their creed with the officials at the time. It was deemed advisable by the leaders of the Church of the Brethren to hold a Special Conference and that a clear statement of the church's tenets on this subject be printed and published in convenient form.

The printed paper was intended for those who are members of the Church of the Brethren and for the information of officials who might desire to know the tenets of the said church in the application of the clause of the Selective Draft Law which provides exemption from combatant service to members of churches whose tenets of faith forbid its members to participate in war.

The use of this paper has always been open. Never has any clandestine or secret use been made of it. There has been no publication of this paper since its first issue in January, 1918.

The other parts of the paper clearly express love and loyalty to our Government indicating according to our understanding entire freedom of the whole paper from any willful intent to obstruct the operation of the Selective Draft Law. The chief purpose of the Goshen Statement was to restate to herself the position of the church which has always been opposed to war.

The General Annual Conference held June 5-12, 1918, passed resolutions of commendation for the liberal provisions provided by the Government for noncombatant service, and these resolutions which virtually supersede the Statement of January 9, 1918, do not contain the paragraph called in question. The Church of the Brethren has steadily sought to avoid any undue publicity, desiring only to be accorded the privilege of living quietly within the realms of conscience as the law provides and the Executive has so graciously made provision.

The Central Service Committee are not the authors of the Statement of January 9, 1918, since a delegated called conference prepared the paper, yet we do pledge our influence and co-operation with the Church of the Brethren at large for the discontinuance of the distribution of this Statement, and humbly pray that any intended prosecution may be withdrawn.

> The Central Service Committee,
> Church of the Brethren,
>
> > W. J. Swigart, Chairman,
> > I. W. Taylor, Vice-Chairman,
> > J. M. Henry, Secretary.

An appointment was made with Judge Guy Goff, the only one of the four Advocate Generals of the War Department who was willing to hear our plea. The others had decided on prosecution. Judge Goff received the Central Peace Committee very kindly, read our written statement, and then discussed the whole matter for nearly an hour. He assured the committee that every effort would be put forth to have the other Advocates consent to call the case off. He succeeded and the Church of the Brethren was saved from the impending tragedy.

The Central Service Peace Committee—guided by wisdom from a gracious heavenly Father—had saved the church from a tragic situation: the church which the peaceful saint, Alexander Mack, had founded, for which Christopher Sower had been persecuted, and for which John Bowman and John Kline had suffered martyrdom in times of war.[32]

Some Church of the Brethren leaders were imprisoned during the Civil War, but this was the nearest the denomination as such came to being prosecuted by the government. J. M. Henry told the writer in a personal interview that F. P. Keppel informed him that the case was clear cut, the Church of the Brethren had violated the "Espionage Law," that three of the Advocate Generals had decided on prosecution, and that they planned to put the officers of the Goshen Conference in prison.[33] The violation of the law consisted in the advice against the uniform and drilling. The open-mindedness of Judge Guy Goff and his belief that the actions of the church were taken in innocence enabled him to persuade the other Advocate Generals to call off the case.

The Goshen Statement was recalled from the mails and camp visitors were urged not to use it in the military camps.

Effect of the Goshen Statement Upon the Attitude of Drafted Men

It is very difficult to tell from the records what the effect of the Goshen Statement was on the attitude of drafted Brethren toward noncombatant service. Before the statement was put under ban, it had been widely publicized and was well known by the church. The church position was defined late in the war, however, and the accepting of noncombatant service had become rather general for Brethren.

It is already noted that G. W. Phillips, from his experience in Camp Taylor, holds that the number of boys taking noncombatant service increased after March, 1918.[34] Charles D. Bonsack further says that "most of the Breth-

[32] Henry, *op. cit.*, pp. 530-532.
[33] Personal interview with J. M. Henry, Bridgewater, Va., March 4, 1943.
[34] Personal letter from G. W. Phillips, Elkhart, Ind., Feb. 5, 1943.

ren boys took noncombatant service, especially after it was clarified.[35]   The President defined noncombatant service through his Executive Order March 23, 1918.   Following the President's statement, conscientious objectors in camps were subjected to more persuasion to accept army service. This had its effect and it seems that the number of Brethren boys taking noncombatant service increased until the end of the war.

P. J. Blough, reporting his visit with W. J. Swigart to Camps Lee and Belvoir, March, 1918, indicates indirectly that the Goshen decision was having some effect. He says, "Those who stand firm from the start, fare the best. Our brethren will simply have to choose between war and the church. . . . It is now plainly evident that the only safe thing to do is as the church urges, and that is, not to uniform. After they uniform, which is the symbol of war, it is hard to take a stand, and refuse what will be required of them."[36]

D. W. Kurtz, writing about his visit to the Brethren boys in Camp Funston, states that "most of our boys are doing some service. One is mess sergeant, another is in the ambulance corps, another is in the kitchen, and another is in the sanitary department."[37]   Further he says:

One thing seems to be certain,—that the officers, especially the superior officers, naturally do all they can, apparently to induce the noncombatants to enter the regular war service. I heard of two cases last week where our Brethren were sent to Funston and had cards from their local boards, stating that they should do only noncombatant service, and they were being delayed from week to week, and in the meantime compelled to carry guns and serve as guards. Upon learning of this, I wrote to the commanding officer and urged that they be transferred at once to the noncombatant service. I also

[35] Personal interview with Charles D. Bonsack. Dec. 30, 1942.
[36] P. J. Blough, article in *Gospel Messenger*, March 30, 1918, p. 199.
[37] D. W. Kurtz, article in *Gospel Messenger*, May 18, 1918, p. 317.

wrote to these boys, urging them to be loyal to the church and to make a plea for their noncombative rights.[38]

The decisions of the Goshen Conference may have helped some Brethren boys to stand more firmly for their peace convictions, but the Conference actions came too late to change the tide toward service in the army. The official position of the Church of the Brethren was against noncombatant service but the functioning position was in favor of it. Some of the leaders of the church took it for granted that a member of the church would not fight, but they failed to realize that something had happened to their people. The young people had not been taught the peace principle. At least they had not been placed in an educational setting where through stimulating discussions they would think through the problem of war. Many of them were not prepared to withstand the pressure of the army officials.

The Conference Resolution of 1918

The last Annual Conference before the close of the war expressed itself in very general and harmless terms. It stated:

We appreciate the generous purpose of our Government in providing noncombatant service for our Brethren called to the colors, and pray that the President and his advisers may be divinely guided through these crises into the paths of righteousness. We renew our pledge of loyalty and urge our people to a liberal financial support of those organizations that are engaged in furthering the moral and religious welfare of the men in camp and in service, the alleviation of suffering, and the reconstruction of devastated lands.[39]

The General Education Board on Militarism

The General Education Board representing the colleges of the Church of the Brethren went on record April 10, 1917, regarding the question of war. The resolution of the Board is as follows:

---

[38] *Ibid.*, p. 317.
[39] *Minutes of the Annual Meeting*, 1918, p. 10.

Whereas, the Church of the Brethren has always maintained the principle of nonresistance, and has always staunchly opposed the militaristic spirit; and

Whereas the present crisis demands a re-avowal of the time-honored principle of peace and reaffirmation of our loyalty to the Prince of Peace; therefore

Be it Resolved, that we, the General Education Board of the Church of the Brethren, deem it proper to make known our position on the question of war.

Resolved that, as representing the educational interests of the church, we hereby voice our opposition to universal military training in the schools.

Resolved, that the members of the Church of the Brethren are hereby strongly urged to patronize our Brethren schools, where the principle of nonresistance is taught and upheld, as against the intense spirit of militarism which pervades our State institutions and country.[40]

This statement is an indication that the Brethren colleges were supporting the peace principle of the church.

Attitudes of Drafted Brethren Toward the Church's Uncertain Position

It is not possible to get a comprehensive overview of the attitude of the Brethren who were drafted toward the position of the church. Some reactions, at least, may be discovered. L. C. Blickenstaff states: "The Brethren ministers didn't give very clear-cut advice about what to do except to do what conscience dictates."[41]   C. Ray Keim writes of his experience in Camp Sherman, "Several well-meaning preachers (at least one of our church) were given an opportunity to talk to our group of C.O.'s in the Detachment, trying to convert us to non-combatant service. Seldom did anyone ask us to take straight military service. Needless to say, the ministers' efforts were quite fruitless."[42]

[40] *Gospel Messenger*, May 5, 1917, p. 277.
[41] Personal conference with L. C. Blickenstaff, Feb. 6, 1943.
[42] Personal letter from C. Ray Keim, North Manchester, Indiana, Feb., 1943.

Kenneth G. Long in his study entitled "Attitudes of the Brethren in Training Camps During the World War," based upon letters from ninety-three Brethren boys from the various military centers, says that there were many pleas for the church to take a more firm and clear-cut stand on the war issue.[43]

Again he states:

It is evident that the Brotherhood's stand was not as united nor as clear as many of the C. O.'s desired. This was to be expected in an organization so democratic as ours. But it would be fair to say that had the church declared herself more clearly and had so instructed her Camp Visitors and the conscientious objectors, those who were weakest might have been stronger while those who were convinced in their own minds would have continued faithful in their beliefs.[44]

The Attitude of the Church Toward Those Who Took Combatant Service

It is generally known that some Brethren boys entered straight military service. There were a few army officers in the group. It was clearly recognized both by them and the church that they had acted contrary to the peace principles of the denomination. However, the local churches generally were very tolerant and very few of them were disciplined. When the Brethren who were soldiers returned from the army, they were welcomed back into the local churches.

ATTITUDE OF THE CHURCH OF THE BRETHREN TOWARD THE STATE

A significant change had come in the relationship of the Church of the Brethren to the state. In the Civil War the Brethren were not voting. In World War I they were voting and a few were holding political offices. In the

---

[43] Kenneth G. Long, *Attitudes of the Brethren in Training Camps During the World War* (unpublished B.D. thesis, Bethany Biblical Seminary, 1939), p. 20.
[44] *Ibid.*, p. 44.

Civil War church members paid the taxes required of them and contacted the government only when their religious convictions were not respected. In World War I the Brethren wanted to be faithful citizens of the nation and maintain their opposition to war. The Annual Conference of 1917, referred to earlier, committed the Brethren to a constructive citizenship of genuine service to the country.

The Goshen Conference declared that the Brethren were loyal citizens; that although governments were ordained of God, when the actions of government conflicted with Christ's teachings, the Brethren had to obey God; and that members of the church because of their favored position under the draft law should contribute liberally through extra sacrifice for the relief of suffering humanity.[45]

H. C. Early, writing in the "Gospel Messenger" of October 13, 1917, gave the same point of view. He said: "We believe that civil government is an institution of God, ordained for man's well-being. Stating it in its lowest and highest terms,—its end is the protection of life and property. We believe that it is our solemn duty to obey the laws of the land, when they are not in violation of New Testament teaching (Rom. 13; Acts 5: 29)."[46]

The Brethren in camps had a definite feeling of loyalty to the government. Kenneth G. Long summarizes the point of view expressed in the letters from the boys:

It is apparent that our church members have been taught to respect and honor our government. Whether the church is directly responsible or not, the fact remains. In no letter do we find disrespect or bitterness against the nation. The absolute objectors may differ violently in their beliefs. The man may dislike the treatment of certain officers and officials. The C. O.'s may become impatient with the seeming slowness in providing transfers and certificates. Yet the nation and government were loved and respected.

---

[45] Minutes of Special General Conference, *Ibid.*, p. 55.
[46] H. C. Early, article in *Gospel Messenger*. Oct. 13, 1917, p. 641.

It was not animosity towards the state that made the C. O.'s refuse to join the army. It was their hatred of war and bloodshed.

Again and again is expressed the desire to find some way in which loyalty to the government may be expressed without disobeying the higher loyalty to one's conscience and one's God. And many of those who refused to do anything and went to Fort Leavenworth did so believing that in this way they were proving most loyal to their country.[47]

The Church's Attitude Toward Holding Office

The Annual Conference of 1918 was asked to redefine the church's position "as regards the propriety of our members holding any office under our Civil Government which would necessitate their using, or causing to be used, physical force, carrying carnal weapons, or administering oaths."[48]

The answer of Conference was:

(1) Annual Meeting reaffirms our position on nonresistance and does not permit the holding of office by members when such office compels them to violate these nonresistance principles or the taking or the administering of oaths. (2) However, we recognize that, in a democracy, it is not wrong for Brethren to serve their communities and municipalities, to promote efficiency and honesty in social and civic life when the nonresistance principles and the New Testament doctrines on this are not violated. (3) Anyone who violates this decision subjects himself to the discipline of the church.[49]

This decision showed that the church was in favor of members serving in government positions when the nonresistant principles of the church were not violated.

A World War Governor

Martin G. Brumbaugh, a minister in the Church of the Brethren, was governor of Pennsylvania during the World War. When he was inaugurated in January, 1915, according to the Brethren practice he "affirmed" instead of taking the "oath." He determined to give Pennsylvania a clean

---

[47] Long, *op. cit.*, pp. 42-43.
[48] Full reports of Annual Conferences (Bound Volume), 1915-1918 (Chicago, Illinois: Bethany Biblical Seminary), p. 83.
[49] *Ibid.*, p. 83.

administration. Penrose was the dominating figure in the state political picture. While Brumbaugh was governor-elect, Penrose phoned him to come over for a conference. Brumbaugh answered, "My office is here and I am willing to see you at any time."[50]   Following that, Penrose fought him.   He was attacked maliciously by his enemies but he ignored all criticisms.   Theodore Roosevelt called him the "woolly little lamb," because of his noncombative spirit. Yet this Dunker minister governed the state during the World War period and was forced by the duties of his office to send the Pennsylvania boys out to fight and die. That this act was inconsistent with the Brethren peace principles cannot be denied.   Martin G. Brumbaugh loved his church, however, and continued as a minister, respected and honored as long as he lived.   After retiring from the governorship, he took up the presidency of Juniata College, a position which he had formerly held, and served the educational interests of his denomination.

The Brethren Bought Liberty Bonds

While no records are available, it is generally known among the Brethren that many members of the church bought Liberty Bonds during World War I.   It was not universally practiced.   Some members refused to help finance the war program.   But the writer recalls the strength of the war propaganda, the community pressure, and the fact that Brethren farmers and businessmen put thousands of dollars into Liberty Bonds.   The church had not analyzed the economic implications of its peace position.   Up to this time in the history of the Church of the Brethren there had been no general and effective protest against helping to finance the war system.

---

[50] Personal interview with Roland Howe of Philadelphia, a friend of M. G. Brumbaugh, Feb. 15, 1943.

How the State Dealt With the Brethren As a Religious Minority Group

The First Draft Law

War was declared by the United States on Good Friday, April 6, 1917. Immediately Congress began to prepare a Selective Service Bill which was passed May 18, 1917. Section 1644 of this bill was quoted earlier. It referred to members of the historic peace churches and exempted them only from combatant service. When the bill was being discussed, Senator La Follette offered an amendment looking in the direction of more comprehensive exemption, but this was defeated.[51] Norman Thomas says, "By actual count, the House spent as many minutes in discussion of the wording of exemption of ministers of the Gospel as on the whole subject of conscientious objection."[52] Secretary Baker had been approached by a committee composed of Miss Jane Addams, Miss Lillian Wald and Norman Thomas regarding the problem of conscientious objectors. Norman Thomas reports that "Mr. Baker had apparently given the matter comparatively little consideration, and was inclined to assume that all objectors would be members of religious sects and that no man was likely to object to anything except combative service. Such objection would be wholly unreasonable. Hence Mr. Baker felt that exemption of bona fide members of pacifist sects covered the case."[53] At the beginning of the war it was evident that neither the law makers nor the Secretary of War had given sufficient consideration to the problem of conscientious objectors.

Brethren Advised to Register

With the coming of the war the Peace Committee of the Church of the Brethren became increasingly active. W. J.

[51] Norman Thomas, *Is Conscience a Crime?* p. 77.
[52] *Ibid.*, p. 78.
[53] *Ibid.*, p. 75.

Swigart wrote in the "Gospel Messenger" of June 2, 1917, about his visit to Washington in early May to study the provisions of the conscription bills. This committee advised the members to register and file their claim for exemption with the local board. Selective Service regulations required local boards to furnish conscientious objectors with certificates of exemption from combatant service. The certificate of exemption read as follows:

Local Board for ....

This is to certify that ....Order No.

..................Serial No. ....has been found to be exempt from combatant service and is eligible only to such military service as may be declared noncombatant by the President of the United States.
                              Member of Local Board.

                              ....[54]

The Law Did Not Exempt Brethren From Military Service

The only exemption provided by the law for members of denominations whose principles were opposed to war was from combatant service. There was no exemption from noncombatant military activities. This point became clear through a letter written by Provost Marshal General Crowder to Rufus Jones, June 28, 1917, in which he informed the Quaker leader that any person granted a permit to go abroad for relief work had to return home if selected by his board for military service.[55]

On August 11, 1917, Provost Marshal General Crowder issued the following ruling on "the drafting of religious sects":

[54] Kellogg, *op. cit.*, p. 140.
[55] Rufus Jones, *A Service of Love in War Time.* p. 48.

Persons considered under paragraph '1' of section 20 of the Regulations will be drafted, will be forwarded to a mobilization camp, will make part of the quota from the state and district from whence they come, and will be assigned to duty in a capacity declared by the President to be non-combatant.[56]

The regulations prescribed by the President for local and district boards, issued June 30, stated in Section 48 that "from the time so specified (i.e., date of reporting at cantonments) each man to whom such notice shall have been mailed shall be in military service of the United States."[57]

F. P. Keppel, at that time private secretary to the Secretary of War, wrote a letter to Rufus Jones, September 10, 1917, in which he stated, "The Selective Service Law exempts adherents to certain creeds from combatant service, but it does not exempt them from military service."[58]

On April 25, 1917, W. J. Swigart, I. W. Taylor and H. C. Early had a conference with Provost Marshal General Crowder regarding the question of what the government would consider as noncombatant service. General Crowder informed them that the only thing that the President had thus far defined as noncombatant was service in the Medical Corps. He told the Brethren in response to their questions that their service would be under the direction of the military, would include care of the wounded and hospital work in war zones, and that refusal to mobilize for it would likely be considered as desertion.[59]

First Drafted Brethren at Mercy of Army Officials

The first general mobilization was made in September, 1917, after the cities of wooden barracks were sufficiently completed. Then the problem of handling conscientious ob-

---

[56] *Ibid.*, p. 53.
[57] *Ibid.*, p. 53.
[58] *Ibid.*, p. 87.
[59] Article in *Gospel Messenger*, Sept. 1, 1917, p. 549.

jectors arose. Local draft boards differed in their attitude toward religious objectors. Some who claimed exemption from combatant service were granted certificates of exemption and some were not. There were objectors to noncombatant service for religious reasons whose cases were not covered by the law. There were religious objectors to war who belonged to churches other than those recognized by the draft law. All of these were sent to camp as regular conscripted soldiers.

The first objectors were clearly at the mercy of army officers. The President had not defined the meaning of noncombatant service and the government had no well-worked-out policy in dealing with those who refused to fight. They were first assigned places in the barracks with the regular soldiers. Some refused to take the uniform and drill, and later refused all service in the army. Others took the uniform but objected to the military service. Still others accepted the uniform, participated for a while in the drill, but objected to carrying a gun and doing combative service. Each objector had to take his stand in the presence of soldiers and under the severe pressure of army officers.

Many army officers tried to persuade objectors to accept regular army duties. If this was refused, the officers urged the taking of noncombatant service. Sometimes coercion was used and occasionally objectors were treated with brutality. The following case happened on the 20th of September, 1917, after the young man had refused to wear the uniform. He had explained his religious convictions earlier in the day to men and officers, but they returned in the evening and demanded again that he wear the uniform. When he objected, they seized him and treated him thus:

They carried me a few rods to the end of the tents and started with their fun. I don't know how long they tossed me up or how high. And I don't know how many had hold of the blanket. But I was told that all took a hold that there was room for. I held to the edge of the blanket a few times with my right hand and I suppose that had a tendency to throw me on the ground. They might of did it on purpose and left me fall on the ground for all I know. I noticed that my arm was broken and I told them that it was. They picked me up and took me to the tent, and called an ambulance. They took me first to the infirmary and then to the hospital. It happened about eight in the evening of the 20th of September. . . . That is about as good as I can tell you about it by writing. I received very good attention since I have been at the hospital.[60]

The mildness or severity with which objectors were treated varied with different camps. At Camp Funston under the command of Major General Leonard Wood, conscientious objectors were treated with such severity that an official investigation was made and it was recommended that five officers be dismissed from the service.[61] The persecution of objectors in Camp Grant was the worst. There the officers seemed to disregard all War Department orders. Conditions for objectors were better in Camps Upton, Sherman and Custer, mostly because of the officers in charge.[62]

L. C. Blickenstaff, who went to Camp Taylor with the first quota of men in September, 1917, gives further illumination on the procedure followed by army officials in dealing with conscientious objectors:

I went to Camp Taylor, Ky., with the feeling that I could accept hospital service providing I was not required to bear arms, my objection being primarily against killing. I made my position clear to the officers and was immediately given a grilling which was intended to humiliate and frighten me into accepting regular service. When this failed other methods were tried, such as giving me kitchen duty, washing windows, cleaning toilets, etc.

Finally after several days of this the Captain of the company called me in and asked me if I were willing to accept a rifle. When I refused he said it would be a waste of time to drill me without a

[60] Long, *op. cit.*, p. 18.
[61] Thomas, *op. cit.*, pp. 161-162.
[62] *Ibid.*, p. 129.

rifle and transferred me to the cooks and bakers school along with other C. O.'s where we learned to cook.

The President had not yet issued his proclamation indicating which branches of service were noncombatant and consequently we could not be assigned.

After enough C. O.'s arrived to form a company of about 150 we were given a barracks of our own where I continued as first cook.

During my spare time I studied the army, reading the manual of arms, visiting the hospital and quartermaster corps and watching the soldiers drill and do bayonet practice. The more I learned the more I was convinced that no part of the army was really noncombatant, but that every branch was a very essential part of the vast fighting machine. When I realized this I felt that I could no longer accept hospital service under army direction. Consequently I refused all service and was sent to Leavenworth.

My experience with officers in camp varied greatly. Some cursed and damned me. Others respected me. One captain said, "If I had an army of men who think they ought to fight as strongly as you think you shouldn't, I wouldn't be afraid of the Devil himself." After a lengthy conference another captain said, "I wish I could see things as you do, but I can't although I respect your position.[63]

C. Ray Keim describes the pressure which was put upon those who refused noncombatant service:

You know in general the arrangement for C. O.'s who would not take noncombatant service. They went to military camps and had to take a stand there, usually beginning by rejecting the uniform. Some were roughly treated in these original companies before being transferred to a C. O. Detachment. Some were put in the guardhouse, some were beaten, and one at least was taken out, stripped and tarred. I was cursed when I refused to take a uniform but not beaten. I served as a K. P. for three weeks and then was transferred to the C. O. group.

I got there just as they were trying them out by asking them to do detail work around the camp which most of them refused to do. I refused because I felt it was just the same as doing noncombatant service. Some were then court-martialed but I was among those who were not. We never were able to decide why some were court-martialed and others were not. Probably it was just a matter of numbers.

---

[63] Personal Letter from L. C. Blickenstaff. Gary, Ind., Jan. 25, 1943.

They argued with us frequently, either singly or as a group, trying to get us to take noncombatant service. It was quite a strain, for we never knew what to expect next. The trouble was the army had not anticipated the problem and had no service worked out for us, outside the army. Finally, in the summer of 1918, they began to furlough us out to farmers. I was furloughed out about September 18, as I recall. Forty-two of us were sent to Proctorville, O. (opposite the city of Huntington, W. Va.) to help pick apples there.[64]

Brethren Leaders Interview Secretary of War Baker

On September 1, 1917, W. J. Swigart, I. W. Taylor, and W. M. Lyon had an interview with Newton D. Baker for the purpose of discussing the problems created by Brethren boys facing the call to army camps. The following paper had been prepared by a committee representing the Mennonite churches and summarized their understanding of what Secretary Baker had said to them verbally:

1. That none of our brethren need serve in any capacity which violates their creed and conscience.

2. When they are called, they should respond at the place designated on their notice.

3. From the place designated on their notice, they should go with others, who are drafted and called, to the training camp.

4. Report to the army officers the church to which they belong, and their belief in its creed and principles.

5. This nonresistant position will place them in detention camps where they will be properly fed and cared for.

6. In these camps, they will not be uniformed nor drilled.

7. A list of services considered noncombatant will be offered, but they need not accept any in violation of their consciences.

8. Those who can not accept any service, either combatant or noncombatant, will be assigned to some other service, not under the military arm of the government.

9. Our ministers will be allowed to visit the brethren at these camps and to keep in touch with them.

10. Our ministers will be privileged to give this information and advice in private or in public meetings.[65]

---

[64] Personal letter from C. Ray Keim, North Manchester, Ind., Feb. 1, 1943.
[65] *Gospel Messenger*, Sept. 15. 1917, p. 581.

This statement was used by the Brethren Committee as the basis for their interview with Baker. The Secretary read it over carefully and agreed that the statement was substantially what he told the Mennonites except that in No. 8 things were specified which he was not ready to state. Mr. Baker said:

It would not be within my province, at this time, to say finally: 'Those who cannot accept noncombatant service will be assigned to some other service not under the military arm of the government.' It may possibly be so, but that would have to be worked out, and on the absolute refusal to obey orders and accept assignments from officers in charge, some might be imprisoned for the time. But provisions will be made for the adjustment. Go as far as you can, and all claims for conscience will be heard.[66]

Secretary Baker visited Camp Meade, September 30, 1917, and questioned Alfred Echroth, a Brethren, why he could not accept army service.

. . . In regard to Secretary Baker's visit, there were only about 25 conscientious objectors in the detention camp at that time. I was one of them. He only spoke to four of us boys. They were Joshua Bailey, Leo B. Galner, a Russian Jew, a Mennonite and myself. He did not talk to us as a whole but took those to whom he did speak to one side. He wanted to get their views.

Major General Kuhn introduced me to him by name and as a member of the Brethren Church. After a hearty handshake he began interrogating me. He asked me whether I couldn't do this or that in the army, so long as I would not be directly engaged in killing. He referred to working in the hospital corps, quartermaster corps, engineering corps and canteens. I refused right then and there to accept any of these branches of service. I explained to him that even engaging in any of these services I would aid in the prosecution of the war, and besides we would have to wear the uniform which would advertise militarism, the very thing we opposed. . . . Previous to Secretary Baker's visit, Major General Kuhn was very unkindly disposed toward us but the Secretary's visit changed this attitude.[67]

---

[66] *Ibid.*, p. 581.
[67] D. C. Moomaw, *Christianity Versus War*, pp. 234-235.

Confidential Order of October 10, 1917

Problems of conscientious objectors in the army increased. The power to make regulations governing their treatment lay with the War Department. Consequently the Confidential Order of October 10 was issued:

1. The Secretary of War directs that you be instructed to segregate the conscientious objectors in their divisions and to place them under supervision of instructors who shall be specifically selected with a view of insuring that these men will be handled with tact and consideration and that their questions will be answered fully and frankly.

2. With reference to their attitude of objecting to military service these men are not to be treated as violating military laws thereby subjecting themselves to the penalties of the Articles of War, but their attitude in this respect will be quietly ignored and they will be treated with kindly consideration. Attention in this connection is invited to a case where a number of conscientious objectors in one of our divisions, when treated in this manner, renounced their original objections to military service and voluntarily offered to give their best efforts to the service of the United States as soldiers.

3. Under no circumstances are the instructions contained in the foregoing to be given to the newspapers.

> (S) H. G. Leonard
> Adjutant General[68]

The statements of Secretary Baker and the unannounced policy of the War Department reported above show that the government had not thought through the problem of conscientious objectors clearly. One thing, however, seems clear as a government policy: conscientious objectors were to be treated in the way that would get the largest number of them to enter military service.

The ruling of October 10 caused the segregation of conscientious objectors into separate barracks, which were called detention camps. On October 20 because of continued reports of mistreatment and nonsegregation, another

---

[68] Kellogg, *op. cit.*, pp. 130-131.

order was issued, insisting that army officials carry out the earlier ruling.[69]   The placing of religious objectors into quarters of their own enabled them to have fellowship with like-minded people and to hold religious services.   But the detention camps were no satisfactory solution to the problem.   Idleness was not good for the boys.   Most of them had come from farms and were used to active work.

Confidential Order of December 19, 1917

There were individuals from churches other than the Friends, Mennonites and Brethren who had personal scruples against war and who made their claims for exemption in camps.   Those young men presented a special problem to the military authorities because their cases were not covered by the law.   The War Department was called upon for a ruling and the Adjutant General, H. G. Leonard, wrote to all camp commanders on December 19 stating:

> The Secretary of War directs that until further instructions on the subject are issued 'personal scruples against war' should be considered as constituting 'conscientious objectors' and such persons should be treated in the same manner as other 'conscientious objectors' under the instructions contained in confidential letter from this office dated October 10, 1917.[70]

This administrative ruling was a definite forward step in recognizing those whom the law did not consider.   The ruling of the War Department was more liberal than the Selective Service Act.

Conscientious Objectors Ordered to Take a Psychological Examination

On March 6, 1918, the Secretary of War ordered that a psychological examination be given to all conscientious objectors and a report furnished to him, and further "that

---

[69] Thomas, *op. cit.*, p. 92.
[70] Kellogg, *op. cit.*, pp. 131-132.

reports be made to him of all trials of Court-martial."[71] Then on April 10, 1918, it was decreed that "in all cases where psychiatric specialists recommend the discharge from the service of such men for mental deficiency or derangement, their discharge for the good of the service should be authorized."[72]

Confidential Order of March 11, 1918

A third Confidential Order from the Adjutant General to the Commanding Generals of the Divisions suggested the segregation even of the different classes of objectors. It stated:

1. You are informed that instructions regarding the segregation of conscientious objectors, contained in the confidential letters from the Adjutant General of October 10th and December 19th, 1917, should not be construed as requiring the mingling in one group of different classes of conscientious objectors, who, for the good of the service, may better be kept apart.

2. Under no circumstances are the instructions contained in the foregoing to be given to the newspapers.[73]

THE GOVERNMENT'S POLICY TOWARD OBJECTORS THROUGH ELEVEN MONTHS OF WAR

The President did not define the meaning of noncombatant service until March 20, 1918, and consequently the objectors lived under constant uncertainty. The government had not anticipated the seriousness of the problems which the conscientious objectors would raise and had no well-thought-out plans. The conclusion that the government tried to get as many objectors as possible to take army service seems to be justified from the evidence. The Confidential Order of October 10 is an indication of this. Having objectors during the early months of the war in the

---

[71] *Statement Concerning the Treatment of Conscientious Objectors in the Army.* Prepared and published by direction of the Secretary of War, June 18, 1919. Page 17.
[72] *Ibid.,* p. 17.
[73] Kellogg, *op. cit.,* p. 132.

barracks with regular soldiers was an influence toward changing their minds. Even the detention camps which permitted segregation and fellowship did not represent any marked protection of conscience. There were army officers over them and many times a definite plan was followed to get the objectors to accept some type of work. G. W. Phillips describes this procedure at Camp Taylor:

> As to the officers' procedures in trying to get the boys to accept service, it usually followed a form something like this: A detail of anywhere up to a dozen C. O. boys would be taken to some work project, usually a very innocent looking job such as raking the lawn at the hospital, or cleaning up some housing quarters, etc. If they accepted the work it was the first step into service. If they refused they were sometimes merely taken back to quarters, but often were given some kind of punishment such as some hard work to do at our living quarters ("busy work." The boys never refused such work given as punishment); solitary confinement for a short period of time on "bread and water," standing attention for a number of minutes, also threats. But ultimately all such would be taken to the guard house, with their privileges greatly curtailed. Guard houses not being large enough to accommodate the supply of inmates; the upper floor of the barracks where we lived was designated as the guard house.[74]

Norman Thomas states that Mr. Baker was much pleased with the number of objectors converted to army service under the supervision of instructors of tact and discretion.[75] Assistant Secretary Keppel, writing after the war, pointed out the gains to the army when 'the policies of Secretary Baker were carried out:

> Where their sincerity was assumed, as for example by Gen. J. Franklin Bell at Upton, out of a division made up from a cross-section of the population of New York City, only thirty-odd men refused to accept military service. At another camp, where it was assumed that they were insincere, 40 men were court-martialed and given long sentences for refusing to sow grass seed and plant flowers around the base hospital, an order obviously framed for the purpose

[74] Personal letter from G. W. Phillips, Elkhart, Ind., Feb. 5, 1943.
[75] Thomas, *op. cit.*, p. 93.

of revealing the insincerity of the objector. At another camp the sanitary regulations regarding these men were interpreted in such a manner as to call forth a severe condemnation from the Inspector of the Army.[76]

The following statements by Newton D. Baker express his attitude toward conscientious objectors:

The so-called "Conscientious Objector" is the residuum left after this appeal is presented in all of its forms and has had a chance to work its effect. In every country in this war this problem was presented. We do not yet know all the answers that were attempted, but we do know that in America out of many tens of thousands who claimed upon one ground or another an irreconcilable objection to bearing arms or serving in military enterprises, there remained at the end a very few hundred who persisted and so found themselves in prison and protesting. To a very large number who presented themselves in this attitude, mere contact with their fellows was enough to enlarge their view and bring them into harmony with the thought of their generation. Other great numbers found it impossible to bear arms, but not impossible to serve in nonmilitary occupations equally necessary and equally arduous. The little residue were of the most various types, and no one can have an intelligent opinion upon the problem presented by the "Conscientious Objector" who does not realize that some one person of his acquaintance can not be generalized so as to constitute the whole class included in the name. One's contempt for the slacker and the coward makes him naturally impatient of a man who refuses to take the risk of battle, and distrustful of excuses based upon conscience when one's own healthy conscience shows the path of duty to lie in the direction of self-sacrifice. But there is no sure way of being just in dealing with a problem of this kind except to take each objector as an individual, consider his antecedents, his opportunities, his limitations; and when these have all been weighed the judgment may be erroneous, but at least it has in it the ingredients of inquiry and patience which make it better than hasty assumptions.[77]

The evidence does not seem to indicate that during the first eleven months of the war the War Department and the army officials were trying to protect the consciences of

---

[76] *Ibid.*, p. 93.
[77] Newton D. Baker, Introduction to *The Conscientious Objector*, by Walter G. Kellogg, pp. xv-xvi.

those who differed with the war program. Their unannounced policy was to persuade and change the consciences of religious objectors.

The President Defined Noncombatant Service March 23, 1918

A different status for conscientious objectors developed as the result of General Order No. 28, issued as an executive order by President Wilson, March 23, 1918. The President defined the various branches of the armed forces which he considered noncombatant. It is easily seen that the majority of the units listed were parts of the war machine:

I hereby declare the following military service in non-combatant service:

(a) Service in the medical corps wherever performed. This includes service in the sanitary detachments attached to combatant units at the front; service in the divisional sanitary trains composed of ambulance companies, and field hospital companies, on the line of communication, at the base in France, and with the troops and at hospitals in the United States; also the service of supply in the Medical Department.

(b) Any service in the Quartermaster Corps in the United States may be treated as non-combatant. Also, in rear zones of operations, service in the following: Stevedore companies, labor companies, remount depots, veterinary hospitals, supply depots, bakery companies, the subsistence service, the bathing service, the salvage service, the clothing renovation service, the shoe repair service, the transportation repair service, and motor truck companies.

(c) Any engineer service in the United States may be treated as non-combatant service. Also, in rear zones of operations, service as follows: Railroad building, operation and repairs; road building and repair; construction of rear line fortifications, auxiliary defenses, etc.; construction of docks, wharves, storehouses and of such cantonments as may be built by the Corps of Engineers; topographical work; camouflage service and forestry service.[78]

The second section of the order gives instructions to local

---

[78] Kellogg, *op. cit.*, pp. 18-19.

draft boards regarding the various types of exemption certificates they are authorized to issue and then directs:

> Upon the promulgation of this order it shall be the duty of each Division, Camp or Post Commander, through a tactful officer, to present to all such persons the provisions hereof with adequate explanation of the character of non-combatant service herein defined, and upon such explanation to secure acceptances of assignment to the several kinds of non-combatant service above enumerated. . . .[79]

The third section provides for monthly reports to the Secretary of War on all persons professing conscientious objections to war. It reads:

> On the first day of April, and thereafter monthly, each Division, Camp, or Post Commander shall report to the Adjutant General of the Army, for the information of the Chief of Staff and the Secretary of War, the names of all persons under their respective commands who possess religious or other conscientious scruples as above described and who have been unwilling to accept, by reason of such scruples, assignment to noncombatant military service as above defined, and as to each such person so reported a brief, comprehensive statement as to the nature of the objection to the acceptance of such noncombatant military service entertained. The Secretary of War will from time to time classify the persons so reported and give further directions as to the disposition of them. Pending such directions from the Secretary of War, all such persons not accepting assignment to noncombatant service shall be segregated as far as practicable and placed under the command of a specially qualified officer of tact and judgment, who will be instructed to impose no punitive hardship of any kind upon them, but not allow their objections to be made the basis of any favor or consideration beyond exemption from actual military service which is not extended to any other soldier in the service of the United States.[80]

Sections four and five recommend uniformity of penalties in sentences of courts-martial and revisions of sentences of courts-martial imposed prior to the Order, if found unfair.

---

[79] *Ibid.*, p. 20.
[80] *Ibid.*, pp. 20-21.

Kellogg comments that "the order, despite certain obscurities, was obviously meant to secure for every objector fair and considerate treatment. Conceived in a broad and liberal spirit of toleration, it is in line with, but more progressive than, the policy adopted during the Civil War."[81]

Kellogg's statement is no doubt true. The executive order was designed to provide fair and just treatment for conscientious objectors. The President's statement was more liberal than the law. There were many different types of services from which noncombatants could choose. But the new rule offered no help for the absolutists and did not provide civilian service for those who refused all orders from the army. Besides that, the President's order led to a testing of all conscientious objectors in the camps and many efforts to persuade them in favor of noncombatant service.

L. C. Blickenstaff, of Camp Taylor, Kentucky, says:

As soon as the President's order was issued, some of our men took noncombatant service. Officers tried to persuade the group to accept work as outlined by the Executive Order. Those who refused were told to do certain types of work in camp. They did that to get them to disobey orders. After that they were arrested and put in the guard house. Then some were court-martialed. When I was being court-martialed one of the officers stepped up to me and said that if I would change my attitude, he could get the charges withdrawn.[82]

Horace Spangler reports the procedure used at Camp Lee, Virginia:

Early one morning we received notice that the Camp Judge Advocate was coming to see us. We all assembled in the mess hall. Colonel Coffee, Colonel Mallery and the Judge Advocate came in very solemnly and courteously as all superior officers do—stated their business and gave us each a letter written from Division Headquarters giving all the President's statement except where farm furloughs are mentioned and where the statement said we "should not be put

---

[81] *Ibid.*, p. 22.
[82] Personal interview, Feb. 6, 1943.

under arrest nor kept in penitentiaries." After carefully reading the letter they gave us the privilege of asking questions. Will we have to wear the uniform, drill, salute, etc., etc., were asked in rapid succession. They assured us that we would have to perform every duty of any other soldier except carry arms. Of course we could not see the noncombatant element in that. They gave us twenty-four hours to select some branch of noncombatant service and told us in absence of choice we'd be assigned to the Medical Department and failure to obey orders would land us in the penitentiary. Nevertheless we know that Mr. Wilson's official statement was quite different. Six of the one hundred accepted some branch of noncombatant service.[83]

Interpretation of the Executive Order

The Secretary of War issued an interpretation of Section Three of General Orders No. 28, April 18, 1918, in which he stated that a conscientious objector "shall not, against his will, be required to wear a uniform or to bear side arms."[84] On April 27, 1918, the Secretary of War directed "that any man classed as a conscientious objector on account of religious belief or personal scruples, (a) whose attitude in camp is sullen and defiant, (b) whose sincerity is questioned, (c) who is active in propaganda, should be promptly brought to trial by court-martial."[85]

The Farm Furlough Law

No solution had been found for those who refused all army service. When the War Department was queried regarding its failure to provide alternative service, it claimed that Congressional action was necessary.[86] Then on March 16, 1918, chiefly because of the shortage of farm labor, the Farm Furlough Law was passed. It provided that:

Whenever during the continuance of the present war in the opinion of the Secretary of War the interests of the service or the na-

---

[83] Moomaw, *op. cit.*, pp. 257-258.
[84] Kellogg, *op. cit.*, p. 23.
[85] *Statement Concerning the Treatment of Conscientious Objectors in the Army*, p. 19.
[86] Thomas, *op. cit.*, pp. 99-100.

tional security and defense render it necessary or advisable, the Secretary of War be, and he hereby is, authorized to grant furloughs to enlisted men of the army of the United States with or without pay and allowances or with partial pay and allowances, and, for such periods as he may designate, to permit said enlisted men to engage in civil occupations and pursuits; Provided, That such furloughs shall be granted only upon the voluntary application of such enlisted men under regulations to be prescribed by the Secretary of War.[87]

In response to requests that the furlough be extended to conscientious objectors, the Judge Advocate General on May 31, 1918, advised the Secretary of War as follows:

If the Secretary of War, in the exercise of his honest discretion, determines that the good of the service and the national security and defense makes it necessary or desirable that these conscientious objectors be furloughed to enable them to engage in civil occupations, he is of course authorized to make regulations providing therefor.[88]

After all the months of idleness for conscientious objectors in detention camps and guard houses, the War Department now had a plan for utilizing their energies in constructive pursuits. They were to be furloughed to farms; but not without a personal examination of each case. Even the farm furlough, however, did not remove the objectors from the supervision of the War Department. There was no place for absolutists. Objectors to war either had to fight, work on farms at private's pay, or go to prison. Those permitted to join the Friends' Reconstruction Unit were the only exceptions to this rule.

The Board of Inquiry Appointed

The Secretary of War, June 1, 1918, appointed a Board of Inquiry composed of Major Richard C. Stoddard, as chairman, a representative of the Judge Advocate General's department; Julian W. Mack, Judge of the United States Cir-

---

[87] *Ibid.*, p. 100.
[88] *Ibid.*, p. 100.

cuit Court of Appeals; and Harlan F. Stone, Dean of the Columbia University Law School. Major Stoddard continued as chairman until about the middle of August, 1918, when he was detailed for duty overseas. Walter G. Kellogg succeeded him. The findings of the Board were advisory to the Secretary of War. Kellogg states:

The Board was instructed to inquire into and to determine the sincerity of conscientious objectors. Its function was primarily to examine all objectors, not under charges, who had declined to accept noncombatant service, or who had not been assigned to noncombatant service by their camp commander, because in the judgment of the camp commander they were insincere.[89]

The order of June 1, 1918, also directed that all conscientious objectors "now segregated in posts and camps . . . shall be transferred to Fort Leavenworth, Kansas."[90] But by a substitute order of July 20, 1918, Fort Riley, Kansas, was substituted for Fort Leavenworth.[91]

On June 10, 1918, a Confidential Order was issued by the War Department authorizing the Board of Inquiry to visit camps and cantonments for the purpose of examining conscientious objectors who had not been court-martialed and were not under charges. It provided for furloughs to be issued by commanding officers under the recommendations of the Board of Inquiry.[92]

Another Confidential Order, issued June 14, 1918, authorized the censoring of mail of conscientious objectors and the refusing of access of political visitors to conscientious objectors.[93]

Instructions of July 30, 1918, Summarized the Government's Policy

The instructions of July 30 from the War Department are

---

[89] Kellogg, *op. cit.*, pp. 27-28.
[90] *Statement Concerning the Treatment of Conscientious Objectors in the Army*, p. 20.
[91] *Ibid.*, p. 20.
[92] *Ibid.*, p. 20.
[93] *Ibid.*, p. 20.

very important in summarizing the government's policy toward conscientious objectors:

From: The Adjutant General of the Army.

To: All department commanders of the United States; commanding generals of all regular Army, National Army, and National Guard Divisions; commanding officers of all excepted places, and all staff departments.

Subject: Conscientious Objectors.

1. Letter of Instruction, dated June 1, 1918, subject, "Conscientious Objectors"; segregation at Camp Leavenworth, Kansas, is hereby rescinded and the following substituted therefor:

2. By the terms of the Presidential order of March 20, 1918, men reporting at the training camps under the provisions of the Selective Service Law who profess conscientious scruples against warfare are given an opportunity to select forms of service designated by the President to be noncombatant in character. Commanding officers are instructed to assign to noncombatant service such objectors as are deemed to be sincere and apply for such service, furnishing such conscientious objectors with a certificate exempting them from combatant service as prescribed in General Orders No. 28, War Department, 1918. Trial by court-martial of those declining to accept such noncombatant service is authorized in the following cases; (a) whose attitude in camp is defiant; (b) whose cases in the judgment of the camp commander, for any reason, should not await investigation by the Board herein referred to; (c) who are active in propaganda.

3. All other men professing conscientious objections, now segregated in posts and camps, I.E., those, who, while themselves refusing to obey military instructions on the ground of conscientious scruples, religious or other, have given no other cause of criticism in their conduct, and all who have been or may be tried and acquitted by court-martial, shall be furloughed as herein directed or transferred to such other stations as may be designated from time to time. Orders for such transfers will be obtained from this office. The commanding officers of all camps or stations will keep these men segregated, but not under arrest, pending further instructions from this office.

. . . .

6. The Secretary of War has constituted a Board of Inquiry com-

posed of a representative from the Judge Advocate General's office, Major General Richard C. Stoddard, Chairman; Judge Julian W. Mack, of the Federal Court, and Dean H. F. Stone of the Columbia University Law School. Under no circumstances will conscientious objectors otherwise qualified to perform military duty be discharged from their responsibility under the Selective Service Law, but all cases of the character referred to in paragraph two, except those under charges or being tried by court-martial, shall be investigated by this board who will interrogate personally each individual whose case is referred to them, and recommend action to be taken. Such men as may be determined by this board to be sincere conscientious objectors as to combatant service, but not as to noncombatant service, shall, on the recommendation of the board, be furloughed without pay for agricultural service, upon the voluntary application of the soldier, under the authority contained in the Act of Congress of March 16, 1918, and the provisions of general orders No. 31, War Department, 1918, provision being made:

(a) That monthly report as to the industry of each person so furloughed shall be received from disinterested sources, and that the furlough may be terminated upon receipt of report that he is not working to the best of his ability; and

(b) That bona fide employment be obtained at the prevailing rate of wages for the class of work in which he engages, in the community in which he is employed.

(c) That no person shall be recommended for such furlough who does not voluntarily agree that he shall receive for his labor an amount no greater than a private's pay, plus an estimated sum for sustenance if such be not provided by the employer, and that any additional amount which may be paid for his services be contributed to the American Red Cross.

7. It is the function of the Board of Inquiry to determine the sincerity of men professing conscientious objections, both as to their refusal to perform noncombatant service and also with regard to the performance of combatant service. When the board upon examination believes any man to be insincere in his protestations against the performance of combatant service it will be so reported to his commanding officer, and such soldier will then be assigned by his commanding officer to any military service and held accountable for its performance.

8. In exceptional cases the board may recommend furlough service in France in the Friends' Reconstruction Unit.

. . . .

By order of the Secretary of War: Signed J. B. Wilson,

Adjutant General[94]

The above order marked the end of the development of the government's policy toward conscientious objectors. Conscientious objectors going to camp were offered noncombatant service. Those deemed sincere in their refusal were furloughed to farms. All who were judged defiant in attitude or insincere were tried by court-martial and sent to prison. Some were recommended for furlough service in France under the Friends' Reconstruction Unit.

Questionable Treatment of Conscientious Objectors Continued in Camps

Because of frequent reports of wide differences regarding the treatment of religious objectors in the various groups, the Adjutant General issued another order, October 2, 1918:

From: The Adjutant General of the Army

To: All Department and Camp Commanders.

Subject: Treatment of Conscientious Objectors.

. . . .

Section 2. There is evidently a wide divergence in the manner in which these men are treated in the different camps and posts. The point at issue is always whether a man is sincere in his professions. If a man brings evidence from his local board, or from other reputable sources, of his membership in a religious body which is on record as opposed to warfare, or gives evidence of his sincerity by his conduct and attitude, it is clearly not the intention, either of the legislation, or of the President's Executive Order, or the instructions issued by the direction of the Secretary of War that men should be treated, either by officers or enlisted men, pending the examination by the Board of Inquiry appointed for that purpose, as if their insincerity and cowardice had already been established. It is not intended or desired that they be pampered or accorded special privileges in any respect not covered by existing instructions;

---

[94] *Ibid.*, pp. 44-45.

on the other hand, they should not be treated, as in a few cases they have been, as men already convicted of cowardice and deceit. It is the experience of the Department that a considerate and tactful attitude toward these men has in many cases resulted in their acceptance, either of noncombatant, or in many cases combatant service, whereas a hectoring and abusive attitude has had an opposite effect.

Section 3. The plans now under way for an enlargement of the Board of Inquiry will make it possible to have these soldiers examined more promptly than had hitherto been the case, and arrangements have also been made for their concentration at points where divisions are not in training.

Section 4. You are directed to notify all concerned,

By order of the Secretary of War:

John S. Johnson,
Adjutant General.[95]

F. P. Keppel, Third Assistant Secretary of War, states that the rulings of July 30, 1918, and October 2, 1918, were typical statements of the War Department's policies.[96] Thus, until the end of the war, the War Department worked to get conscientious objectors to enter army service.

The United States Disciplinary Barracks, Fort Leavenworth, Kansas, were designated, September 21, 1918, as the place of confinement for those who were sent to prison.[97]

How the Board of Inquiry Classified Objectors

The following classifications were drawn up as a basis for the Board's considerations:

1-A Those found to be sincere religious objectors, and recommended for farm or industrial furlough.

1-B Those found to be sincere non-religious objectors, and recommended for farm or industrial furlough.

1-C Those found to be sincere conscientious objectors, who are recommended for the Friends' Reconstruction Unit.

---

[95] Kellogg, *op. cit.*, p. 139.
[96] *Statement Concerning the Treatment of Conscientious Objectors*, p. 8.
[97] *Ibid.*, p. 22.

2-A Those found to be sincere conscientious objectors as to combatant but not sincere as to noncombatant service, and who are therefore recommended to be assigned to noncombatant service.

2-B Those found to be sincere conscientious objectors who are willing to accept, and who are therefore recommended for, noncombatant service.

2-C Those found to be sincere conscientious objectors, who are willing to accept service in and who are assigned to, reconstruction hospitals.

3- Those found to be insincere and assignable to military duty.

4- Those objectors who are recommended to be sent to Fort Leavenworth, Kansas, for further examination.

5- Those objectors who, upon examination, withdraw their objections.

6- Those found to be sick or unfit for examination, and recommended to be sent to a hospital for treatment.

7- Alien enemies or neutrals.

8- Those objectors who are recommended for mental examination and discharge, if not found competent.

9- Not in camp—not seen by the Board.

10- Under criminal charges—the Board expresses no opinion until the decision of the court.

11- Tried by court-martial, therefore no opinion is now expressed.[98]

The War Department in its statement June 18, 1919, summarized the Board of Inquiry's recommendations regarding conscientious objectors:

The disposition of the 3,989 men who claimed exemption at camp on account of religious or other conscientious objection were disposed of as follows:

Originally accepted, or
    were assigned to noncombatant service 1,300
Furloughed to agriculture 1,200
Furloughed to Friends' Reconstruction Unit 99
Class 1 remaining in camp after the armistice 715

---

[98] Kellogg, *op. cit.*, pp. 31-32.

Class 2 remaining in camp after the armistice 225
General court-martial prisoners 450
                                                    ———
                                                  3,989

From the foregoing it appears that of the 3,989 inducted men who claimed exemption at camp, 2,600—about equally divided—went into noncombatant service and on furlough. About 1,000 or more than 70 per cent of those who went into noncombatant service did so voluntarily and without examination by the Board of Inquiry. Nine hundred and forty found by the Board of Inquiry to be sincere in their objections remained in camps unassigned at the time of the armistice and 504 were court-martialed.

The class 1 and class 2 objectors remaining in camps after the armistice were discharged in accordance with the orders of November 29, and December 11, 1918.[99]

The following table compiled by Lieutenant Mark A. May, Division of Psychology, Surgeon General's Office, shows the religious denominations of 1,060 conscientious objectors in twelve camps:

Mennonites 554
Friends 80
International Bible Students 60
Dunkards 37
Israelites of the House of David 39
Church of Christ 31
Church of God (colored) 20
Seventh Day Adventists 20
Pentecostal Assembly 13
All other denominations ....206[100]

This report does not represent the complete number of Brethren boys in camps who refused army service. It is another indication, however, that the larger number of Dunkers accepted some form of military work.

[99] *Statement Concerning the Treatment of Conscientious Objectors in the Army,* p. 25.
[100] Kellogg, *op. cit.,* pp. 128-129.

Court-martial Cases

The War Department also analyzed the results of the trials by courts-martial:

From the beginning of the draft to the present time (June 7, 1919), there were 504 trials by general court-martial of conscientious objectors. . . . Some, but a small proportion of the cases involved disloyalty, sedition, and propaganda. The general results of the trials were as follows:

Trial by courts-martial	504
Acquitted	1
Convicted and Sentenced	503
Disapproved by Reviewing Authority	3
Disapproved on the Recommendation of the Judge Advocate General	50
Effective Sentences	450

Of these, 113 were granted clemency on January 17, 1919.[101]

The original sentences as given by the courts are as follows:

Death	17	2 years	3
Life	142	50 years	3
10 years	89	8 years	1
20 years	73	11 years	1
25 years	57	12 years	1
15 years	47	13 years	1
5 years	29	18 years	1
30 years	19	28 years	1
3 years	5	45 years	1
1 year	4	99 years	1
40 years	4		—
Less than 1 year	3	Total	503[102]

These long sentences were not carried out but they show the severity with which the objectors were dealt. Many of those who went to prison had to experience hard tribulations before their sentences were modified.

---

[101] *Statement Concerning the Treatment of Conscientious Objectors in the Army*, p. 25.
[102] *Ibid.*, p. 52.

Eighty per cent of Objectors Changed Their Minds

Another evidence of the War Department's policy to influence conscientious objectors to enter army service is the fact that eighty per cent changed their minds and the War Department attributed it to the treatment of objectors prescribed by Secretary Baker. The following report explains:

From the second report of the Provost Marshal General which covers the whole period of the administration of the Selective Service Law from its enactment May 18, 1917, to December 20, 1918, and further subsequent data furnished by the boards but not included in the second report of the Provost Marshal General, it appears that there were 64,693 claims made for noncombatant classification, of which 56,830 were recognized by the boards. Of these, 29,679 were classified in Class 1 and found physically fit for general military service of whom 20,873 were inducted into the service from the beginning of mobilization to the termination thereof on November 11, 1918. During the entire period of the draft the total number of inductions into the Army was 2,810,296.

So far as statistics are available it appears that only about 4,000 men inducted into the military service made any claim in camp, either by presentation of a certificate or otherwise, for exemption from combatant service or from all military service. It would therefore appear that more than 80 per cent of religious objectors whose claims were recognized by the local boards and who were furnished with noncombatant certificates changed their minds before or shortly after reaching camp and failed to claim the advantage of exemption from combatant service. Undoubtedly this was due in a large measure to the character of treatment prescribed by the order of the Secretary of War of October 10, 1917.[103]

Secretary Baker wrote a memorandum to the Chief of Staff, December 8, 1918, in which he admitted the difficulties and inequalities experienced in administering the regulations concerning conscientious objectors. It is quoted in part:

The so-called conscientious objectors present a novel problem in military administration. . . .

Because of the novelty of the question, and the difficulty of con-

---
[103] *Ibid.*, p. 16.

veying explicitly the directions of the President to the widespread and scattered military organization, a number of cases have arisen in which that direction has not been complied with. Moreover, the order of the Commander in Chief on this subject came after a number of cases had been disposed of upon an entirely different theory. In addition to this it not unnaturally happened that as the administration of the principle proceeded, larger experience led to modifications of the practice. The net result of the whole situation is that we have among this group of people some who have been subjected to one theory of discipline, another large group who have had the benefit of the principle as modified by the fullest experience, and between these two groups, persons who have been caught up by the principle in process of modification, and instead of having military discipline administered in a uniform and consistent way, for which the Judge Advocate General so properly pleads, we have a variegated and spasmodic ad personam application of that phase of the principle either uppermost at the time, or believed to be uppermost by the particular tribunal which undertook to apply it.

To permit such a result to continue would, of course, be discreditable to the entire system of military justice, as well as at variance with the positively expressed wishes of the President as Commander in Chief. Fortunately, we are not obliged to continue the results of such a system. The Secretary of War, acting for the President, had the final power of review and of clemency. Therefore, all the power necessary to correct any inequality in the application of the law and the executive order is in the Secretary of War. If the Secretary of War had time he would personally review each of the persons in this class, or by assembling all the records in the cases would attempt personally to see that uniformity of procedure and principle obtained. To aid him in this task he had secured the co-operation of Dean Stone and Judge Mack, whose peculiar qualifications for the task are obvious. . . .

Newton D. Baker
Secretary of War.[104]

Attitude of Secretary Baker Toward Conscientious Objectors

The writer lived under the impression until very re-

---

[104] *Ibid.*, p. 29.

cently that Newton D. Baker had a sympathetic understanding of the religious objectors and wanted to see that
their conscientious convictions against war got adequate
consideration. It has been mentioned in Brethren circles
and even suggested to the writer by Rufus Jones that Secretary Baker had some connection with the Brethren people
and that this may have accounted for his understanding of
the peace churches. The writer found upon investigation
that Newton D. Baker's wife's grandfather, Jonus Leopold,
was an active member of the Coventry Church of the
Brethren, Pennsylvania.[105] Whether this had any influence upon the Secretary of War cannot be determined.
Charles D. Bonsack, one of the Brethren who dealt with the
Washington officials, says: "It seemed that Secretary Baker
wanted to be fair with the conscientious objectors. He was
more sympathetic with them than most of the other officials. He had a better understanding of our position."[106]
J. E. Miller says, "Secretary Baker was friendly to our people. He had some connection with the Brethren."[107]

The Secretary of War may have had more of an understanding of the religious objectors than most government
officials at that time. He gave orders against brutal treatment in the army. But his handling of the conscientious
objector problem does not show constructive and far-
sighted statesmanship; neither does it reveal any marked
efforts to safeguard religious objectors in the exercising
of their convictions against war. The War Department
followed a deliberate policy to get as many objectors as
possible to take army service. For those who refused, there
was nothing but idleness in detention camps with court-
martial proceedings and much abuse. A farm furlough
law early in the war would have saved many hardships.

[105] Personal letter from Rev. Trostle P. Dick, Pottstown, Pa., Jan. 12, 1943.
[106] Personal interview with Charles D. Bonsack, Dec. 30, 1942.
[107] Personal interview with J. E. Miller, Elgin, Ill., Dec. 31, 1942.

It came late and then not on the invitation of the War Department. Mr. Baker allowed sincere religious objectors to be tried as disobedient soldiers. After the Executive Order of March 23, 1918, both Baker and Keppel became more impatient with objectors who refused service in the army. Court-martialing cases increased and many sincere church people were sent to Leavenworth.

The Attitude of President Wilson Toward Conscientious Objectors

The Brethren felt that President Wilson was a little more liberal toward conscientious objectors than many other government officials. How much initiative the President took with reference to objectors is not known. It is thought that the order abolishing manacling in prisons came as a result of an interview between Wilson and Baker before the President sailed for the peace conference.[108] Why the President hesitated so long before defining noncombatant service is difficult to determine. He hints at it in a letter to Rufus Jones August 28, 1917, which is quoted in part:

The varieties of conscientious objection developed in the application of the selective conscription law have been so numerous as to make it necessary to delay the establishment of a policy until we can be sure that we have both satisfied the requirements of the law and gone just as far as we can justly go in the recognition of the rights of individual conscience in such a matter. When the total number of persons interposing conscientious objection to military service has been ascertained, I hope to be able to work out with the Secretary of War a plan which will give the nation the benefit of the service of these men without injustice to the great company of young men who are free to accept their country's call to military duty.[109]

The President led the country into a war in which he declared, "We fought for the right of men everywhere to

[108] Thomas, *op. cit.,* pp. 256-257
[109] Jones, *op. cit.,* p. 52.

choose their way of life and obedience."[110] He was rated as a liberal, but the handling of the conscientious objector problem during his presidency was not in harmony with his lofty idealism.

Attitude of F. P. Keppel Toward Conscientious Objectors

In the War Department, Assistant Secretary F. P. Keppel had general charge of the matters dealing with men professing conscientious objections to war. He seemed to have a clearer understanding of the problems than Mr. Baker and tried to obtain for the conscientious objectors tolerance and fair treatment. It is known that he personally rectified many wrongs when they came to his attention.

Mr. Kellogg's Testimony Regarding Conscientious Objectors

Mr. Kellogg, as a member of the Board of Inquiry, described his impressions of the objectors whom he helped to examine:

> My first trip as a member of the Board upset most of my ideas regarding the objector. I began to see him in a new light. And an examination of over eight hundred objectors in twenty widely distributed military camps and posts has convinced me that they are, as a rule, sincere—cowards and shirkers, in the commonly accepted sense, they are not. Their sincerity, however, makes them no less a national problem.[111]

Again he says, "A sovereign government must not oppress the honest objector, nor assuredly, should it grant him such special privileges that it thereby discriminates against its patriotic soldiery."[112]

Conduct of the Objectors

Kellogg as a member of the Examining Board testifies regarding the conscientious objectors:

> The conduct of the majority of objectors cannot seriously be criti-

---

[110] Thomas, *op. cit., p.* 255.
[111] Kellogg, *op. cit.,* Preface, p. 5.
[112] *Ibid.,* p. 6.

cized. They realized that the administration had endeavored to be fair with them, and they, in their turn, tried to be fair with the administration. Although they refused to work they seemed desirous of avoiding any action which would embarrass the camp authorities.[113]

MORE EXPERIENCES OF THE BRETHREN IN ARMY AND PRISON

The War Department reported that nearly ninety per cent of the objectors were religious.[114] The larger part of them came from churches whose teaching forbade participation in war. Their experiences during the war have already been partly described in discussing the relationship of minority groups to the state. The Brethren who were unwilling to accept noncombatant service, like others from the Friends and Mennonites, suffered the embarrassments of abuse, misunderstanding and the guard house. The mentioning of a few more experiences may throw light on the treatment accorded to religious objectors.

Roy E. Peters describes his experiences during the first days at Camp Greenleaf:

My turn came. The captain stood there beside a large pile of uniforms; he ordered me to take up mine. I refused to touch it; he ordered me the second time to pick it up, at the same time menacing me with his automatic. Again I refused; he then ordered me under arrest. It was now 7:30 P. M. I was confined to the barracks until 10 A. M. the following day. Meanwhile, a corporal brought in my uniform and other army equipment and threw them down on my bunk.

Next day at 10 A. M. I was released. The Sergeant then ordered me to come with him to the bath house. There was no one else present except him and me. He ordered me to put on the army uniform. I refused. He then proceeded to strip off my civilian clothing and then to dress me up in a new uniform; he forgot to button me up properly as a sudden inspiration struck him to take away all my own clothes and let me finish the buttoning myself.

They couldn't say now that of my own free will I had donned the

---

[113] *Ibid.*, p. 83.
[114] Thomas, *op. cit.*, p. 19.

uniform; but against my will they forced the uniform on me and required me to wear it, or else go without any clothes. This was all done in direct opposition to Secretary of War Baker's order.

After they had gotten the uniform on me I was then ordered to go and work in the kitchen. I went to the kitchen and worked there all afternoon.

Saturday, March 23. Company ordered out for drill exercises in afternoon. I stepped out of the line and stayed until the lieutenant caught sight of me. He ordered me back into line; I went. He then gave the command 'forward march.' I remained behind standing still, lieutenant watching me closely, commanded 'company halt,' caught me by the shoulder and shoved me up into line, told me to stay there. He ordered 'company march.' I stood still as before, he came back exasperated and wanted to know what was wrong with me. I explained to him my status in brief. He ordered me to quarters. I complied with his order most willingly.[115]

Maurice A. Hess, a member of the Old German Baptist Church (frequently called Old Order Brethren), told his court-martial judges why he chose the path of suffering:

I do not believe that I am seeking martyrdom. As a young man, life and its hopes and freedom and opportunities for service are sweet to me. I want to go out into the world and make use of what little talent I may have acquired by long and laborious study. (Mr. Hess is now a college professor.)

But I know that I dare not purchase these things at the price of eternal condemnation. I know the teaching of Christ, my Savior. He taught us to resist not evil, to love our enemies, to bless them that curse us, and do good to them that hate us. Not only did he teach this, but he also practiced it in Gethsemane, before Pilate, and on Calvary. We would indeed be hypocrites and base traitors to our profession if we would be unwilling to bear the taunts and jeers of a sinful world, and imprisonment, and torture or death, rather than to participate in war and military service. We know that obedience to Christ will gain for us the glorious prize of eternal life. We cannot yield, we cannot compromise, we must suffer.

Two centuries ago our people were driven out of Germany by religious persecution, and they accepted the invitation of William Penn to come to his colony where they might enjoy the blessing of

---

[115] Moomaw, *op. cit.*, pp. 296-297.

religious liberty which he promised them. This religious liberty was later confirmed by the Constitution of Pennsylvania, and the Constitution of the United States.

If the authorities now see fit to change those fundamental documents and take away our privilege of living in accordance with the teaching of the scriptures of God, then we have no course but to endure persecution as true soldiers of Christ.

If I have committed anything worthy of bonds or death, I do not refuse to suffer or to die.

I pray God for strength to remain faithful.[116]

The writer knows Maurice A. Hess personally. He has been a college professor since the war and is a man of intelligence and character. He gives his own judgment of the justice of the court-martial proceedings:

In relation to our court-martial trials, I may say that they did not have the slightest resemblance to justice. They were a mere formality on carrying out the policy of the camp commander . . . or possibly of certain officials at Washington, for the suppression or extinction of the conscientious objector idea. We were prejudged.[117]

Hess was one of those who suffered severe treatment at Leavenworth, including solitary confinement.

As a result of frequent protests to President Wilson and Secretary Baker regarding the cruel treatment to which some of the objectors were being subjected in prison, the War Department on December 6, 1918, issued the following order:

The Secretary of War authorized the following statement: Disciplinary regulations in force in military prisons have been modified by the War Department Order. Fastening of prisoners to the bars of cells will not longer be used as a mode of punishment. . . .[118]

The Church of the Brethren had at least sixteen members to reach military prisons.[119] A few were punished severely but the records indicate that most of them after a short time were able to win considerate treatment from their

---

[116] Thomas, *op. cit.*, pp. 25-26.
[117] *Ibid.*, p. 169.
[118] Paul French, *We Won't Murder*, p. 104.
[119] Moomaw, *op. cit.*, p. 325.

officers. L. C. Blickenstaff says, "At Leavenworth C.O.'s were respected by both officers and other prisoners; at first we were treated as any prisoners, but we rapidly won the confidence of our jailors and were soon given responsible jobs and some special privileges."[120]

William Warren Sweet says:

It is an important fact that the World War produced practically no heroes of high military rank, as did the Civil War. To a large degree it was a sergeants' and second lieutenants' war and there were many Sergeant Yorks. But undoubtedly among the greatest heroes produced by the war were the conscientious objectors. Some of them may not have been sincere, but there are enough of the other variety to warrant an appraisal of the part they played.[121]

THE PROGRAM OF RELIEF AND RECONSTRUCTION

The Church of the Brethren carried on an active program of relief during World War I. The church members were asked to contribute liberally because of the suffering in the world and out of gratitude to God because of their favored position with the government. Relief work was considered as a kind of alternative service. The Special General Conference at Goshen, Indiana, appointed a Relief and Reconstruction Committee composed of J. E. Miller, Galen B. Royer and Clarence Lahman. The committee was authorized to plan a program of relief and reconstruction work for the church, to appeal for funds and disburse them. The report of the committee, February 28, 1919, shows that $91,859.98 had been received up to that time. During the next year the church responded with $162,885.87, and the third year with $34,384.00. Most of the money was appropriated for Armenian and Syrian Relief through the administration of the Armenian Committee, but donations were made to the Red Cross, Belgian Relief, the French Children's Relief Fund, China Famine Relief and to many

---

[120] Personal letter from L. C. Blickenstaff, Jan. 25, 1943.
[121] Sweet, *The Story of Religion in America*, p. 562.

other needs. The members as a whole gave liberally in Red Cross drives. The point of view of the church was that since Brethren could not destroy life, they should do all they could to save life.

Co-operation With the Friends and Mennonites

There was more co-operation between the historic peace churches in World War I than during the Civil War. The Brethren had come to see the need and value of working together. There were frequent conversations between the leaders of the Friends, Mennonites and Brethren and an interchange of helpful experiences. While there was no united committee to deal with the government, some meetings were called for the joint consideration of problems relating to the draft. There was united action, however, in planning for reconstruction work in France and the peace churches agreed that concerted action would best serve the interests of each body. The Church of the Brethren co-operated with the Friends in this foreign service project.

Effect of World War I Upon the Church of the Brethren

J. E. Miller says that World War I set the Brethren "to re-evaluating their peace position."[122] Many Brethren leaders were disillusioned regarding noncombatant service. There was a general feeling of dissatisfaction regarding the church's war record. The church saw that its teaching program on peace had been a failure. Some of the strongest peace leaders of the church came out of disillusioning war experiences. The denomination was committed toward more co-operation with other churches in peace work.

Summary

The Church of the Brethren opposed the United States entering World War I. The church had passed general

---

[122] Personal interview with J. E. Miller, Elgin, Ill., Dec. 31, 1942.

peace resolutions, but had offered no effective program for teaching its peace doctrines to the young people. Brethren boys faced the draft unprepared to defend their peace convictions before military officers. During the first half of the war Brethren leaders were uncertain as to the position the church should take regarding noncombatant service. Many ministers advised the young men to accept this service and the church officially did not advise against it. Consequently, most Brethren boys entered noncombatant activities and a small number went into straight army service. There were several hundred, however, who refused all work under army domination. These were finally placed in detention camps, lived under constant pressure from army officials, and were later either furloughed to farms or sent to prison. The Church of the Brethren defined its position at the Goshen Conference in January, 1918, and advised against putting on the uniform and drilling. This more definite and clear-cut attitude was taken because of the disillusioning experiences the church leaders were having with army officers who were continually trying to persuade Brethren boys to accept military service. It was thought that the young men should have some definite church decisions upon which to stand. The general feeling was also developing that noncombatant assignments were in reality military service, as the statement of General Kuhn, quoted in the Goshen letter to the President, implied. The Goshen Statement had to be withdrawn from circulation and the Annual Conference officials narrowly escaped prosecution. The records indicate that the number of Brethren boys entering noncombatant branches of the army increased. While the official position of the church after January, 1918, was against noncombatant military service, the functional position was in favor of it. The church waited for the government to say what it could or

could not do, and did not look ahead. It had no plan to offer to the government.

The government, likewise, was not prepared to handle
the conscientious objector problem. The draft law recognized only members from churches whose tenets of faith
were opposed to participation in war. The law provided
for exemption from only combatant service and not from
military service. There was no provision for absolutists,
nor for those who would not take their orders from the
military. The President did not define noncombatant service until the war was half over. In the meantime, conscientious objectors in camps were being persuaded to accept military assignments, and those who refused were
being detained in detention camps or guard houses. Detention camps without constructive work were not wholesome for young men. The many confidential orders and
regulations from the War Department and the statements
from Secretary Baker which have come to light since the
war make it clear that the unannounced policy of the War
Department was to get as many conscientious objectors as
possible to accept useful army service. Neither the War
Department nor the army was trying to protect the consciences of those who differed from the military program.

After the President's executive order outlining noncombatant service, conscientious objectors in camps were
placed under persuasion again to accept army service. The
Farm Furlough Law was passed because of the need for
farm help. This offered one solution for the objector problem. Many court-martial proceedings were being carried on in camps for those who refused all military activities. A Board of Inquiry was appointed to examine those
with conscientious objections to war. The objectors had to
fight, work on farms at a private's pay, or go to prison.
The record of court-martial proceedings and the punish-

ments in prison for sincere religious objectors is not a bright page in American history. Neither the Church of the Brethren, nor the government, nor the army, showed any far-sighted statesmanship in handling the conscientious objector problem. The effect of the World War upon the Brethren was to set the church to the task of re-evaluating its peace position.

Chapter VIII

THE DEVELOPMENT OF THE BRETHREN PEACE
PHILOSOPHY AND ACTIVITIES BETWEEN
WORLD WARS I AND II

World War I stimulated the Brethren to re-evaluate their peace position. There was a strong revulsion against war. Some of the strongest peace leaders of the denomination, like M. R. Zigler, Dan West and C. Ray Keim, were persons who had disillusioning war experiences.

The period between the world wars was one of marked increase of interest in Christian educational activities. Strong church programs for children, young people and adults were planned and promoted. Church leaders co-operated freely with county and city councils of churches, the International Council of Religious Education, the Home Missions Council of North America, the Foreign Missions Council, and the various commissions of the Federal Council of Churches of Christ in America. Summer camps for young people were carried on in regions and many districts. Young people went to college in great numbers and entered a large number of the professions. Among Brethren youth there were many farmers but also a large number of schoolteachers, doctors, and business leaders. More young people went to graduate schools and took higher degrees. There was a strong missionary enthusiasm in the church program, and also a continual growth of interest in relief and reconstruction projects, which led to the formation of the Brethren Service Committee. During the period under review the Church of the Brethren looked out of itself, overcame in a large degree its inferiority complex and focused its attention upon the needs of the world. Education, co-operation, and world service were leading ideas in Brethren thought. During this time of a widening church horizon, what significant developments occurred in the Brethren peace philosophy?

ANNUAL CONFERENCE RESOLUTIONS

Practically every Annual Conference between the world wars made a strong declaration on peace. The Conference of 1919 came out strongly in opposition to universal military training and asked for the release of conscientious objectors in Leavenworth prison.[1] In 1920 the General Peace Committee called for more peace teaching throughout the denomination, asked that the Goshen Conference Statement be re-published and distributed, and that the church favor "a Court or League of Arbitration for the settlement of differences."[2] In 1921 the Central Service Committee made a strong appeal to President Harding for disarmament.[3] The problem of members joining the American Legion was not long delayed. The Conference of 1922 stated: "Our members should not affiliate themselves with the American Legion or kindred ex-service organizations."[4] However, it is known that some Brethren joined the American Legion and they were not disciplined for it.

Revision of Brethren's Card

The Brethren's Card is a brief statement of the ideals and teachings of the church. This card was revised in 1923 and a part of section 5 which states the teaching of the church on war is quoted as follows:

Opposes on scriptural grounds: War and the taking of human life (Matt. 5: 21-26, 43, 44; Rom. 12: 19-21; Isa. 53: 7-12; violence in personal and industrial controversy (Matt. 7: 12; Rom. 13: 8-10). . . .[5]

---

[1] *Minutes of the Annual Conference of the Church of the Brethren*, 1919. p. 34.
[2] *Ibid.*, 1920, pp. 31-32.
[3] *Ibid.*, 1921, pp. 30-31.
[4] *Ibid.*, 1922, p. 3.
[5] *Ibid.*, 1923, p. 9.

Peace Position Still Biblical

The Brethren's Card shows clearly that the foundation of the church's peace convictions was still Biblical. This is further confirmed by the Annual Conference Resolution of 1924 which was drawn purposefully for an authoritative peace statement. It is quoted in part:

1. The Testimony of the Fathers. At the organization of our church, when a few Brethren, as reformers, divesting themselves of all previous teaching and of all preconceived opinions, prostrated themselves in prayer and supplication, with the New Testament alone open before them; desiring the Holy Spirit to interpret to them its teachings—desiring thus to be led and influenced in the determination and formation of their religious beliefs and tenets, among the findings is that the New Testament, in letter and spirit, is clearly and definitely committed against war and in favor of peace; and that the follower of the Lord Jesus should not engage in war or learn the arts thereof.

2. The Continuance of this Teaching. This same principle has been diligently and persistently taught by our people throughout our course and history by faithful preaching, writing and teaching—both in public and in personal presentation of the subject. So entirely has this been the case that every applicant for membership in the church had been instructed on the subject and asked to assent to it as a Christian principle and teaching of the New Testament. Adherence to this principle has generally been held as a test of membership.

. . . .

4. Reasons for This Position Taken and Maintained by the Church:

(1) The teachings and precepts of Jesus while here upon earth.

(2) All the teachings and precepts of our Lord on the subject of nonresistance in personal conduct or in attitude towards militant service were exemplified by him in his contact with men and authorities.

(3) The Acts of the Apostles, setting forth the teachings of the apostles and their successors—and their own conduct—during the organization of the church.

(4) The epistolary writings harmonize throughout with the teaching and example of our Lord.[6]

---

[6] *Ibid.*, 1924, p. 10.

The Conference Resolutions of 1931 and 1932

A study of the general peace statements reveals a gradual trend following World War I for the Brethren to exercise more pressure for political action. They no longer take the position that they will accept what the government requires of them. The denomination is acting more as a pressure group. The Conference pronouncement of 1931 is an illustration:

The Board of Religious Education petitions this Conference to pass the following special resolutions:

First, That this Conference urges the President of the United States to take steps to bring about a drastic reduction in armament expenditures in both land and naval forces, and that the United States take the initiative step at the Geneva Disarmament Conference in 1932.

Second, That the Church of the Brethren disapproves the aggressive policy of the War and Navy Departments through their channels of propaganda to militarize this nation.

Third, That the church reaffirms its position on peace and goodwill and refuses to sanction or take any part in war.

Fourth, That the church vigorously opposes the passage of any laws which will authorize universal conscription in peace times.

Answer of Conference: Resolutions approved.[7]

The special resolution of 1932 is very significant. A part of it is quoted:

Therefore, we feel bound to avow our conviction that all war is out of harmony with the plain precepts of the Gospel of Christ, and that no plea of necessity or policy, however urgent, can be set up to release either the individual or any nation from the paramount duty which they owe to Jesus who enjoined all men to love their enemies. We express, in all humility, our firm persuasion that all problems, questions and exigencies incident to the well being of civil government and the social order can be settled under the banner of the Prince of Peace in strict conformity to His commands.

. . . .

The fundamental ground of our opposition to war is religious and

_____
[7] *Ibid.*, 1931, p. 45.

ethical. Our position is one which attaches to the inherent nature of right which grows out of an abiding consciousness of the individual's obligation of what the enlightened soul ought to be. The Christ way of life revealed in the Holy Scriptures, the voice of conscience revealed in the soul, make our participation in war under any and all circumstances impossible.[8]

This statement marks a development in Brethren peace philosophy. *All war is declared to be "out of harmony with the plain precepts of the Gospel of Christ."* The peace teachings of Christ are applied to the state as much as to the church. *The whole war system is considered to be wrong.* The church's opposition to war is both "religious and ethical." And the ethical note is significant. For more than two hundred years the Brethren opposed war because the Bible said it was wrong. "Thus saith the Lord" was enough for them. Now other reasons for war's wrongness are appearing. The "social gospel" emphasis with its optimism for the building of a better world is increasingly gripping the church.

Brethren Protest Against Military Taxes

A query came to the Conference of 1933 from the First District of West Virginia asking how to protest most effectively "against paying taxes for military purposes."[9] The next year the following action was taken:

J. All lawful taxes should be paid. As Christians we differentiate between taxes for constructive and taxes for destructive purposes. Because war is unchristian, taxes for military and naval purposes should be protested.

Not less than 70% out of our taxes paid to the federal government goes directly or indirectly for military and naval purposes. Some of these federal taxes are: income taxes, estate taxes, federal stamp taxes, and the federal tax on gasoline, etc.

II. Ways of protesting against taxes for military and naval purposes.

---

[8] *Ibid.*, 1932, pp. 47-48.
[9] *Ibid.*, 1933, p. 39.

1. Paste a small sticker on your income tax returns and other payments made to the federal government, which reads as follows: "That portion of this tax devoted to armaments and war preparedness is paid under protest." The Board of Christian Education will furnish these stickers.

2. Write a letter once a year to your congressmen protesting against the appropriation of funds for military and naval purposes.

3. Protest personally when paying federal taxes, such as the federal gasoline tax.

4. Protest through resolutions from local churches, district and Annual Conferences.

III. We favor a further study of this problem with the purpose of helping to develop a sound theory of taxation.[10]

How general these protests were carried out is not known. The writer at that time was in the office of the Board of Christian Education and the correspondence with interested members would indicate that there was a growing church consciousness that paying taxes for military purposes was wrong. Some strong protests were made through letters and personal conferences with congressmen but there is no indication that any large number of church members carried out the instructions of Annual Conference.

A Growing Interest in Neutral Relief

The young people of the church asked the Conference of 1932 to outline a church program for international goodwill and neutral relief work in the event of war. In 1934 the Brethren took the following action:

1. War can be prevented if all who love peace give their best to that end. Then no relief plan would be necessary.

2. If a major war is allowed to occur, in a mobilized nation neutrality is not really possible.

3. We can not co-operate with any nation in war, either directly in military or naval service, or indirectly in service in organizations under military command. "Above all the nations is humanity." We can give relief to sufferers on both sides of any conflict, particular-

---

[10] *Ibid.*, 1934, pp. 39-40.

ly to women and children. We dare not cloud our testimony against
war.

4. In our efforts to oppose war we must guard carefully our love
for our country. We may be classed as enemies of our country, but
we must give no valid reason for being so classed. Where we can
not co-operate, we must try to compensate.

5. Because we can not know ahead of time the conditions of any
possible war in the future, we can not build an adequate relief plan
now. Any plan we might outline would have to be changed in the
actual emergency. However, if we are ever to have an adequate relief plan we must begin building it now.

6. We want to develop in our church the state of mind which, if
written large, will prevent war and bring peace; then if our efforts
should fail to prevent the outbreak of hostilities, we shall have a
background of experience out of which to construct an adequate
neutral relief plan. This will involve—

a. A commitment to the way of life that makes war impossible.

b. A knowledge of the essential New Testament teaching on the
subject; also of our national history on the peace and war question,
and of the major problems in the modern world.

c. A plan for passing on the truths that we have learned to those
who have not heard.

d. A program of training in subsistence homestead projects, areas
of conflict such as strikes, and other conditions of civilian suffering
and need. These might include classes in dietetics for mothers,
milk and vegetables for under-nourished children, guidance of the
leisure time for under-privileged boys and girls, and extra self-
denial on our part to help build up a relief chest.

A program of this nature will tend to develop the emotional stability that will hold us steady under whatever strains may come.[11]

The above statement is important because it indicates
the desire of the church for a worthy program of alternative service in the event of war. It also shows that church
leaders were recognizing the need of carrying on special
service projects in peacetime so that alternative service in
war might be a continuance of what was already being
done.

---

[11] *Ibid.*, 1934, pp. 41-42.

The Church Declares That All War Is Sin

Another comprehensive restatement of the church's position on war and peace was made by the Annual Conference of 1935. It is more definite and specific than the 1932 pronouncement and for the first time in history the Brethren declared that "all war is sin." The statement is as follows:

Conscious of the growing danger of war in the world today and feeling the need of a reaffirmation of our stand on peace and war, we, the Peace Commission of the Church of the Brethren, through the Board of Christian Education, recommend to the Annual Conference of 1935 the adoption of the following statement, which statement shall be submitted to the proper officials of our federal government and to the leaders of other churches in America:

As a people we have opposed wars at all times throughout our entire history of over two hundred twenty-five years and we have stood with equal consistency for constructive peace principles in all relationships of life. We hate war because we love peace, our way of life at all times. It has been the practice of the church through the years to require of applicants for membership a pledge not to engage in war nor learn the art of war. In our constant attempt to be truly devoted to the highest interests of our country, we have recognized that our supreme allegiance is to God, and we believe that recognition commits us to the highest standard of Christian citizenship by which we can serve our country and our God. We believe a Christian regard for other peoples increases rather than decreases our respect for and our attachment to our own nation.

We believe that all war is sin; that it is wrong for Christians to support or to engage in it; and that war is incompatible with the spirit, example and teachings of Jesus. We believe that war is not inevitable. Those beliefs are not based upon a popular peace doctrine of our own; they arise from our application of Christian standards to all human relations, whether individual, group, class, or national. To settle conflicts in any of these relationships by war is not efficient, not constructive, not permanent, and certainly not Christian. We believe that nonviolence, motivated by goodwill, is more powerful than the sword, making possible the survival of both parties, while warfare insures the ultimate destruction of both. War is a far greater calamity to victor and vanquished alike, than would be the hazards incidental to a renunciation of war by a nation and the settlement of all their disputes by peaceful means.

We believe that armaments for nations, like weapons for private defense, do not bring security, but rather intensify the dangers of conflict, as present world conditions tragically testify. We do not believe in the expenditure of our substance for those instruments which endanger our peace and safety. We believe in the only preparedness for our nation—goodwill, and the agencies through which it may be expressed and maintained.

We believe the whole war system is futile, always leaving more problems than it settles, if it settles any. Today, only a few years after winning the "war to end war," the United States is in the midst of the greatest of war preparation, and our country shares with other nations the general feeling of insecurity throughout the world. We believe that true democracy, "government of the people, by the people and for the people," is consistent with the spirit and principles of Christianity. But the fruit of war is not democracy; war destroys democracy as the prevalence of dictatorships of the communist, fascist, or other varieties, testifies. We can not "make the world safe for democracy" by war.

Consequently, we are committed to such interests as a program of peace education for all people; the development and support of the necessary international institutions to settle the disputes between nations by means other than war; the promotion of better relations between conflicting social or economic groups within our country; and honesty and a spirit of public service in our government.

Likewise we are committed in our active opposition to all such interests as appropriations for military purposes; the manufacture of munitions of war either for private profit or by the government; the teaching of the doctrines of military preparedness which are so unsound and so unchristian; voluntary or compulsory military training in our secondary schools and colleges; the challenges of our so-called "war games" to other nations; the enactment of laws conscripting men or property for military purposes; neutrality laws that permit our citizens to profit from the trade of belligerents and draw us into wars; and the secret influence of munitions makers and military officials in conferences called to reduce or abolish armaments.

Therefore, as Christian citizens, we are devoted in principles and in action to the furtherance of every effort by our own nation or any other nation to promote peace in the world, and we are equally devoted in our opposition to those forces within or without our country which make for war, for class struggle, for civil disorder, or for personal conflict.[12]

This pronouncement was printed and circulated as the official position of the Church of the Brethren. A committee composed of C. C. Ellis, M. R. Zigler, V. F. Schwalm and Rufus D. Bowman took this peace resolution to the secretary of President Roosevelt, and Cordell Hull, Secretary of State. The President's secretary assured the committee that Mr. Roosevelt would read it. Cordell Hull was very appreciative of the fact that the church people were supporting measures for peace. The historic peace position of the church was explained and these government leaders were requested to file this statement as the official position of the Church of the Brethren on war. *Six years before the war came the Brethren had informed the government what its basic convictions were.*

The Church and International Relationships

The Conference of 1936 dealt with the problem of international relationships. It applied the Christian theory of life to nations as well as individuals. It is quoted thus:

We believe that the Christian theory of life demands that Christians should learn to live together as friends and neighbors. We deplore the fact that hatred, suspicion, fear, and rivalry so completely dominate our international life. The rulers and people of the world need the mind and spirit of Christ. We reaffirm our position on peace and pledge ourselves to a renewed attack on war and international strife. We again register our unreserved opposition to all wars, our purpose not to participate in any war, and our protest against the application of such a large proportion of our taxes to military purposes. We urge the establishment of a department of peace in our government, the universal disarmament among the nations of the world led by the United States, the exemption of conscientious objectors of all Christian bodies from military service,

---

[12] *Ibid.*, 1935, pp. 40-41.

the exemption of our youth from military training in high schools, colleges and universities, the complete control of the manufacture of munitions by the federal government and the removal of all profit from war materials of whatever character.[13]

Statement Sent to the Oxford Conference

M. R. Zigler represented the Church of the Brethren at the Oxford Conference. With him was sent the following statement of the church's position on peace, an action of the Conference of 1937, calling for that great world conference of Christian leaders to take definite steps toward world peace. The resolution is quoted in part:

We share the feeling of many Christians today that the church is facing a momentous crisis. Racial, economic, and political tensions threaten us with another world-wide war. Too often the answer to these tensions has been more guns. But the peoples of the world can not maintain for long a spiritual unity if beside our cathedral spires we build mountains of hate—our ever-increasing armaments. We feel that the church in many of our lands is facing two alternatives. The church may renounce war, oppose the prostitution of the spiritual life of the church to militarist purposes in the state, and endure the persecution consequent upon that position; or, the church may furnish the spiritual dynamic of the warring state and receive the staunch support of the same, but lose her own soul.

Our sincere hope is that out of this great conference of Christian leaders will come the spiritual impetus necessary for definite steps .in the leadership of the church toward world peace. The problem is not one of good intentions alone; it is one of changing the spirit and character of international policies, of race relations, and of economic systems. To the solution of this great problem of Christendom today, we dedicate ourselves and stand ready to join hands with our fellow Christians everywhere in bringing peace among men.[14]

Resolutions of 1938

A query came to the Annual Conference of 1938 asking what the attitude of the church should be toward a mem-

---

[13] *Ibid.*, 1936, p. 47.
[14] *Ibid.*, 1937, pp. 43-44.

ber who enlists for military service. The Conference answered:

It is evident according to Annual Meeting Minutes, Art. 9, 1840, (page 204), and Art. 7, 1886 (page 131), Sec. (1) that one who enlists in military service is not in full accord with the faith and practice of the general brotherhood. The attitude of the church toward such, however, should be one of brotherly love and forbearance, endeavoring by faithful teaching to restore him to full accord as long as he expresses desire to continue membership in the Church of the Brethren.[15]

Thus, while members who enter straight army service go against the advice of the church, they are not to be disfellowshiped. They are to be brought back through brotherly love into harmony with the Brethren teachings. *This position of tolerance and forbearance is in great contrast to the strict discipline of the Civil War period when persons lost their church membership if they entered military service.*

Another resolution of 1938 was an action "deploring the military nature of many toys in use" and asking the Board of Christian Education to instruct the church members regarding this matter.[16]

The same church Conference applied the peace principle to the area of industrial conflicts and showed the responsibility of the church to help relieve industrial tensions. The Conference stated:

In this day of industrial strife and clash of economic systems the church can not piously fold her arms and stand aloof from these conflicting groups. Thousands of our people are looking to our church for guidance in these conflicts in which they are directly or indirectly involved. The church can not be for one group or another, regardless of their merits or grievances. In many cases both contending parties are quite unchristian in spirit and conduct. The church must labor to bring into these areas of industrial conflict the spirit of Christ, thereby making possible the dissolving of these tensions.

---

[15] *Ibid.*, 1938, p. 41.
[16] *Ibid.*, 1938, p. 42.

The church stands for the redemption of all. This is the only true basis upon which industrial and other problems can be solved. Christians need to be intelligent concerning industrial conflicts so that their efforts made in the spirit of Christian love may be effective in a given situation. The Society of Friends are to be commended for the fine work they are doing in areas of conflict. Here are vast opportunities for us to bring healing to a world of strife.

We need to be deeply concerned that labor groups feel the church has neglected them and they are to an alarming degree anti-Christian. In the face of this challenging condition and the fact that increasing numbers of our people are entering the ranks of organized labor, we urge that the church without prejudice study and act upon the problem in keeping with the Gospel of our Lord who was ever the champion of the underprivileged and who put human welfare and brotherhood above selfish profits.[17]

In the Shadow of Conscription

In 1939 the Brethren reaffirmed again their time-honored peace position. The Annual Conference of 1940 was held during the period of increasing armaments and when there was much talk of conscription. Much time was given to the consideration of the peace problem. The following resolution shows the strong position which the church maintained against conscription, preparation for war and efforts to militarize the nation.

With Respect to a World at War:

We are saddened beyond power of expression by the widespread wars now raging. As followers of Jesus, we have the burden of the world's suffering and sin on our hearts. The failure of our world wide profession of Christianity to prevent these tragedies humbles us. Therefore we resolve to do the following:

1. To commend our government for whatever efforts have been made to keep us out of the present war, and, constrained by the love of Christ, to pray that the United States may not enter into any war; to protest earnestly:

(1) The program of armament so feverishly being carried on now by our own country;

---

[17] *Ibid.*, 1938, p. 45.

(2) The increasing tendency at present to militarize the CCC and NYA programs;

(3) The current proposals for universal military conscription.

Furthermore we strongly urge our government to take any possible measures consistent with and in the spirit of Christianity for the securing of peace between the warring nations and for the prevention of any further spreading of the war.

2. To reaffirm our positive conviction that all war is sin and that we cannot participate therein.

3. To urge our members to refrain from war hatreds so that we may have a redemptive attitude toward all nations, in the spirit of love and expressed in impartial humanitarian service to the needs of all lands.

4. To redouble our efforts, locally and otherwise, to teach our Christian peace principles and to find therein the Christian way in the emergencies of the current conflicts. May these principles be demonstrated daily in our personal and group relationships.

5. To commend our newly-formed Brethren Service Committee for their task in the fields of refugee aid, relief and rehabilitation. We ask the churches for the most liberal support possible in carrying on this work, both in terms of money and of personnel.

6. To make clear to the government under which we live our earnest desire to assume all responsibilities and opportunities of citizenship which do not conflict with our supreme allegiance which is to God. We cite the Resolutions of the Conference of 1938, and preceding pronouncements, on the relation of church and state.

7. To re-emphasize previous statements that Christianity must not be identified with nor limited to any one race, nation, ruler, system of government, or social class. We need to stress the unity of all mankind under God (Acts 17: 26).[18]

In addition, the Conference of 1940 sent a letter to President Roosevelt and Secretary Hull:

Ocean Grove, New Jersey, June 10, 1940.
Honorable Franklin D. Roosevelt, President of the United States,
Honorable Cordell Hull, Secretary of State,
Washington, D. C.

Honorable Sirs:

The 154th Annual General Conference of the Church of the Breth-

---

[18] *Ibid.*, 1940, pp. 50-51.

ren here assembled wish to express to you our deep appreciation for your most courteous reception given our representatives in several personal interviews, through which our convictions on peace and war have been made known to you.

We commend you and other responsible officials for all policies and measures which have been taken to keep our country out of the wars now raging. We feel that our involvement in these wars would be a calamity, serving no constructive purpose, and that all policies and measures of our government should be in harmony with the maintenance of our position of strict neutrality.

It is the sense of this meeting that the recent indirect sale of supplies from our army and navy to the Allies is not conducive to nor consistent with our neutral position. Therefore, we disapprove of this practice.

We note with great apprehension suggestions being made to introduce universal military training in our country and other suggestions relative to the militarization of our CCC and NYA services. As a church, we stand opposed to any such measures.

We fervently pray that you may continue your constructive statesmanship in efforts to make peace and prevent the further spread of the present wars. We heartily endorse any such measures, consistent with Christian principles, that may be taken to restore peace to this distressed world. To this end we are praying for you and all others responsible for government throughout the world.

> Rufus D. Bowman, Moderator
> J. E. Miller, Secretary
> C. Ernest Davis, Reader[19]

The Church Advises Against Noncombatant Service

The coming of conscription and the emergency situation confronting the church made it necessary to call a special meeting of Standing Committee, representing all the districts of the brotherhood, to face the many new problems. This meeting was held in Chicago, December 18 and 19, 1940. Among other things, the church made the following definite pronouncement regarding noncombatant service:

Reaffirmed that we continue to advise our young men that non-

---

[19] *Ibid.*, 1940, pp. 51-52.

combatant service within the army is inconsistent with the teachings of the Bible and the Church of the Brethren. Further, that it cannot be reconciled with our historic peace position.[20]

While the functioning position during World War I was in favor of noncombatant service, *the Church of the Brethren faced World War II advising against all service within the ranks of the army.*

The Relationship of Church Members to Labor Unions

The increasing number of Brethren working in the industrial field brought the labor problem to the attention of the church. The Annual Conference of 1941 applied the peace principles of the denomination to labor union practices. The church stated:

As a church, we do not represent any one social or economic group, but attempt to build an inclusive fellowship of all men. We appreciate the problems that grow out of the attempt to integrate the various groups in the social order. On the one hand, there are Christian tenets that should guide us in our relations to others, such as the principles of the scriptures relating to oaths (Matt. 5: 33-37); the principles involved in our relations to our fellowmen (Matt. 5: 38-48 and other scriptures); nonviolence in times of strife (Rom. 12: 18-21); and the fact that we are Christian brethren (Matt. 23: 8). These principles and the spirit of brotherhood should be observed by capital, labor, and the consumer and efforts at common understanding should be made by all involved.

Therefore, we recommend: That no oath of membership be taken, that an appeal be made to the unions that attendance at meetings be not made a test of membership, and that no violent part be taken in any difficulties, and that the ways of Christian brotherhood be followed.[21]

An Appeal for Peace

The Conference of 1941 reaffirmed that "war is sin, unconditionally and always" and "an utter repudiation of all that Jesus taught and exemplified in his life."[22]   It

[20] *Ibid.*, 1941, p. 54.
[21] *Ibid.*, 1941, p. 49.
[22] *Ibid.*, 1941, p. 55.

lamented the drift of our government toward war and sent a special message to the President and the Secretary of State appealing for peace.[23]

The Conference resolutions reveal a development in the Brethren point of view regarding war. The church declared that all war is sin, that the whole war system is futile, and even advised against noncombatant service. The peace principle was applied to industrial and labor situations. The church protested against war taxes, war toys, the increasing of armaments, conscription and the coming of war.

Organization and Program of Activities

The Central Service Committee was created during World War I to meet an emergency situation. It functioned from 1918 to 1921 and dealt chiefly with the problems related to conscription. Following the war this committee made strong pleas in favor of the disarmament of all nations. The General Peace Committee was comparatively inactive during the life of the Central Service Committee. However, in 1921 and 1922, the Peace Committee became active again in advocating a peace educational program for the church. The Goshen Conference Statement was printed and circulated as the basis for the church's peace teaching program.

General Welfare Board Created

The Conference of 1924 combined the "Temperance and Purity," "Dress Reform," and "Peace" committees into a General Welfare Board.[24] In 1925 this Board appointed J. M. Henry to represent the Church of the Brethren on the National Council for the Prevention of War. He was soon chosen as a member of the executive committee of that organization. In 1926 peace oratorical contests were

---

[23] *Ibid.*, 1941, p. 57.
[24] *Ibid.*, 1924, p. 9.

started among young people. J. M. Henry worked with the
Friends' Peace Committee in placing Japanese students in
American colleges, and peace literature was widely dis-
seminated. The following year local churches were urged
to organize study classes on peace, and peace oratorical contests were carried on in districts and colleges. In 1928 J. M.
Henry visited the Brethren colleges in the interest of peace
education and the organization of an intercollegiate peace
oratorical contest. He also prepared twelve peace studies
to be used as the basis for local church study groups.

Board of Religious Education Organized

The Annual Conference of 1928 took action merging the
General Sunday School Board, the General Welfare Board,
and the Music Committee into the Board of Religious Education.[25] Peace became one of its activities. During the
summer of 1929 two peace caravan teams of young people
were put into the field and study courses on peace were
carried on in summer camps. There was a feeling, however, on the part of some members of the Board of Religious
Education and others, that because of the many activities
of this Board, peace work was not being cared for adequately. The Board petitioned Annual Conference for the
privilege of placing in the field a full-time peace worker.[26]
The request was granted but the same Conference made it
practically inoperative because no increased budget was
granted. No special peace worker was appointed until
1937. During 1930 special appeals for disarmament were
made, youth peace contests were encouraged for local
churches and districts and during the summer two caravan
teams of young people were sent to churches and other organizations to speak for goodwill.

[25] *Ibid.*, 1928, p. 3.
[26] *Ibid.*, 1929, p. 33.

Peace Commission Appointed

In order to help in building and promoting the educational program of the church, the Board of Religious Education appointed a Peace Commission. The work of this Commission was advisory and it functioned largely through recommendations to . the Board. The Peace Commission served until 1934 when the Manchester College faculty was asked to serve as the Commission. The faculty committee carried on many valuable activities. Several conferences of the historic peace churches were called. In 1932 the Foreign Relations Committee of the Senate was petitioned to enter the World Court. The repeal of the Japanese Exclusion Act was requested in 1934. Efforts were made to train some outstanding young people to be effective peace leaders in the church by sending them to institutes of international relations. In 1935 the following recommendation was brought to the Council of Boards looking toward a comprehensive peace program:

In order to meet effectively the present world crisis, we approve

a. An intensive education program in the Church of the Brethren to mobilize its members for peace in the calendar year 1936.

b. A united plan with Friends, Mennonites, and peace loving groups in other church bodies toward developing the peace way of life.

c. A co-operative plan with the American Friends Service Committee and the Committee on International Goodwill of the Federal Council of Churches for peace education outside our own church.

d. At least one new missionary who can help to integrate peace and missions in America and on the field.

e. A co-operative plan with the National Council for the Prevention of War for effective political action.

f. A campaign to insure adequate finances for this work.[27]

This program was endorsed and became the basis for a comprehensive peace action program which was sent to all

[27] *Minutes of the Board of Christian Education,* June, 1935. The Board of Religious Education was changed to Board of Christian Education in 1932.

the churches of the denomination, and local and district leaders were asked to carry out its suggestions.[28]

The Board of Christian Education appointed Rufus D. Bowman to represent the denomination at the conference on "Christ and the Peace of the World" which was held at Cambridge University, England, July 28 to August 4, 1936. During that same year the Brethren took part in the Emergency Peace Campaign, whose purpose was to counteract the drift òf the country toward war. This organization was created at the initiative of the Peace Section of the American Friends Service Committee. Dan West represented the Church of the Brethren on the staff of this campaign and gave his full time to its program. Rufus D. Bowman served on the executive committee as the general plans were formulated.

Spanish Relief Work

In 1937 the Church of the Brethren decided to work with the Friends and Mennonites in helping to feed and clothe the children of Spain. Dan West was sent to Spain September 4, 1937, to spend five months in getting the work started. David Blickenstaff was sent to Spain in December of the same year and continued until July, 1939. Leaders of the American Friends Service Committee state that he did an outstanding piece of work in winning the goodwill of Franco's officials and in administering the program. Paul Bowman, Jr., was sent to work with David Blickenstaff and to carry on after his return. Paul Bowman carried on the work with the same effectiveness until conditions in Spain made relief work no longer possible. He returned to this country in June, 1940. Martha Rupel was another Church of the Brethren relief worker in Spain who served on the Loyalist side.

---

[28] Pamphlet entitled *Peace Action Program for the Church of the Brethren, 1936-37.*

The response of the church to this relief project was gratifying. The report of the Board of Christian Education, June, 1939, states that 5,391 pounds of clothing, shoes and soap, valued at $3,686.50, and $19,719.75 in money were given for Spanish Relief up to February 28, 1939, and during that winter the church contributed $1,000.00 per month to the work on the field.[29]

The personnel from the various churches working in Spain numbered about one dozen and the $150,000.00 from America was multiplied by twenty governments into a one and a half million dollar program.

China Relief Work

The Annual Conference of June, 1938, issued a call for $3,000.00 for China and $1,000.00 for Spain per month to be used to relieve the suffering people. By another year $26,336.69 had been given by the churches for China Relief. Leland Brubaker was sent to China for a few months to help organize the relief program. Howard Sollenberger went over to work with the Church of the Brethren missionaries in administering relief funds. He did relief work in both occupied and free China. Forest Eisenbise carried on a relief program with the Friends' Center in Shanghai. The Conference of 1940 showed that the congregations had given $13,513.52 more for relief purposes. The Church of the Brethren felt that since it could not fight, it had an added responsibility for helping to care for suffering people.

The Brethren Service Committee Formed

In November, 1939, the Board of Christian Education and the General Mission Board decided to handle the program of relief though the united action of the two boards. This was necessary because the General Mission Board had charge of China Relief while Spanish Relief was carried on through the Board of Christian Education. The Annual Conference of 1940 took one step further and authorized these two Boards to administer jointly the peace and relief work of the church through an executive committee to be known as the Brethren Service Committee.[30] This organization worked only fairly well. These boards had heavy responsibilities and the work of the Brethren Service Committee was multiplying. Consequently the Conference of 1941 saw the necessity for a Brethren Service Committee appointed and functioning like any other general board or committee. Consequently, a new Brethren Service Committee was appointed.

This committee led out in developing the program of Civilian Public Service, and in organizing and financing C.P.S. camps. In addition, relief work was continued in China, David Blickenstaff was sent abroad to work with the American Friends' Service Committee in giving relief to the refugees in unoccupied France, and John Barwick was sent to England to work with German war prisoners. The Brethren Service Committee has been notified that Barwick is one of the most valuable men in war prison work in England. The placing of refugees was one of the most outstanding elements of the program carried on cooperatively with the Friends. Refugees were cared for in hostels and many were located in colleges and business enterprises.

With the organization of the Brethren Service Committee, the Board of Christian Education remained in charge of peace education within the denomination. The Brethren Service Committee became the service arm of the church in relation to the war emergency, relief and reconstruction work, and international goodwill.

[30] *Ibid.*, 1940, p. 43.

Independent Peace Organizations

In 1932 under the leadership of Dan West, a movement known as the "One Hundred Dunkers for Peace" was organized. The purpose was to get at least one hundred young people who had the potentiality to become key peace workers in the Church of the Brethren and lead them through a series of discussions to the place where they would become wholeheartedly active for peace. It was the conviction of Dan West that a Dunker should give as much for peace as a soldier gives for war, and that points of view are conditioned through a process of sharing. He was in favor of the peace program of the church as it was stated on paper but felt that the great lack was in counseling with individuals. His movement was short-lived but the idea which he had is worthy of attention.

In the same year a movement known as the "Twenty Thousand Dunkers for Peace" was organized. This name was kept until the Annual Conference of 1935, when it was changed to "Brethren Peace Action" and the slogan became "Two Hundred Thousand Dunkers for Peace." This organization was sponsored by young people who wanted to see more real peace activity on the part of the church. They asked the members of the church to sign the following pledge:

> I ...., as a Christian citizen, hereby declare my love for my country, my purpose at all times to be a good citizen, and my willingness to lay down my life in the service of humanity. I further declare that, because of conscientious convictions, I cannot engage in war, and do protest the appropriation of my taxes for military purposes.[31]

Several thousand members signed the statement. This movement, too, was short-lived but it is another evidence that there were interested persons in the church who were not satisfied with the peace program.

---

[31] *Brethren Peace Action* (a pamphlet), p. 1.

Weaknesses of the Brethren Peace Program Between World Wars I and II

There were many peace activities, and comprehensive peace programs were recommended to local churches and districts. Strong pronouncements were made practically every year. It seems on the surface that the peace teaching of the church must have been widespread and thorough. But there were several outstanding weaknesses. First, too many changes were made in the general organizations responsible for peace education. Over a period of twenty years there were ten changes in boards and committees dealing with peace education, government problems and international relationships. No one organization had time enough to do its work well. Consequently the programs developed were too largely paper programs without functioning effectively in local churches.

Second, there was no general field supervision to see that the local churches carried out the recommendations. The Church of the Brethren has no administrative offices to see that the decisions of the Annual Conference are carried out. The Board of Christian Education did not employ a peace worker until 1937. Even then one worker could not effectively cover a church territory spread over most of the United States. Regional workers generally were not appointed until after the Annual Conference of June, 1942. Some of the districts had field workers and during recent years these have been called together annually for coaching regarding the total church program. But this was not the procedure during most of the years between the world wars. There was not enough effective supervision of local churches and districts.

Third, peace literature was widely distributed, sermons and lectures on goodwill were delivered throughout the church, but the records of the Board of Christian Education do not indicate that many discussion groups on peace were carried on in local churches. Young people became acquainted with the church's position, but as a whole they were not placed in an educational setting where points of view are challenged and changed through stimulating discussions. The Brethren peace program was one more largely of literature, with some strategic centers in colleges, summer camps and other interested groups, where vital discussions took place. The great masses of young people were not effectively reached.

ADVISORY COMMITTEE FOR CONSCIENTIOUS OBJECTORS

There came to the Conference of 1936 a request from the Board of Christian Education and also a query from the Eastern District of Maryland calling for the appointment of a committee to give advice to conscientious objectors in the event of war. The Conference appointed a committee with the following duties:

1. To study the question of compulsory military training as it relates to State colleges and to release information to our young people clarifying this issue.

2. To offer young people advice regarding attendance at schools where military training is compulsory.

3. To study existing laws and to secure legal opinion regarding the status of conscientious objectors in the event of war.

4. To study carefully with competent legal counsel in co-operation with the Friends, Mennonites and other peace loving bodies, the position that our young people should take in the event of war.

5. To discuss this question with our young people in colleges, camps, conferences, and help prepare them to meet war crises.

6. To offer advice to young people if or when a war comes.

Committee: Rufus D. Bowman, Paul H. Bowman, F. S. Carper; ex officio members; C. Ray Keim, Peace Committee; M. R. Zigler, Board of Christian Education; Dan West, Young People's Work; Ross D. Murphy, Pastoral Association.

The above committee shall appoint advisory members in different sections of our brotherhood to carry out the above duties.[32]

The committee secured legal advice concerning the status of conscientious objectors under existing laws, gave help to young Brethren attending state schools where military training was required, and studied the problem regarding the types of service which would be consistent with the historic position of the church in the event of war. A preliminary report was brought to the Conference of 1936, but the report of 1938 shows further thinking and marks a distinct development in the Brethren peace philosophy. It is quoted thus:

The Committee on Counsel for Conscientious Objectors desires to make the following recommendations to the Conference of 1938 on the positions that our people should take in the event of war:

I. Types of service considered consistent with the historic position of the church.

1. Constructive service under church or civilian direction, such as housing, road making, farming, forestry, hospitalization, and recreational work.

2. Relief work under the church or civilian direction in and outside of the war zone, or in neutral zones, either as a denomination or in co-operation with the Friends and the Mennonites.

II. Types of service considered not consistent with the historic position of the church:

1. Chaplaincy in the army or navy.

2. Red Cross service if this organization is definitely committed to render active service under military command in the event of war.

3. Hospital service if under military command.

4. Y.M.C.A. work if under military command.

5. Services of any kind within the ranks of the army, all of which are without question under direct military command.

III. Types of peace testimony to register our convictions and to avoid our participation in war-related activities:

1. The refraining from the purchase of such as Liberty Bonds to finance war.

---

[32] *Ibid.,* 1935, pp. 34-35.

2. The renunciation of, or the sacrificial use of, profits derived from industry, farming, or invested securities as a result of war; sacrificing always during war periods to build a fund for the furtherance of goodwill and for the support of families who suffer because of their conscientious objections to war.

3. The protesting against federal taxes if used for military purposes.

IV. Plan of action to meet war crises:

1. That as a denomination we present our historic position on war and peace in the form of memorials to the President of the United States and to the governors of states in which we have members located. We urge that influential members of our churches present, informally and unofficially, our position to local governmental officials who might by their position become part of the mobilization system.

2. That in local congregations the pastor or the minister in charge of the congregation shall prepare those members subject to the military call to meet the crisis.

3. That in the event of a war crisis the minister in charge of the congregation shall consult with the Conference Committee or a regional or district representative of the committee on any situation not covered by previous church decisions or situations in which, in the judgment of the minister, their counsel and advice would be helpful. The minister shall counsel with those subject to military conscription and advise with them regarding the position of the church in terms of any particular problem.

4. That the local congregations of the brotherhood be urged to declare their purpose to give relief to bona fide cases of suffering on account of their conscientious objection to war in either peace time or war time and that they have the privilege of calling upon the district and the brotherhood for assistance when the burden becomes too heavy for the local churches to bear. In the event that an appeal for assistance is made to a district or to the brotherhood this shall only be done after approval by the Board of Christian Education of the district or brotherhood respectively, and all funds received shall be subject to the supervision of the appropriate board.

5. That in states where teachers' oath laws have been enacted, or proposed, our districts or our local churches, or both, express our convictions in opposition to such laws. Also, that in cases where

members object because of conscience to such laws and suffer loss thereby, the recommendation just preceding be carried out.

6. That in case of federal action in the direction of conscription in war time, or of state legislation favoring compulsory military training in state colleges or high schools, our districts or local congregations, or both, express our convictions against such laws to those responsible for the legislation in question. Likewise, that protest be made against existing regulations providing for compulsory military training in state high schools or colleges.

Rufus D. Bowman, Chairman
C. Ray Keim, Secretary[33]

These recommendations were adopted and still represent the official position of the church. Any service under military command was not considered consistent with the historic position of the church. Members were to refrain from purchasing war bonds and if they received extra profits because of the war situation, these profits were to be used for a program of goodwill and for the relief of suffering families. Members were also to protest the payment of taxes for military purposes. This is the farthest the church had gone in considering the economic implications of its peace position and in advising against all service under military control.

This 1938 Conference action was sent with a comprehensive letter to all the churches advising study groups with young people, suggesting materials for reading, outlining the procedure to take in a war crisis and urging ministers to begin coaching their young people regarding their convictions on war. Some pastors responded but many of them thought that there was plenty of time for this sort of thing. Regional workers were selected who could go into action immediately in the case of war to see that local churches received the advice of the brotherhood. But there were few individual discussions with local pastors

---

[33] *Ibid.*, 1938. pp. 39-40.

to help them to see the need of conferences with young people before the coming of war so that their convictions would be mature. Once more, the peace position of the church was taken for granted. If Annual Conference decisions, the writing of letters and the circulation of pamphlets are sufficient education to produce a peace-minded church, then the Church of the Brethren during World War II should make a great peace testimony. If the preaching of peace sermons, and the giving of lectures on goodwill, and the holding of peace oratorical contests are sufficient to help church people mature their thinking, then most of the Brethren should not be vitally affected by war propaganda. However, sermons and lectures were not generally followed by creative group discussions in the Church of the Brethren. Preaching was a one-way process without the opportunity for members of the congregation to ask questions. Adult education was very largely a pouring-in process.

The Advisory Committee for Conscientious Objectors in summarizing its work to the Conference of 1940, and realizing that conscription was coming, asked that a committee of three be appointed to carry on the program. The committee needed to have time to assume heavy duties and to be located strategically so as to work with the Friends and Mennonites and to be able to contact government officials. Paul H. Bowman of Bridgewater, Virginia, Ross D. Murphy of Philadelphia, Pennsylvania, and M. R. Zigler of Elgin, Illinois, were appointed. The general boards of the church were asked to release M. R. Zigler from other duties so that he would have time for this work. This committee served faithfully for a year and worked with government officials in developing Civilian Public Service for conscientious objectors. Its work was merged with that of the Brethren Service Committee by the action of the Annual Conference of 1941, and since that time the

Brethren Service Committee has been in charge of the entire Brethren program in behalf of objectors to war.

The committee's 1940 report is significant in that it recommended the attitude the church should take toward absolutists and those who accept combatant and noncombatant services. It stated:

What ought to be the attitude of our church toward (1) those of her members who may, in case of war, accept non-combatant, or, even combatant service, and (2) those who are absolute objectors, refusing to register for conscription and refusing all alternatives to military service? In dealing with all of these cases, the church ought not deny spiritual fellowship and ministry, her aim always being redemptive. Recognizing the first group above as persons who have not followed the general position of the church, she ought to encourage them to lead exemplary lives. She ought to do all possible to get consideration for the absolutists at the hands of the government.[34]

THE KIRBY PAGE QUESTIONNAIRE TO MINISTERS

In "The World Tomorrow" of May 10, 1934, Kirby Page gave the summary of replies from 20,870 clergymen to his questionnaire concerning war and peace and economic justice. Out of two thousand, six hundred and sixty Church of the Brethren ministers receiving the questionnaire, five hundred and twenty-seven responded. This latter group represented approximately one sixth of the Brethren ministers. It would be easy to exaggerate the findings of the questionnaire. It is possible that those ministers replied who were most interested in the question of peace and international relationships. Then, too, opinions on complex problems cannot be given by yes and no answers. However, the opinions of five hundred and twenty-seven clergymen to the following questions have some value in revealing the Brethren point of view in the period between the wars:

---

[34] *Ibid.*, 1940, pp. 45-46.

	Yes	No	In Doubt	No An- swer	Per cent Yes	Per cent No
1. Do you favor the immediate entrance of the United States into the League of Nations?	233	106	165	23	44	20
2. Do you favor military training in our public high schools and civilian colleges or universities?	3	520	1	3	1	99
3. Do you favor substantial reductions in armaments even if the United States is compelled to take the initiative and make a proportionately greater reduction than other nations are yet willing to do?	478	26	15	8	91	5
4. Do you believe that the policy of armed intervention in other lands by our Government to protect the lives and property of American citizens should be abandoned and protective efforts confined to pacific means?	453	27	35	12	86	5
5. Do you believe that the churches of America should now go on record as refusing to sanction or support any future war?	508	11	5	3	96	2
6. Are you personally prepared to state that it is your present purpose not to sanction any future war or participate as an armed combatant?	501	11	13	2	95	2
7. Could you conscientiously serve as an official army chaplain on active duty in war time?	45	399	73	10	9	76
8. Do you regard the distinction between "defensive" and "aggressive" war as sufficiently valid to justify your sanctioning						

	Yes	No	In Doubt	No Answer	Per cent Yes	Per cent No
or participating in a future war of defense?	31	421	51	24	6	80
9. Do you favor the drastic limitation, through the inheritance tax, of the amount of wealth that may be inherited by an individual?	352	50	68	57	67	9
10. Do you favor the drastic limitation, through the income tax and the removal of tax exempt sources, of the annual income that may be legally retained by an individual?	346	50	70	61	66	9
11. Do you favor a system of compulsory unemployment insurance under government administration?	194	118	155	60	37	22
12. Do you favor national unions of workers (instead of local company-unions) in an endeavor to bring about a more equal distribution of the proceeds of industry?	190	85	185	67	36	16
13. Do you favor a system of private ownership of banks, under government regulation (instead of a system of socialized banking as a public service)?	176	119	152	80	33	23

14. Which economic system appears to you to be less antagonistic to and more consistent with the ideals and methods of Jesus and the noblest of the Hebrew prophets?

Capitalism	28
Co-operative Commonwealth	455
No Answer	44
Percentage selecting Capitalism	5
Percentage selecting Co-operative Commonwealth	86

15. If you favor a co-operative commonwealth, which political system seems to you to offer the most effective method of achieving this end?

Drastically Reformed Capitalism	257
Fascism	1
Communism	1
Socialism	136
Some other Political System	46
No Answer	86
Percentage selecting:	
Drastically Reformed Capitalism	49
Communism	
Fascism	
Socialism	26
Some other Political System	9[35]

The results show that 44 per cent of the Brethren ministers replying favored the entrance of the United States into the League of Nations, while 20 per cent did not; 99 per cent opposed military training in public schools and colleges; 91 per cent favored substantial reductions in armaments; 86 per cent thought the United States should abandon armed protection of property and lives in other lands; 96 per cent believed that the churches should go on record as refusing to sanction or support any future war; 95 per cent thought they were personally prepared to state that they would not sanction any future war or participate as an armed combatant; 76 per cent stated that they could not conscientiously serve as an army chaplain; 80 per cent did not regard a defensive war as justifying their sanction or participation; 67 per cent favored the drastic limitation through an inheritance tax of the wealth an individual could inherit; 66 per cent favored the limitation of the annual income which an individual could legally receive; 37 per cent expressed approval of compulsory employment in-

---

[35] Kirby Page, "20,870 Clergymen on War and Economic Justice," *The World Tomorrow*, May 10, 1934, pp. 228-231.

surance under the government; 36 per cent were in favor
of national unions of workers instead of local company
unions; 33 per cent voted for private ownership of banks
instead of socialized banking as a public service, while 23
per cent did not, and the rest were in doubt; 86 per cent
favored the co-operative commonwealth instead of capitalism as the best economic system; and in order to achieve
the co-operative commonwealth, 49 per cent voted for a
drastically reformed capitalism, 26 per cent for socialism,
and 9 per cent for some other political system.

The answer to the specific questions regarding war and
peace were generally consistent with the church's historic peace position, *but their answers showed that many
of them were not applying their peace principles to social
and economic problems.*

Co-operative Work With the Friends and Mennonites

During the period under review, the Friends, Mennonites and Brethren had a number of conferences together.
The experiences of World War I taught these churches the
necessity of close co-operation. In August of 1923 a conference of these churches was held at Bluffton College,
Bluffton, Ohio.[36] Another meeting of representatives from
these churches was held December 28-31, 1923, at Juniata
College, Huntingdon, Pennsylvania.[37] The purpose of this
meeting was to study the New Testament teachings concerning war and peace. Some years later joint conferences were held at Mount Morris, Illinois, and at Manchester College, Indiana, and several smaller group meetings
took place in Chicago. These gatherings promoted fellowship and gave opportunity for valuable discussions.

The most important meeting, however, in its far-reaching

---

[36] *Minutes of the Annual Conference*, 1923, p. 40.
[37] *Ibid.*, 1924, p. 43.

results was the one held at Newton, Kansas, October 31 to November 2, 1935. The three churches were well represented with delegates. After several days of fellowship and intensive discussion of common problems, the conference drew up the following statement of position and plan of procedure:

I. Statement of Position.

We, Friends, Brethren, and Mennonites, assembled in the Conference of the Historic Peace Churches, at Newton, Kansas, October 31—November 2, 1935, remembering in gratitude to God the historic war testimony of our churches, desire, in absolute renunciation of war for the wholehearted practice of peace and love, to state the basis of our Committee's position.

1. Our peace principles are rooted in Christ and his Word.

2. Through Jesus Christ, who lived among men as the incarnation of the God of love, we become partakers of the spirit and character of our Lord, and thereby are constrained to love all men, even our enemies.

3. Christ has led us to see the value of human life and personality, and possibilities in all men, who by a spiritual birth from above may become sons of God.

4. The spirit of sacrificial service, love, and goodwill, promotes the highest wellbeing and development of men and society, whereas the spirit of hatred, ill will, and fear, destroys, as has been demonstrated repeatedly in human experiences.

5. Since good alone can overcome evil, the use of violence must be abandoned.

6. War is sin. It is the complete denial of the Spirit, Christian love and all that Christ stands for. It is wrong in spirit and method, and destructive in results. Therefore, we cannot support or engage in any war, or conflict between nations, classes, or groups.

7. Our supreme allegiance is to God. We cannot violate it by a conflictory lesser loyalty, but we are determined to follow Christ in all things. In this determination we believe we are serving the interests of our country, and are truly loyal to our nation.

8. Under God we commit ourselves to set forth in this true way of life this statement of position and assume the obligations and sacrifices attending its practice.

II. Our Concept of Patriotism.

The members of the Historic Peace Churches love this country and sincerely work for its highest welfare. True love for our country does not mean a hatred of others. It is our conviction that only the application of the principles of peace, love, justice, liberty, the international goodwill, will make for the highest welfare of our country; and that the highest welfare of our country must harmonize with the highest welfare of humanity everywhere. Our faith is security through love, protection through goodwill; and for such we are willing to make the necessary sacrifice. We are opposed to war as a method of settling disputes because it is unchristian, destructive of our highest values and sows the seeds of future wars. We feel that we are true patriots because we build upon the eternal principles of right which are the only foundation for stable Government in our world community.

III. Joint Committee of the Historic Peace Churches.

We recommend that the American Friends Service Committee, the Mennonite Central Committee, and the Peace Commission of the Church of the Brethren, each appoint a representative on the Joint Committee of the Historic Peace Churches. We recommend that this Committee be empowered to add to its members and to appoint such sub-committees as may seem necessary

We recommend that this Committee meet as early as possible and be charged with formulating its own plan of procedure and with the duty of conserving and perpetuating our co-operative program.

We recommend that the representative appointed by the American Friends Service Committee be requested to call the first meeting, at which time the Committee will organize itself.

IV. Exchanging Our Literature.

We recommend that the Joint Committee create a Joint Sub-Committee on literature for the purpose of exchanging and disseminating literature of mutual interest and value.

V. A Program of United Action.

We recommend:

1. Co-operative peace conferences.
2. Exchange of speakers in our educational program.

3. Peace work for our own young people, especially in our colleges.

4. That we encourage the Historic Peace Churches to be diligent in the presentation of their peace message to others than their own members.

VI. A Plan of Unified Action in Case the United States Is Involved in War.

We recommend the following plan of unified action to be entered upon at such time as the United States government may officially decide to enter upon organized warfare, or at such a time as the churches are convinced that the United States is certain to become involved in war.

1. That each of the Historic Peace Churches shall reinstruct its members in the position of the Historic Peace Churches relative to war.

2. That each of the Historic Peace Churches shall urge its members to observe the peace position of these churches, which means no co-operation with war, or the acceptance of any service under military control.

3. That the Historic Peace Churches continue their peace testimony as long as possible.

4. That advice and counsel be given all who need help relative to their position regarding participation in war.

5. That members of these Churches be encouraged to refuse co-operation in financing of war.

6. That these Churches provide for conscientious objectors who become involved in the draft as follows:

(a) Furloughs from army and navy for alternative service of non-military nature and not under military control.

(b) Spiritual care for those who are confined in camp under government jurisdiction.

(c) Spiritual care and counsel for those who refuse to register.

(d) Financial support for dependents of conscientious objectors deprived of their income because of their position toward war. This is not limited to men involved in the draft.

7. That spiritual advice and counsel be provided for members of the Historic Peace Churches who accept service under the control of the army.[38]

---

[38] *Secretary's Report of the Conference of Historic Peace Churches*, Oct. 31— Nov. 2, 1935, Newton, Kansas. (Mimeographed document.)

The outline for a program of united action was adopted. A joint committee, later called the Continuation Committee, was appointed, composed of one representative from each of the churches. Robert W. Balderston represented the Friends, Orie O. Miller, the Mennonites, and C. Ray Keim, the Church of the Brethren. The Continuation Committee became very active. The secretary of the committee, C. Ray Keim, summarized its work as follows:

The following ways of co-operating were set forth in the minutes of the first meeting:

1. Maps to be prepared, showing the locations of our respective churches in the United States and elsewhere.

2. Conferences. Later a conference on Peace Literature and one on Peace and Missions were held. About a half dozen conferences were held, most of them taking up problems of interest to all.

3. Exchange of fraternal delegates between the three churches in their conferences. This was actually done in several cases.

4. Frequent meetings of the Continuation Committee, usually about four per year. In case of a conference the committee often met in connection with it.

5. Committees on peace literature, pooling our resources in this field. The Pacifist Handbook was an outgrowth of this movement.

6. Common delegations to outside groups, as to the Methodist Conference at Dayton, Ohio, and the Congregational Conference in the East, at Northampton, Massachusetts, in 1936.

7. Sending of joint delegations to foreign countries, as South America, by the groups, to give testimony there.

8. Relief work—in Spain, for example.

9. Refugee work—in Europe, then in the United States.

Other interests which developed later included:

1. Summer work camps.

2. Student-faculty conferences of the three churches. Colleges in Ohio and Indiana (two colleges of each church) were represented.

3. Delegation to interview President Roosevelt and other officials. Roosevelt was interviewed twice before the draft act of 1940. Some state and local officials were interviewed by joint delegations.

4. Consideration of such cases as that of Dr. Workentin of Bethel College, who was denied citizenship because of his pacifism.

5. With Methodists and others, we gave much attention to compulsory military training in universities, especially at Ohio State University, where two Methodists were expelled for refusing it.[39]

Not only did representatives of the historic peace churches make united decisions regarding what the churches should do in case of war; they decided that the government should be made aware òf their peace convictions and testimony. Consequently, they asked for a conference with President Roosevelt and were granted an interview February 12, 1937. Rufus M. Jones, Alvin T. Coate and Patrick M. Malin represented the Friends; A. J. Neuenschwander and C. L. Graber, the Mennonites; Paul H. Bowman and Rufus D. Bowman, the Church of the Brethren. The representatives of each church presented a separate paper which was read to the President. After the writer read the Brethren statement, Mr. Roosevelt asked where the Church of the Brethren originated. He was told that the church started in Germany and that the members came to America because of religious persecution. Then he wanted to know whether the position of the Church of the Brethren on war had been the same as that of the Quakers through the years. He was assured that the three churches represented there had the same central convictions on war. This may have been Mr. Roosevelt's first introduction to the Church of the Brethren as an historic denomination opposed to war. The Brethren statement is as follows:

Feb. 12, 1937.

The Honorable Franklin D. Roosevelt
The White House
Washington, D. C.

Dear Mr. President:

The Church of the Brethren numbers approximately one hundred sixty thousand members in the United States. We are chiefly a

---

[39] Personal letter from C. Ray Keim. North Manchester, Ind., Feb. 15, 1943.

rural people, emphasizing the sanctity of the home, honest toil, plain spiritual living, and our duty toward helping humanity.

We love our country and endeavor to be worthy citizens by living honorable lives and working for that which makes for the highest welfare of our country. It is our conviction that true love for our country does not mean a hatred of others, and that only the application of the principles of peace, love, and international goodwill will make for the highest welfare of our country. Our faith is in security through love.

As a people we have consistently opposed war throughout our entire history of over two hundred and twenty-five years. Our opposition to war is based upon the plain teachings of the Gospel of Christ. It is our conviction that all war is incompatible with the spirit, example, and teachings of Jesus; and that it is wrong for Christians to support or engage in it. We give our supreme allegiance to God, and believe that this allegiance commits us to the highest standard of Christian citizenship by which we can serve our country and our God.

We are actively interested in the prevention of war, and are doing our utmost through peace education and service to foster goodwill between individual citizens, groups of citizens, and nations. We strongly favor all efforts of our government to keep the United States out of war, to pass a strong neutrality law, and to establish peace in the world.

We earnestly solicit your co-operation, Mr. President, now, and if, or when a war comes in discussing and dealing with the types of service in which those of us with deep religious convictions on peace may serve in the spirit of Christ with constructive benefit to humanity and without compromise of conscience.

> Signed: Rufus D. Bowman
> Chairman, Advisory Committee on Peace
>
> Paul H. Bowman
> Moderator 1937 Annual Conference[40]

In response to the above statement, the following reply was received from the Department of State:

---

[40] Taken from a carbon copy of the original.

Department of State

Washington

In reply refer to
WE 7000.0011 Peace/204

February 24, 1937

Reverend Rufus D. Bowman
Washington City Church of the Brethren
Fourth and North Carolina Avenue, Southeast
Washington, D. C.

Sir:

The receipt is acknowledged, by reference from the White House, of your letter to the President, dated February 12, 1937, expressing, on behalf of the Church of the Brethren, your deep devotion to the cause of peace and conscientious objection to war or service in war.

Very truly yours,

For the Secretary of State:

James Clement Dunn,
Chief, Division of Western European Affairs.[41]

There were other important developments in the united program of these three churches. A Missions-Peace Conference was held at John Woolman Hall, Chicago, March 11 and 12, 1938. The problems of registration in the event of conscription and alternative service to war were considered together a number of times. The gradual drift of the country toward war led the Mennonites, Brethren and Friends to feel that they should go back again to the President with more specific proposals. They were motivated by the idea that the churches should do everything possible to solve their own problems, that they should think ahead of the government and outline what they could and could not do if war came, and that they should suggest to the government an acceptable procedure in dealing with conscientious objectors.

A second conference was sought with President Roose-

---

[41] Copied from the original in the possession of the writer.

velt, which was granted for January 10, 1940. This time the representatives of the churches presented two joint statements. The first statement was of a general nature, calling attention to the conference of February 12, 1937, the peace convictions of the historic peace churches, and the concern of the churches for peace. The second statement was a confidential memorandum suggesting a procedure to be used in dealing with conscientious objectors. The two statements are as follows:

January 10, 1940

The Honorable Franklin D. Roosevelt
The President of the United States
The White House
Washington, D. C.

Dear Mr. President:

On February 12, 1937, you graciously received representatives of the Society of Friends, the Mennonite Church, and the Church of the Brethren, who presented to you statements expressing the historic and unbroken convictions of these groups against war, and their devotion to peace and goodwill. These attitudes grew out of deep religious convictions, based on the spirit and teachings of Jesus, and are a part of a way of life which we believe cherishes the highest values for all men. Today we again submit to you our concern in view of present world conditions.

We desire, first of all, to express our deep appreciation for your repeated effort to prevent the European war, our warm support of your confident insistence that the United States shall not be drawn into this conflict, and our hope that opportunity will arise for our nation to co-operate with other neutral nations in offering mediation or other peace-promoting techniques toward the earliest possible establishment of peace. We have also warmly appreciated your personal interest in the large number of political and racial refugees whose relief and resettlement are so urgent a present obligation for all men of goodwill. Your recent challenging appeal for humanitarian relief to European war sufferers has likewise won the hearty response of our groups. Our own organizations are definitely planning to contribute to such projects in the future, as in the past, not only with the desire to minister to human need, but also to keep vivid the vision of a better way of life than that of intolerance, persecution and war.

Opportunities and responsibilities of relief and rehabilitation for the war sufferers in Spain and elsewhere have come to us recently through the American Friends Service Committee and the service agencies of the Mennonite Church and the Church of the Brethren. Our Spanish relief program, after more than two years, is probably drawing to a close, but relief responsibilities in China continue. Refugee colonies in Paraguay and Brazil still require our care and support. Just now we are being asked by interested American groups to assume important new responsibilities for the many tragic Polish war sufferers, and our representatives are now in Europe to investigate, and if possible, to inaugurate this project.

If, in spite of all efforts to maintain neutrality, the tragic day should come when our beloved nation is drawn into war, we should expect to continue our work for suffering humanity, and to increase its scope because of the greater need at home and abroad. Such service would permit those whose conscientious convictions forbid participation in war in any form to render constructive service to their country and to the world. We appear today chiefly to discuss with you plans to provide for this alternative service as it may relate to possible conscription, reserving the privilege to offer at a later date a supplementary memorandum dealing with other types of conscientious objectors.

As you know, in the last war the United States Government finally authorized such non-military humanitarian service to be substituted for military service, and furloughed conscientious objectors to this relief work or to farm labor. But this arrangement was provided only after months of confusion and distress, and only after repeated conferences between our representatives and officials of the War Department, because of the lack of any previously established policy. Since we understand that plans are now being formulated for mobilization of the nation's man power if war should come, and since the need for dealing with conscientious objectors would again emerge to confront Government agencies, we venture to suggest the advantage of advanced discussion of the problem with the appropriate officials. We should much appreciate the opportunity for such discussion and are prepared to make concrete proposals to such officials regarding procedures for handling conscientious objectors and types of service which might be provided. In this connection we also venture to suggest the desirability of again setting up a civilian agency for dealing with this problem. There is a precedent for this in the action of President Wilson in 1918.

We have come to you, Mr. President, with these requests, because our previous conversations with you have persuaded us that you both understand and appreciate the position of the Historic Peace Churches. Our desire is to co-operate in finding the best solution to the problem of the conscientious objector, and it is even more to render as loyal citizens the highest type of constructive service we can to our country and to the world.

Faithfully yours,

For the Society of Friends
Rufus Jones
Walter C. Woodward

For the Mennonite Church
P. C. Hiebert
Harold S. Bender
E. L. Harshbarger

For the Church of the Brethren
Rufus D. Bowman
Paul H. Bowman

A Memorandum to the Government regarding a plan of procedure for providing alternative service for conscientious objectors in case of military conscription.

The undersigned representatives of the three historic peace churches—the Society of Friends, the Mennonite Church, and the Church of the Brethren—addressed a communication to the President on January 10, 1940, suggesting that it might be helpful at this time to discuss certain forms of non-military service which might be substituted by conscientious objectors for military service if military conscription should again be instituted by law. It is often more satisfactory, however, to discuss a general proposition when it has been reduced to rather concrete proposals. Therefore, to facilitate such discussion, we should like to submit the following as a possible procedure for dealing with those whose consciences will not permit them to engage in military service, but who would welcome some form of constructive service in the interests of humanity.

We should like to suggest:

1. That a civilian board be appointed by the President to serve under him or under a cabinet officer, to judge the sincerity and weigh the claims of conscientious objectors, to assign to them a definite status, and to consider and authorize non-military service projects to which they might be assigned.

2. That draft boards be directed to route conscientious objectors directly to this civilian board, leaving them at all times under civilian direction and control. This might be facilitated by the issuance of certificates by our church organizations regarding the status of members who might be drafted.

3. That appropriate organizations of the historic peace churches be permitted to set up and administer, through their own personnel, service projects to which conscientious objectors might be assigned. The following forms of service might be considered as representative of the sort of projects we might undertake:

> Relief of war sufferers
> Relief of refugees of evacuated civilian populations
> Reconstruction of war-stricken areas
> Resettlement of refugees
> Reclamation or forestry services in the United States or elsewhere
> Relief and reconstruction work in local communities in the United States
> Medical and health services in connection with any of these projects
> Farm service

In submitting the above proposals we realize that our organizations would have to be prepared to undertake difficult tasks and assume heavy burdens, but the type of projects we are suggesting are closely related to tasks in which we have been long engaged in times of peace. We would be willing to undertake an extension of these tasks up to the limit of our abilities to carry out those proposals and to offer our co-operation in working out details with the proper government agencies if occasion should arise.

We should like to call attention, however, to the fact that the procedures we have outlined apply only to those whose convictions permit participation in some form of alternative service. There are some whose consciences are unable to conform to the demands of any type of military conscription, however modified. These we should like to commend to the consideration of the responsible government officials, trusting that the consciences of such persons may receive due recognition.

We have spoken here as representatives of the three historic peace churches with particular reference to our own constituencies, but we are concerned that any arrangements which might be worked out would also be extended to all conscientious objectors who act from similar convictions, whatever their affiliation.

Submitted on behalf of the Historic Peace Churches

> For the Society of Friends
> Rufus Jones
> Walter C. Woodward
>
> For the Mennonite Church
> E. L. Harshbarger
> Harold S. Bender
> P. C. Hiebert
>
> For the Church of the Brethren
> Rufus D. Bowman
> Paul H. Bowman[42]

Mr. Roosevelt received the delegation in a friendly spirit. General Watson, his assistant, admonished the group that not more than two or three minutes could be expected out of the President's crowded schedule. The President, however, did not appear hurried. He had the delegates to stand around his desk, giving an opportunity for directness and the free exchange of conversation. Instead of three minutes, the interview consumed about thirty minutes. After the statements were presented, Mr. Roosevelt commented: "I am glad you have done it. That's getting down to a practical basis. It shows us what work the conscientious objectors can do without fighting. Excellent! Excellent!"[43]

---

[42] Both statements were copied from the original letter and memorandum.
[43] From notes written by the writer immediately following the interview.

The President gave approval for this matter to be laid before Attorney General Frank W. Murphy. Consequently the same day the delegation interviewed Mr. Murphy. He is a man who weighs his words carefully and gives the impression of sincerity. He told the group how he, who had been a captain during the World War, had worked to secure fair treatment for conscientious objectors to war. He made these significant statements: "The country is not hurt by the people who exercise conscience. We need to think this through now so that good people aren't declared traitors. I will give it serious consideration and present it to the Cabinet."[44]

Attorney General Murphy had already been appointed to the United States Supreme Court and Robert H. Jackson had been chosen as his successor. Therefore, the delegates interviewed Mr. Jackson, who at that time was outspoken in his conviction that the United States should not enter into another European war.

In these interviews with government officials, those representing the historic peace churches asked for the same consideration for all conscientious objectors to war regardless of their denominational affiliation. This matter was discussed by the group before the meeting with the President. It was considered when the statements were prepared. The memorandum stated: "We should like to submit the following as a possible procedure for dealing with those whose consciences will not permit them to engage in military service, but who would welcome some form of constructive service in the interests of humanity." The denominations concerned were in favor of a program of constructive service. They did not desire a preferred status under the law, but rather consideration for all religious objectors. Again the memorandum stated: "We are con-

---

[44] *Ibid.*

cerned that any arrangements which might be worked out would also be extended to all conscientious objectors who act from similar convictions, whatever their affiliation." Even political objectors and those who would refuse all government service were not forgotten. The memorandum called attention to those whose consciences were opposed to any type of conscription and asked the government officials to give them due consideration.

There may be some grounds for the criticism that the historic peace churches went alone to the government officials and offered a procedure for dealing with conscientious objectors in a war situation which would involve conscientious objectors of other denominations; and that the case for political objectors and religious objectors to all forms of conscription was not adequately represented. The reasons for the action of the church may be understood when one considers these facts: First, these churches had suffered persecution together and periodically had worked jointly with government officials for over two centuries. Second, conscription laws until World War II had recognized only members of churches whose tenets of faith forbade participation in war, and these churches recognized by the laws were trying to liberalize future legislation. Third, the Mennonites, Friends, and Brethren through a process of years were beginning to work closely together. Co-operative planning with other churches was a next step. While they asked the government to respect the consciences of all sincere objectors, these churches felt themselves directly responsible for the program involving religious objectors to war. The members of the Church of the Brethren generally have not been absolutists in the way of refusing all government service. The church has held that members should serve their country in peaceful enterprises instead of armed conflict. The government was notified ahead of war that alternative service would be acceptable.

The Newton conference, the work of the Continuation Committee, the conferences with government officials, and the joint planning of these churches laid the foundation for the National Service Board for Religious Objectors.

THE OXFORD CONFERENCE ON CONSCIENTIOUS OBJECTORS

M. R. Zigler, who represented the Church of the Brethren at the Oxford Conference, 1937, informed the Brethren that it was only after a great deal of discussion that the delegates in the section on "The Church and State" were willing to include conscientious objection to all war as one of the positions which true Christians could hold. The fact, however, that this position was recognized in a world conference of Christians is significant. The statement regarding conscientious objection to war is as follows:

(1) Some believe that war, especially in its modern form, is always sin, being a denial of the nature of God as love, of the redemptive way of the cross, and of the community of the Holy Spirit; that war is always ultimately destructive in its effects, and ends in futility by corrupting even the noblest purpose for which it is waged; and that the church will become a creative, regenerative, and reconciling instrument for the healing of the nations only as it renounces war absolutely. They are therefore constrained to refuse to take part in war themselves, to plead among their fellows for a similar repudiation of war in favor of a better way, and to replace military force by methods of active peace-making.[45]

ATTITUDE OF THE CHURCH OF THE BRETHREN TOWARD THE STATE

Three outstanding pronouncements were made between World Wars I and II which show the attitude of the Brethren toward the state. The first statement was that of the

---

[45] From the Oxford report, *The Universal Church and the World of Nations*, p. 83.
[46] *Minutes of the Annual Conference*, 1938, p. 45.

Newton conference of 1935, quoted earlier, which emphasized the love for country, that true patriotism did not mean a hatred for others, and that "the highest welfare of our country must harmonize with the highest welfare of humanity everywhere."

The second statement was made by the Annual Conference of 1938, and shows that the supreme allegiance of the church was to Christ rather than to the state. The report stated:

We recognize that government is essential to the maintenance of orderly living and performs many social services for society. Government is a necessary means but never ought to become an end in itself. We are Christians; we are also citizens of the land in which we live. We ought to labor constantly to put the ideals of Christ into our government so that it will serve our people better and maintain with other people relationships that are Christian in spirit. As a church we strive to make the state Christian in principles and conduct; as citizens we help formulate ways and means of accomplishing these ends.

We love our country and are willing to sacrifice to her best interests. We love her none the less because of our Christian regard for all peoples, for true patriotism is not based upon hatred for others. By the very nature of things a government cannot claim the spiritual allegiance of men since it does not transcend men. Our supreme allegiance is to Christ. Today many Christians are finding themselves faced with a conflict between this allegiance and the demands of the state. We believe that in such a conflict a Christian must be true to his faith, accepting in meekness, without violence or rebellion, whatever penalty may be imposed, thereby giving a witness through which men may be drawn to Christ. Our prayers and sympathies go out to all who are suffering today because of their steadfastness in refusing to do that which is contrary to their faith.[46]

The third statement was made by Paul H. Bowman on behalf of the Church of the Brethren before the Committee on Military Affairs, House of Representatives, July 30, 1940, in opposition to the Burke-Wadsworth bill for Selective Compulsory Military Training and Service. The statement in part is as follows:

The Brethren regard their supreme citizenship as being in the commonwealth of God to which they yield their greater loyalty, but they do accept constructive and creative citizenship in the state. They exercise the right of suffrage and approve the holding of public office where the principles of love and nonviolence are not violated. Political government is regarded as ordained of God through the collective judgment of its citizenry but the Brethren deny the right of the majority to conscript or suppress the conscience of the minority. They are not obstructionists but refuse to bear arms or learn the art of war. They pay their taxes faithfully as imposed by the Government; they obey the laws of the land as loyal citizens; they lay little burden upon the Government for settling their disputes, and rarely has the Government found it necessary to charge against them any part of the enormous crime bill of this country. They build stable homes and foster permanent family ties in harmony with the best American traditions. In times of war, as well as peace, they proclaim a social order based on love and brotherhood and seek to practice those eternal principles of life revealed by the Master.

．　．　．　．　．　．　．

In times of war the Brethren believe that they must still be creative and not destructive. They want to serve in those enterprises which are removed in purpose so far as possible from war and bloodshed, and which are calculated to help the nations more easily to forgive and forget the bitterness and hatred which war engenders. To these enterprises the Brethren expect to bring a spirit of courage and self-sacrifice and a willingness to face physical hazard comparable to that of the soldier in the ranks of the military forces. They desire to keep alive in American life a spiritual glow and a sense of world mission which shall make this nation virile and strong throughout the world in the cause of justice, righteousness and peace.

It therefore follows from the above statement that we could scarcely be true to our profession and the historic position of our church without protesting against any legislation which seems to violate these principles of our faith and departs radically from the spirit and tradition so long held by our Government. We desire to file our objection to House Bill No. 10132, otherwise known as the

Burke-Wadsworth bill. The grounds of our objections have already been amply covered in the testimony of other historic peace groups, particularly in that of the Friends and Mennonites.[47]

The expression of Paul H. Bowman was printed in a pamphlet entitled "Creative Citizenship" and sent to the churches. It was well received by the church as a whole and was accepted as a valid statement of the point of view of the denomination.

In offering their loyal citizenship, the Brethren have not interpreted it as meaning their participation in war. Some members of the church from other countries have been denied citizenship by the courts because they would not promise to "support and defend the constitution of the United States of America against all enemies, foreign and domestic."[48] Mr. Niels Bendsen, of the First Church of the Brethren of Chicago, is one who was refused citizenship because of his conscientious objection to war.

THE BRETHREN FACE PEACETIME CONSCRIPTION

The Annual Conference of June, 1940, held at Ocean Grove, New Jersey, anticipated the coming of conscription and set apart the Brethren Advisory Committee for immediate work with the government. The committee in early summer began to contact government officials and church groups. During July and August, 1940, hearings were held on the Burke-Wadsworth bill— S. 4164. Many peace organizations and churches testified against the passage of the conscription bill.

The First Bill

The original bill introduced in the Senate, June 20, 1940, was patterned after the conscription law of World War I. It recognized only members of the historic peace churches

---

[47] *Hearings Before the Committee on Military Affairs, House of Representatives,* pp. 369-371.
[48] Oath of allegiance in the application for citizenship, U.S. Dept. of Labor, Washington, D.C.

and offered no exemption except from combatant service. Section 7 (d) stated:

> Nothing contained in this act shall be construed to require or compel any person to be subject to training or service in a combatant capacity in the land and naval forces of the United States who is found to be a member of any well recognized religious sect whose creed or principles forbid its members to participate in war in any form, if the conscientious holding of such belief by such person shall be established under such regulations as the President may prescribe; but no such person shall be relieved from training or service in such capacity as the President may declare to be non-combatant.[49]

This proposed legislation was not satisfactory to the Friends, Mennonites and Brethren. At once these churches began to work for a more liberal bill. They centered their efforts toward broadening the original exemption to include noncombatant service, to get consideration for conscientious objectors regardless of their church affiliation, to win government approval for a program of civilian service, to gain recognition for conscience on the grounds of "belief" as well as "religious training and belief," to secure complete exemption for absolutists, and to have the administration of the law regarding conscientious objectors in the hands of the Justice Department.

Paul French Tells the Story

Paul Comly French summarizes the activities of the peace groups until the enactment of the law:

> The Burke-Wadsworth Bill, which later became the Selective Training and Service Act of 1940, was introduced in the Congress in the summer of 1940 by Congressman Wadsworth of New York and Senator Burke of Nebraska. Its provisions for conscientious objectors were the same as those of the Draft Act of 1917 and covered only members of the Historic Peace Churches. At that time representatives of the Friends, Brethren and Mennonites talked with officials of the War Department and members of the House and Senate

---

[49] Memorandum No. 14, *Friends War Problems Committee*, Philadelphia, Pa., Jan. 27, 1943, p. 6.

Military Affairs Committees and expressed their opposition to conscription but suggested that provisions should be made for all sincere conscientious objectors without regard to organizational affiliation if Congress approved such an act. We felt that conscience was an individual, not a corporate, matter.

We discussed the provisions which had been made for conscientious objectors by the British government and urged that persons who felt unable to accept any service be granted complete exemption. We asked joint committees to change the wording of the Act to read "religious training and/or belief" so that a man's individual convictions would be recognized regardless of his training. That phrasing would have made belief stand alone. Both committees gave us sympathetic attention, but neither felt willing to consider absolute exemption for persons other than regular or ordained ministers and divinity students.

As summer moved toward fall and the final passage of the bill, the original group was joined by representatives of the Methodists, Episcopalians, Catholics, War Resisters, F. O. R., Baptists, Presbyterians, Disciples of Christ and others who felt concerned that the rights of individual conscience should be preserved.

Frequently it has been said that the Historic Peace Churches agreed to a program without consulting the men involved. I do not think that this is entirely true. My recollections of that summer are filled with memories of the discussions and meetings directed toward learning what the groups concerned felt was right. Individuals throughout the country were not consulted because no one had any record of individual persons who held the pacifist position, and because all of the groups of pacifists were in and out of Washington during that period, and we assumed that they were representing their constituency. Most of us felt, too, I think, that those who were deeply interested would make their wishes known. There were many men of married age in the groups in Washington in that summer; obviously men in C. P. S. camps were not consulted because the camps did not exist, or at that moment were not even envisioned.

When the bill finally became a law, most of us felt that America had made a real advance in religious liberty and the recognition of conscience. It marked the first Congressional approval of an organized program of tolerance in the United States. We knew that many problems of administration were ahead, but we approached them with the faith that a way would open to solve them as they developed.[50]

Paul French in another statement describes more in detail the initial work of the peace groups in behalf of satisfactory legislation:

In the late part of July, 1940, Raymond Wilson came down from the AFSC and within a very short time Amos Horst and Orie Miller representing the Mennonites and M. R. Zigler of the Brethren; there were representatives of the Episcopal groups, the Presbyterian groups, Disciples of Christ, Congregational Churches and Jewish groups. A fairly wide representation came down to Washington during the summer and fall.

Raymond and I stayed here pretty close to the scene and pretty consistently, and established a sort of travel agency in our rooms at the Commodore Hotel where all the groups coming in would tell us whom they were going to see during that period.

I believe we talked to better than seventy-five Senators and more than 250 members of the House. We also talked with a committee which had been constituted by the Army and Navy to prepare a draft in the event of war or if a draft ever became necessary again. General Hershey, who is now director of Selective Service, then a major, was the executive officer of that group, with Colonel O'Keliher. They had offices down at the Army War College then. Raymond and I talked with both of them and the members of the House and Senate Military Affairs Committees. We told them that if a draft was coming there would be the problem of the conscientious objectors and that it might be faced on a more intelligent basis than in 1917 and 1918, and we found everybody we talked to quite willing to accept that viewpoint. It had not been handled too satisfactorily in 1917 and 1918 from the standpoint of the Army, the individuals or religious groups, and they were quite prepared to do it a little differently this time.

During that time we had ten, twelve, or fifteen different drafts of the proposed sections of the act. They ranged all the way from what we urged on both House and Senate Military Affairs Committee, absolute exemption of conscientious objectors, which neither committee would support, to the provisions which finally went into the act. We talked with General Shedd, who was then Deputy

[50] Paul Comly French, *Civilian Public Service*, National Service Board for Religious Objectors, pp. 4-6.

Chief of Staff of the Army, and found him quite sympathetic to the problem and willing to face it. We found, with one exception in the House Committee, both the Senate and House Committee quite understanding of the difficulty. The one member of the House Committee had a perfect solution of the problem. He said they should take everybody out and shoot them. But after we had discussed that at some length he agreed that maybe it wasn't the most practical solution and might be reconsidered, and he finally voted for the provision as it was stated in the act.[51]

The Senate Committee Proposal

As a result of the many conferences and discussions, the Senate Military Affairs Committee reported the bill out of committee on August 5, 1940, with the following wording:

Sec. 5 (d) Nothing contained in this Act shall be construed to require any person to be subject to combatant training or service in the land or naval forces of the United States who, by reason of religious training and belief, is conscientiously opposed to participation in war in any form. All persons claiming such exemption from combatant training and service because of such conscientious objections shall be listed on a Register of Conscientious Objectors at the time of their classification by a local board, and the names of the persons so registered shall be at once referred by such local board to the Department of Justice for inquiry and hearing. After appropriate inquiry by the proper agency of the Department of Justice, a hearing shall be held by the Department of Justice in the case of each person with respect to character and good faith of his objections, and such person shall be notified of the time and place of such hearing. The Department shall, after such hearing, if the objections are found to be sustained, recommend (1) that the objector shall be assigned to noncombatant service as defined by the President, or (2) if the objector is found to be conscientiously opposed to participation in such noncombatant service, that he shall be assigned to work of national importance under civilian direction. If, after such hearing, the objections of any such person are found not to be sustained, the objector and the local board shall be immediately notified thereof, the name of the objector shall then be removed from the Register of Conscientious Objectors, and such objector shall thereafter be liable to training and service as provided by this Act. If, within

[51] *Proceedings of the Assistant Directors Training Institute*, National Service Board for Religious Objectors, Nov. 9 to Dec. 1, 1942, pp. 38-39.

five days after the date of such findings by the Department of Justice, the objector or the local board gives notice to the other of disagreement with such findings, the local board shall immediately refer the matter for final determination to an appropriate appeal board established pursuant to section 10 (a) (2). [52]

The above text of the bill was passed by the Senate on August 28, 1940. From August 5 to September 13 there was much activity in Washington on behalf of the peace groups. Paul H. Bowman, M. R. Zigler, Ross D. Murphy and A. W. Cordier represented the Brethren. Raymond Wilson and Paul French represented the Friends. In addition there were interested workers from the Mennonites, Methodists, Disciples of Christ, Fellowship of Reconciliation, War Resisters League and others who joined in efforts to secure legislation acceptable to the various kinds of conscientious objectors. Even though the Senate bill had endorsed civilian service there was no guarantee that the whole provision would not be thrown out. Raymond Wilson says that the peace groups organized and saw "about two-thirds of the Senators and over one-half of the House Members." [53] Besides that, members from the peace groups worked constantly with the members of the Senate and House Committee on Military Affairs. Efforts were centered upon securing complete exemption for absolutists and broadening the provisions to include "belief" as well as "religious training" as grounds for consideration.

Absolute Exemption Defeated

M. R. Zigler says:

> An effort was made by everyone to get absolute exemption. Individuals on the Committee of both House and Senate were contacted. We used the law of England as a precedent. We had private conferences with members of Congress. I saw personally about two dozen members. Total exemption was turned down. [54]

---

[52] Memorandum No. 14, *op. cit.*, p. 9.
[53] Personal interview with Raymond Wilson, Philadelphia, Pa., Feb. 16, 1943.
[54] Personal interview with M. R. Zigler, Elgin, Ill., Dec. 31, 1942.

The House bill as it was being discussed for passage contained the provisions of the Senate bill providing for the establishment of a registry of conscientious objectors so that every member of draft age would register at an independent register, and that the administration of the provision of the law relating to conscientious objectors would be under the Justice Department. Before the bill was passed the Attorney General offered objection to it on the grounds that the Justice Department had neither the funds nor the personnel to administer this work. Paul French states that one afternoon about forty-five seconds before the House adjourned for the day, the chairman of the House Judiciary Committee, Congressman Walters, of Pennsylvania, moved that the provision be stricken out which would provide for a separate register for the conscientious objectors and which would have provided for tribunals under the Justice Department.[55] Without a roll call the section was eliminated. The next morning Jerry Voorhis of California asked the members if they knew what they had done and that a plan, carefully worked out, to which the War Department had agreed, had been eliminated without any discussion at all. But the bill was passed September 7, 1940, and went to the Joint Committee of the House and Senate for final wording.

The Selective Training and Service Act of 1940

The bill reported by the Conference Committee to the House and Senate, September 13, 1940, which became a law the next day, is as follows:

Section 5 (g)

Nothing contained in this Act shall be construed to require any person to be subject to combatant training and service in the land or naval forces in the United States, who, by reason of religious training and belief, is conscientiously opposed to participation in war in

---

[55] *Assistant Directors' Institute, op. cit.,* p. 41.

any form. Any such persons claiming such exemption from combatant training and service because of such conscientious objections whose claim is sustained by the local board shall, if he is inducted into the land or naval forces under this Act, be assigned to noncombatant service as defined by the President, or shall, if he is found to be conscientiously opposed to participation in such noncombatant service, in lieu of such induction be assigned to work of national importance under civilian direction. Any such person claiming such exemption from combatant training and service because of such conscientious objections shall, if such claim is not sustained by the local board, be entitled to an appeal to the appropriate appeal board, provided for in section 10 (a) (2). Upon the filing of such appeal with the appeal board, the appeal board shall forthwith refer the matter to the Department of Justice for inquiry and hearing by the Department or the proper agency thereof. After appropriate inquiry by such agency, a hearing shall be held by the Department of Justice with respect to the character and good faith of the objections of the person concerned, and such person shall be notified of the time and place of such hearing. The Department shall, after such hearing, if the objections are found to be sustained, recommend to the appeal board (1) that if the objector is inducted into the land or naval forces under this Act, he shall be assigned to noncombatant service as defined by the President, or (2) that if the objector is found to be conscientiously opposed to participation in such noncombatant service, he shall in lieu of such induction be assigned to work of national importance under civilian direction. If after such hearing the Department finds that his objections are not sustained, it shall recommend to the appeal board that such objections be not sustained. The appeal board shall give consideration to but shall not be bound to follow the recommendation of the Department of Justice together with the record on appeal from the local board in making its decision. Each person whose claim for exemption from combatant training and service because of conscientious objections is sustained shall be listed by the local board on a register of conscientious objectors.[56]

The draft law did not grant exemption for absolutists and stated "religious training and belief" instead of "religious training" or "belief" as grounds for exemption from

[56] *Congressional Record,* LXXXVI, Pt. II, Sec. 5(g) (76th Cong., 3rd Sess.), p. 12157.

combatant service. *Although the law was not as liberal as the peace groups had hoped for, it was certainly more reasonable and considerate of conscientious objectors than it would have been had the churches and other organizations not worked so constantly with the government.*

Formation of the National Service Board for Religious Objectors

The National Service Board was formed to unite the independent C. O. bodies in their work with the government and to be the liaison committee between the conscientious objectors and the government. After the Selective Service Law was passed these peace groups realized that they needed some organization to speak with a united voice to the government. General Hershey indicated that he would deal only with some kind of a centralized organization and not with individual groups.[57] A preliminary meeting was held in Washington to consider the question. The Society of Friends presented a plan to take over the whole administration of the conscientious objector program on behalf of everyone. The Mennonites and Brethren indicated their desire for a co-operative program. A larger group was called together in Chicago on October 4, 1940, to consider a co-operative plan of action. Once more the Friends presented their proposal to assume the administrative responsibility. Orie Miller of the Mennonites, M. R. Zigler of the Church of the Brethren, and Charles Boss of the Methodists indicated their preference for a joint organization and the group decided upon the co-operative method. The National Council for Religious Objectors was organized at Washington, D. C., October 11, 1940.[58] Those present were Orie Miller and Henry Fast, representing the Mennonite Central Committee; Paul Comly French, temporarily

---

[57] *Assistant Directors' Institute, op. cit.,* p. 127.
[58] *Minutes of the Brethren Service Committee,* Oct. 22, 1940.

representing the Friends War Problems Committee and the American Friends Service Committee; M. R. Zigler representing the Brethren Service Committee. In a consultative capacity, Charles Boss, Jr., represented the World Peace Commission of the Methodist Church, and Roswell Barnes represented the Federal Council of Churches. M. R. Zigler was named as chairman, Orie Miller as vice-chairman, and Paul Comly French as executive secretary. Paul J. Furnas was appointed to represent the Friends on the Council.

On November 26, 1940, the name was changed from the National Council for Religious Objectors to the National Service Board for Religious Objectors. By this time the Fellowship of Reconciliation had joined the participating organizations and was represented by Arthur L. Swift. Soon Charles Boss, Jr., of the Methodists, Walter W. Van Kirk of the Federal Council of Churches, and James A. Crain of the Disciples of Christ became participating members.

The work of the National Service Board grew rapidly. Many churches and peace organizations were interested in representation. For the sake of efficiency the Board limited its membership to seven but organized a Consultative Council. By July 1, 1942, there were twenty-seven members of the Consultative Council.

Planning for Work of National Importance

Major Lewis B. Hershey, who had been executive of the joint Army and Navy Committee on Selective Service, was first placed in charge of the administration of the law. The opening discussions regarding "work of national importance" were with him. The National Service Board found Major Hershey friendly and understanding and willing to take time to consider the problems of conscientious objectors. Later the President called C. A. Dykstra, president of the University of Wisconsin, as Director of Selective

Service, promoted Hershey to a colonel, and named him as Assistant Director. Later he became General Hershey and was appointed Director of Selective Service after the resignation of Dr. Dykstra.

The history of the development of camp projects is well told by Paul Comly French:

Now came the question of projects. We suggested to Dr. Dykstra that there might be three types. One would be financed solely by the Government; the second would have the work program financed by the Government and the administration and educational program by the religious agencies; the third would be financed and administered solely by the religious groups. Dr. Dykstra agreed to our proposal and investigated the question of Government funds for the operation of the first type and for the Government's share of the second type. Inquiry revealed that sufficient funds were not available for Type One project and that it would be necessary to ask the Congress for an appropriation. At that point four representatives of Selective Service—Dr. Dykstra, Colonel Hershey, Colonel William Draper, Jr., and Major Guiton Morgan—met with Lowell Mellett, then director of the office of Government Reports, and Clarence Pickett and me to discuss the situation.

Dr. Dykstra said they could ask the Congress for the funds, but he felt that if they did, it would be unlikely that they would be granted on any basis that would permit the religious groups to share in the program. All of the Government representatives agreed that this was true and it was suggested to us that the Historic Peace Churches might be willing to assume the cost of operating the whole program on the basis of the second type of project for an experimental period.

We recognized that the Congress had established "religious training and belief" as the basis for judging sincerity and felt that the majority of the men who took the conscientious objector position would do so from religious conviction and motivation. As a result of this reasoning it seemed to the majority of us that it was right that religious groups, which had stood for the nonresistant and pacifist approach to Christianity, should participate in the program. Even with this belief, however, we obviously could not make any commitment at that time because it involved the assumption of a real financial burden and an agreement that we would accept all men certified as sincere by local draft boards regardless of whether they, or their churches, could aid in the financial program. After consultation and consideration representatives of the Historic Peace Churches told Dr. Dykstra that they would agree to his suggestion and assume the responsibility within the limits of their financial ability, for an experimental period of six months. That period, following conversations with General Hershey, has been extended three times and is now in force until January 1, 1944.

We worked out together an understanding of the responsibilities of Selective Service and the National Service Board, as representatives of the administrative agencies, and the program started. We are still operating on the basis of that understanding between General Hershey and the General Service Board for Religious Objectors. It is a co-operative agreement under which we are mutually concerned about the success of the program. The scope of authority which Selective Service has delegated to the operating agencies is clear and the National Service Board and the administrative agencies are consulted before any change takes place in the relationship. We all recognize that the ultimate authority rests with the Director of Selective Service under a Presidential Executive Order and that he can, if he feels it is in the public interest, withdraw the delegation of authority he has given us in the operation of the program. But while the agreement continues in force we have certain defined responsibilities and authority.[59]

It seemed clear to the leaders of the historic peace churches that asking Congress to finance the civilian camps would mean government control of them without any definite sharing of these religious groups in the program. The big question was this: Should the Friends, Mennonites and Brethren assume responsibility for the operation of these camps with the financial burden which it involved? Obviously some financial help would come from other churches desiring to finance their own conscientious objectors. But the commitment to assume the responsibility for the operation of the camps meant a tremendous undertaking. And the agreement also included the acceptance of all conscientious objectors judged by their local draft boards as

---

[59] Paul Comly French, *Civilian Public Service*, pp. 8-10.

being sincere. The representatives of these churches went to their respective denominations to ask for counsel and advice.

Special Standing Committee Meeting

The special Standing Committee meeting held in Chicago, December, 1940, considered the serious problem of whether to endorse and recommend to the church the support of the Civilian Public Service program. After two days of discussion the group voted unanimously to undertake the responsibility of administering and supporting this program in co-operation with the other churches. There was not a delegate who spoke in favor of government-controlled camps. The Brethren Service Committee was authorized to outline plans for the raising of the necessary funds. The meeting asked the various delegates to call special district and local meetings to discuss the program of alternative service with the members. Within a few months the church as a whole was informed regarding this new undertaking. The church began to respond with funds. For the twelve months ending February 28, 1941, the Brethren Service Committee received $88,963.51. For the same period ending February 28, 1942, the receipts were $198,196.09. For the next year the offerings from the churches amounted to $340,222.97 for the Service Committee. This means that the members have more than doubled the amount which they had been giving to general church work. There has been no hesitation on the part of the church in its efforts to support Civilian Public Service.

The President Defines Noncombatant Service

On December 6, 1940, President Roosevelt issued an Executive Order defining the branches of the army which are considered as noncombatant and providing for the assignment of those conscientious objectors who are able to accept such service. The Executive Order reads:

Definition of Noncombatant Training and Service

1. By virtue of authority contained in section 5 (g) of the Selective Training and Service Act of 1940, approved September 16, 1940, whereby it is provided:

"Nothing contained in this Act shall be construed to require any person to be subject to combatant training and service in the land or naval forces of the United States, who by reason of religious training and belief, is conscientiously opposed to participation in war in any form. Any such person claiming such exemption from combatant training and service because of such conscientious objections whose claim is sustained by the local board shall, if he is inducted into the land and naval forces under this Act, be assigned to noncombatant service as defined by the President, or shall, if he is found to be conscientiously opposed to participation in such noncombatant service, in lieu of such induction, be assigned to work of national importance under civilian direction. . . ."

I hereby declare that the following military service is noncombatant service:

(1) Service in any unit which is unarmed at all times.

(2) Service in the Medical Department wherever performed.

(3) Service in any unit or installation the primary function of which does not require the use of arms in combat, provided the individual's assignment within such unit or installation does not require him to bear arms or to be trained in their use.

I further declare that noncombatant training consists of training in all military subjects except marksmanship, combat firing, target practices, and those subjects relating to the employment of weapons.

2. Persons inducted in the military service under the above act whose claim to exemption from combatant training and service because of conscientious objection has been sustained will receive noncombatant training and be assigned to noncombatant military service as defined in paragraph one.

Franklin D. Roosevelt

The White House
December 6, 1940.[60]

Thus noncombatant work was clarified before the declaration of war by the United States, which represents an

---

[60] *The Conscientious Objector under the Selective Service Act of 1940*, National Service Board for Religious Objectors, Washington, D.C., pp. 3-4.

improvement over the postponed definition of noncombatant duties by President Wilson in World War I. Mr. Roosevelt's order was so specifically worded that everyone could
easily understand that noncombatant service meant genuine military activities. The choice for conscientious objectors, a year before the war began, was between military
service and work of national importance under civilian
direction.

An Agreement Reached With Selective Service

Paul French had secured sufficient approval from the
historic peace churches to write the following letter to the
Director of Selective Service on December 20, 1940:

December 20, 1940

Dr. Clarence A. Dykstra, Director
Selective Service System
21st and C Streets N. W.
Washington, D. C.

Dear Dr. Dykstra:

This will confirm our recent conversations in which we discussed a
program of "work of national importance" for conscientious objectors judged sincere by local boards. The groups I represent—the
American Friends Service Committee, Brethren Service Committee,
Mennonite Central Peace Committee, and the Fellowship of Reconciliation—are prepared to organize and finance, within the limits
of their ability, a program under which conscientious objectors
could perform "work of national importance."

If our proposal is accepted, we would be prepared to handle conscientious objectors by the middle of January in the first of the units
we would establish. We understand that this plan would be experimental from the standpoint of the Government and from ours and
that we would both re-examine it in July to see whether its continuation was desirable from either of our viewpoints.

We feel that this is an opportunity for us to serve our country in a
way which, though insignificant in its immediate results, may in the
long run be of great value to it.

It is our understanding that certain unused C.C.C. camps might possibly be made available to us at a nominal rental. It would seem unwise for us to engage in a comprehensive camp construction program while the plan is experimental.

We wish to assure you that we deeply appreciate the understanding and the intelligent co-operation we have received from the Selective Service administration in working out this program. We feel that the spirit in which you and your associates have met these problems is of great significance in the development of democratic institutions and in proving the ability of our nation to protect her religious minorities.

Cordially yours,

Paul Comly French
Executive Secretary[61]

In return Dr. Dykstra accepted the proposal of the peace groups:

December 20, 1940

Paul Comly French, Executive Secretary
National Service Board for Religious Objectors

1205 National Press Building
Washington, D. C.

Dear Mr. French:

I am very glad to have your letter of December 20th which brings the news that the groups which you represent are prepared to go along with us within the limits of their ability to prosecute a program of work of national importance under civilian direction, and to take such heavy responsibility in connection with it.

The proposal as discussed and tentatively accepted has been approved by the President of the United States and by those members of the Cabinet whose Departments may be somewhat involved in preparing and planning for this work. Here at Selective Service headquarters, we shall give this program our heartiest co-operation and general supervision. We all realize that for the time being all of our plans for this work must be experimental. I have a definite feeling myself, that together we shall work out a sound and sane program which will appeal to the whole Nation.

---

[61] *Ibid.*, pp. 4-5.

Will you convey to your National Council my heartiest thanks for this tender of great service to our Country?

With my kindest regards and best wishes, I am

Yours very sincerely,

C. A. Dykstra, Director[62]

On February 6, 1941, the President issued an Executive Order authorizing the Director of Selective Service to establish Civilian Public Service:

Executive Order

On February 6, 1941, the President signed the following Executive Order:

Authorizing the Director of Selective Service to Establish or Designate Work of National Importance Under Civilian Direction for Persons Conscientiously Opposed to Combatant and Noncombatant Service in the Land or Naval Forces of the United States.

By virtue of the authority vested in me by the Selective Training and Service Act of 1940 (Pub. No. 783, 76th Congress), it is hereby ordered as follows:

1. The Director of Selective Service, hereinafter called the Director, is authorized to establish, designate, or determine work of national importance under civilian direction to which may be assigned persons found under section 5 (g) of the Selective Training and Service Act of 1940 to be conscientiously opposed to participation in combatant and noncombatant training and service in the land or naval forces of the United States.

2. The Director shall make the necessary assignments to such work, shall determine the agencies, organizations, or individuals that may provide civilian direction thereof, and shall have general supervision and control over such work.

3. To the extent that he may deem necessary to carry out the provisions of this order, the Director may utilize the services of the Departments, officers and agents of the United States; accept the services of officers and agents of the several states, territories, and the District of Columbia, and the subdivisions thereof; and accept voluntary services of private organizations and individuals; and may

---

[62] *Ibid.*, p. 5.

obtain, by purchase, loan or gift, equipment and supplies from Federal and other public agencies and private organizations and individuals, with or without advertising or formal contract.

4. The Director is authorized to prescribe such rules and regulations as may be necessary to carry out the provisions of this order.

Franklin D. Roosevelt.

The White House
February 6, 1941.[63]

Major General Lewis B. Hershey in his report on Selective Service, covering the period from the enactment of the law until the declaration of war, December 8, 1941, gives the following interesting report regarding Civilian Public Service, in which he quotes from the secretaries of the committees of the historic peace churches:

The Work Program

The plan as worked out provided that the work program would be developed and supervised by the same governmental agencies as were directing the CCC projects, while the internal or housekeeping part of the camp activities would be under the control of the religious group. They agreed to provide food, clothing, medical care, recreation, and education, for all men assigned to them, and to maintain the camp. In return they were to be allowed to provide the administrative staff and to carry on religious training and education programs. The assignees to the camp would not receive pay and, where financially able, could be asked to contribute to the support of the camp. Each of the three churches would sponsor and operate a camp individually, through their own administrative machinery. However, to coordinate activities, act as a clearing house, and maintain liaison with the Selective Service System, they established an unincorporated, not for profit, organization known as the National Service Board for Religious Objectors with offices and an executive secretary in Washington, D. C.

* * * * * *

Assignees had same Responsibility as to the Length of Service as Inductees

In keeping with the Selective Service Act, it was expected that assignees would serve one year in camp and then be released. How-

---

[63] *Ibid.*, p. 6.

ever, congressional action extended the term of service for men in the Army. It was interpreted to apply to assignees as well, so that their term of duty was increased to 18 months. Similarly, when the Army released men over 28 years old, the Camp Operations Division did the same. The general rule has been to follow Army policy in matters of this kind as closely as possible, not because the assignees were considered to have a military status, but with the idea of making the conditions of their service comparable wherever this could be done. It was felt that assignees should be neither favored, nor punished because of their beliefs, but as far as the law allowed, they should undergo the same inconveniences and receive the same benefits as the men in service.

The Selection of Projects

With changing conditions, the value of different projects changes. Continuous exploration for new projects, which were considered to be of more benefit to the Government, was made. This involved a continuous problem of education of both the objectors and the public.

The following factors had to be considered in selecting projects:

1. Is the project important to the government in the emergency considering the manpower available, and is the project the most important thing that can be done at the time; and will it continue to be important with the probable changes in the situation?

2. Will the conscientious objectors do it? It would be useless to select projects which the conscientious objectors would not do wholeheartedly, because filling the jails would not solve the problem.

3. Will the public tolerate the objector in the community where the project is located? It is useless to attempt a project in a community where the local population so threatens or harasses the objector that he cannot do a creditable job. In many cases, the cooperation of the citizens of the community is necessary. Veterans' organizations have usually been the leaders in opposition to attempted projects.

4. Will other employable labor be displaced? No projects were attempted which would displace labor already employed, or where funds and labor were available for the project.

5. Will it raise political controversy? An attempt was made to keep the conscientious objectors out of the community where their

presence might become a political issue. This was done in order to maintain unity by not creating cause for dissension. Some of the projects under consideration are: farm labor, sanitation, attendants in hospitals, research work for forestry, soil conservation, and fish and wildlife.

An Effort at Sympathetic Understanding

We have tried to understand the position of the conscientious objector, and to give him assignments consistent with his conscience, and generally to administer sympathetically the will of the American people in the difficult problem of wartime. The representatives of the conscientious objectors are appreciative of this effort of Selective Service. In a letter to the Director of Selective Service dated November 27, 1941, they say:

This will confirm our conversation of yesterday when we told you, as representatives of the American Friends Service Committee, the Brethren Service Committee, and the Mennonite Central Committee, that we were prepared to continue the present program within the limits of our financial ability until January 1, 1943. If convenient with you, we would discuss the whole program again in September 1942, to see whether the arrangement is still mutually satisfactory and should be continued.

We wish you to know that we appreciate the sympathy and understanding with which you have faced this problem during the past year or more and assure you that we are hopeful that the same relationships can continue during the coming year so that jointly we can demonstrate the ability of a democracy to respect minority religious groups.

Cordially yours,

M. R. Zigler
Brethren Service Committee

Clarence Pickett
American Friends Service Committee

Orie Miller
Mennonite Central Committee[64]

Agreement Regarding the Operation of Camps

One of the first duties of the newly organized National Service Board was to work out a policy with Selective

---

[64] Lewis B. Hershey, *Selective Service in Peacetime,* pp. 196-201.

Service for the operation of Civilian Public Service camps. The President's Executive Order of February 6, 1941, authorized the Director of Selective Service "to establish, designate, or determine work of national importance under civilian direction."[65] Legally the Director of Selective Service has the right to declare any kind of a project he wants to as being work of national importance. The only limitation upon him is that the project must be under civilian direction. Further, the Executive Order placed the responsibility for general supervision and control over such camps in the hands of the Director of Selective Service.[66] How were the peace groups to secure a measure of authority to operate their own camps and help in choosing their own projects even though the government maintained final control? Obviously, the working out of satisfactory relationships depended somewhat upon the goodwill and understanding of General Hershey. The administrative agencies, the organizations designated to operate camps, worked through the National Service Board toward a co-operative plan with the government in dealing with camps and projects. Through a gentleman's agreement the National Service Board was delegated the authority by Selective Service to operate camps. The Mennonites, Friends, and Brethren are in charge of camps as the administrative agents of the National Service Board. There are constant contacts with Selective Service and the problems are worked out co-operatively.

The technical relationships were outlined by Lewis B. Hershey, April 11, 1941, in the Selective Service regulations:

2. Civilian Direction and Responsibility.

a. Assignees, as defined in paragraph 1 above, will be assigned to camps and engaged on work of national importance under civilian

---

[65] *Selective Service Regulations,* April 11, 1941, p. 2.
[66] *Ibid.,* p. 3.

direction of the Department of Agriculture, of the Department of the Interior, or such other agencies as may be designated from time to time by the Director of Selective Service.

b. The responsibility and authority for general supervision and control over such work and such camps is vested in the Director of Selective Service. The supervisory and administrative functions of the Director will be performed by the Camp Operations Division of National Headquarters, Selective Service System, hereinafter referred to as the Camp Operations Division. Such camps will be designated by an appropriate geographical location, as follows: "San Dimas Camp."

3. National Service Board for Religious Objectors.

The National Service Board for Religious Objectors is a voluntary unincorporated association of religious organizations which has agreed, in the absence of Federal funds specifically allocated by the Director of Selective Service, to take care of the expenses of the rehabilitation of necessary buildings at camp sites; wages for camp directors and other employees of the National Service Board for Religious Objectors; camp physicians; clothing; medical care; hospitalization; feeding and housing of the assignees and the cost of operation and maintenance of equipment required by and belonging to the agency engaged in the technical direction of the work project.

4. Camp Responsibility.

a. Camp Director: The National Service Board for Religious Objectors, through its camp director, is responsible for the maintenance of the camp and its environs in accordance with standards acceptable to the governmental agency involved; maintenance of discipline; recreation, education, health and camp life of the assignee; and such watchman service as is required.

b. Project Superintendent: The agency whose responsibility it is to carry out the work program shall provide a project superintendent and such other personnel as it deems necessary. Such personnel will be governed by the personnel regulations of such agency. The project superintendent shall be responsible for all phases of job planning and direction; for the direction of technicians detailed to the camp; for the on-the-job training; and for the safety program while the assignees are under his direction. The project superintendent will issue drivers' permits in conformity with the regulations set forth by his agency.[67]

---

[67] *Ibid.*, pp. 3-4.

The most recent rules of Selective Service state:

The Director of Selective Service may authorize the National Service Board for Religious Objectors, a voluntary unincorporated association of religious organizations, to operate camps. The work project for assignees of such camps will be under the civilian direction of a technical agency. Such camps and work projects will be operated under such rules as may be prescribed by the Director of Selective Service.[68]

The camps are still operated upon the basis of the gentleman's agreement between the churches and Selective Service. It is a co-operative program based upon understanding and willingness of the churches and government to work together. The Church of the Brethren has moved from non-co-operation to co-operation with the government in a program for conscientious objectors.

Official Attitude of the Selective Service Officers

Those in charge of Selective Service issued a memorandum in December, 1940, to all state directors, in which they expressed their concern for a just administration of the law. Part of the memorandum reads:

The Congress of the United States, in the passage of the Selective Training and Service Act of 1940, recognized the importance of individual conscience in a democracy and made a provision for deferment from combatant military service of those registrants judged by local boards to be sincere in their conscientious opposition to participation in war. The Act specifically provides consideration for all such persons on a basis of their individual conscientious convictions and does not require membership in a religious organization or sect as evidence of the sincerity of their convictions.

This provision is important and illustrates one of the fundamental principles of a democratic form of society in that it recognizes that a democracy respects the conscientious convictions of individuals representing a very small minority, even though the great majority of our citizens cannot agree with their position.

Local boards should make an attempt to understand the viewpoint of those registrants who claim deferment from military service on

---

[68] *Selective Service Manual, Second Edition,* Section 653.2, p. 653-3.

the grounds of conscientious objection, and to see that all sincere persons receive proper classification. On the other hand, every care should be taken to prevent any registrant from being so deferred whose claim is based on a desire to evade and avoid service, rather than on a sincere religious belief opposing participation in war.

And another section of the memorandum defines broadly the meaning of "religious training and belief":

Religious training or discipline may be considered as having been received in the home, in the church, or other organizations whose influence is religious though not professionally such, in the school, or in the individual's own personal religious experience and conduct of life. Any and all influences which have contributed to the consistent endeavor to live the good life may be classed as "religious training." Belief signifies sincere conviction as to the supreme worth of that to which one gives his supreme allegiance. ". . . conscientiously . . . opposed to participation in war in any form" may be interpreted as meaning that a person may have become a conscientious objector to war, either by specific teaching, as for instance, the Quaker tenet of nonparticipation in war, or by specific application of fundamental doctrines, as for instance, the Christian doctrines of reverence for life, "non-retaliation," "brotherly love," expressed in phrases such as "Love your enemies"; "Render to no man evil for evil"; etc.[69]

This statement made it clear that conscientious objection to war was an individual matter and did not depend upon membership in any church. "Religious training and belief" was given a rather broad interpretation. The different interpretations of this memorandum by local draft boards together. with the fact that the administrative agencies were to accept all persons designated for work of national importance, led to a great many people of divergent points of view in C.P.S. camps.

Brethren Boys Advised to Register

The Advisory Committee for conscientious objectors early in 1940 sent a program to the churches in which young

---

[69] *The Conscientious Objector under the Selective Training and Service Act of 1940, op. cit.,* pp. 2-3.

men were advised to register when called upon to do so. As the registration day approached, no general advice was issued, but Brethren leaders over the denomination practically without an exception advised registration. The Brethren Service Committee has no record of any Brethren member who refused to register.

How the Conscientious Objectors Claim Exemption

As in the case of World War I, local draft boards are given much authority. The treatment of conscientious objectors differs greatly with the various draft boards. On the registrant's main questionnaire is a place for him to designate his conscientious objection to war. This designation gives him the legal right to call for Form 47 upon which he states his willingness to accept noncombatant service or his opposition to all service under the direction of military authorities. Form 47 requires a statement of the registrant's peace views, religious training, general background, and activities. Upon this basis the local board classifies the registrant, usually I-A-O, noncombatant service, or IV-E, work of national importance under civilian direction. When a registrant is not satisfied with his classification he may appeal to the Board of Appeal, at which time his case is investigated by the Department of Justice and a recommendation is given to the Appeal Board. If the vote of the Appeal Board is negative, the registrant may appeal to the President. Appeals to the President are made to General Hershey. The National Service Board prepares the appeal cases and presents them to Selective Service. They first go to the office of Colonel Simon P. Dunkel where he and Major Wherry consider them. The officers investigate the cases carefully. If they consider them worthy cases they are sent to the President's Appeal Committee for final action.[70]

---

[70] Personal interview with Guy West of the National Service Board staff, February 23, 1943.

ATTITUDE OF THE CHURCH OF THE BRETHREN TOWARD YOUNG
MEN IN MILITARY CAMPS

Even though the position of the church was against service in the army, the Brethren from the beginning of conscription held that a spiritual ministry should be provided
for members in the armed forces. Paul H. Bowman, who
was then in charge of Civilian Public Service for the
Church of the Brethren, wrote in the "Gospel Messenger"
of April 12, 1941:

> There are, even among Brethren, divergent points of view. We
> are not all conscientious objectors. Not a few young men of the
> church have volunteered for military service; others have gone to
> the combatant forces under the Selective Service Act; and still oth-
> ers have accepted noncombatant service within the army. These
> last two groups are assigned to classes I-A and I-A-O and are now
> being inducted into military camps throughout the country. They
> are in the ranks of the army as full-fledged soldiers.
>
> Our interest and concern for the young men who support the po-
> sition of the church and go to Civilian Public Service camps must
> not overshadow the spiritual needs of men who go into the army.
> We must go with them too with our spiritual administration. They
> need the counsel and nurture of the church even more than others.
> A chaplain service is being maintained within the army, and the
> Federal Council of Churches is undertaking a large program in this
> connection. But the Church of the Brethren will certainly follow
> these men personally with her prayers, her sympathy and whatever
> other service she can offer.[71]

The Annual Conference held at La Verne, California,
June 18-24, 1941, authorized "pastoral visitation in military
camps where Brethren are located.[72] Pastors located near
military camps were appointed as visitors and H. L. Hart-
sough, a pastor of unusual tact and ability, was appointed
as a special representative from the denomination to contact both C.P.S. and military camps. He served effectively

---

[71] *Gospel Messenger,* April 12, 1941, p. 12.
[72] *Annual Conference Minutes,* 1941, p. 52.

until the rapid movement of troops and gas rationing made his work extremely difficult.

THE PHILOSOPHY OF CIVILIAN PUBLIC SERVICE CAMPS

It has been noted how the Brethren following the first World War endeavored to prepare the way for a program of alternative service through relief and reconstruction projects and that they wanted to be creative citizens. With the coming of conscription the Brethren leaders felt that it was more righteous for them to do something constructive for the nation than to refuse all service. They also thought that the peace testimony of the church would be stronger if they refused army service but co-operated with the government in working out valuable civilian projects. Thus, the philosophy of Civilian Public Service is that of co-operation with the state in working out mutual problems. It holds that conscientious objectors are citizens of the state and have a responsibility for serving their country in harmony with conscience. When conscription comes, even though they oppose it, rather than do nothing they will choose creative alternatives to war. C. L. Graber, a Mennonite, and administrative assistant to Paul French, says, "Paul French has built up the National Service Board on the theory that you need mutual confidence between the National Service Board and the Government."[73] Paul French states his philosophy of Civilian Public Service:

Civilian Public Service was conceived as a way of giving the state-community the service which it asked of all its citizens and then going beyond that and paying for the privilege of serving. I think that most of the people who participated in the decision to accept the responsibility felt that it would give them an opportunity to prepare men for the tasks that would come with the ending of the war and the reconstruction period that would face us at home and abroad. All of the groups who agreed to the present church-financed program saw those values clearly when the suggestion was

---

[*] Personal interview with C. L. Graber, Washington, D. C., Feb. 23, 1943.

made to us that we might be willing to operate the program without Federal financial assistance on an experimental basis. We were so sure of this fundamental ideal that we agreed on three different occasions to continue on that basis for additional periods. What I have said may be an over-simplification, yet I am satisfied that the fact that people believe in a thing sufficiently to pay for it has worth in making our testimony clear in a society in which material things are predominant and the basis on which values are judged.

Civilian Public Service, as I see it, has two values. The first is the worth to the nation as a whole, engaged in a war for the preservation of the individual rights and democratic political forms, in permitting some of its citizens to remain outside the scope of military action because of religious convictions. At the moment it is impossible to evaluate the ultimate service to all of the people of the nation and the world in this recognition and tolerance of individual conscience. Another value to the country comes from the ability of the Government to work with a religious-pacifist minority in a time of total war and opens the way for closer association between Government and private agencies in the realms of reconstruction, relief and social service at the conclusion of the conflict.

The other contribution that Civilian Public Service has to make is in a demonstration of the irresistible power of constructive goodwill as against force and violence. We have the opportunity of proving that good ends cannot be achieved by evil means—that you cannot sow barley and reap corn.

We have the opportunity to see whether men of varying backgrounds can live and work together and create a pattern of life that will demonstrate the way that nations can live together in peace and harmony. We all know that one of the fundamental problems of the world is the apparent inability of men to work and live together. Civilian Public Service has the chance to develop the new Third Order—not by formal educational courses nor by idealistic pronouncements, but by the ability to live and work together.

• • • • • •

And the final value, as I see it, is in the co-operation and the developing sense of unity among the religious groups and communities which hold to the fundamental Christian philosophy of nonresistance and pacifism.[74]

---
[74] Paul French, *Civilian Public Service*, pp. 10-13.

Harold Row, Director of Civilian Public Service for the Church of the Brethren, states the Brethren point of view:

This is the first time in our church's history (indeed in world history) that we have been allowed to give a positive testimony of our peace doctrines in time of war. The Civilian Public Service program was established by the Selective Training and Service Act of 1940 to provide those draftees who by "reason of religious training and belief" were opposed to military service an opportunity to do "work of national importance, under civilian direction." (The government first designated such work as soil conservation and forestry service, but now new types of service, such as hospitals, farm furlough, public health, foreign relief and rehabilitation, are opening up.) It was an attempt upon the part of our government, encouraged by leaders of the historic peace churches and others, to respect conscience and to safeguard minority rights. It is our first opportunity during a war crisis to demonstrate that Brethren, who refuse to kill, love their country deeply and are willing to sacrifice for its good. Until now, for Brethren youth to be true to the peace teachings of the church meant to defy the law of the land and to go to prison, suffering the stigma of bad citizenship. Today a Brethren youth may be loyal to his church's heritage of peace and at the same time be a creative citizen.

This is something new in our development. The peace position of our church has been a succession of new insights. Each crisis in our history has advanced us toward a more positive expression of our peace conviction, and each advance has been possible only because of our accumulating heritage.

Civilian Public Service is the latest and clearest affirmation of our doctrine. It implements our peace attitude with a program of action. Hundreds of our young men are leaving homes, positions, and wages for induction into the several camps administered by the Brethren Service Committee. Here they are making a concrete witness against war and at the same time preparing themselves through the disciplines of work, study, and fellowship for active participation in the Christian reconstruction of the local and worldwide community. Our members at home are supporting this program by gifts of food, clothing and money.[75]

In an interview with the writer Paul French stated brief-

---

[75] Harold Row, *Fulfilling Our Heritage* (a pamphlet), pp. 6-8.

ly the philosophy under which the National Service Board operates:

That of co-operation. The government has demanded service of its citizens. We cannot perform the military service which they ask. We tell the government that if it will let us do what we can in harmony with conscience, we will sacrifice for it and pay for it.[76]

SUMMARY

The development of the Brethren peace philosophy and activities in the period between World Wars I and II is very significant because of its bearing upon the peace position of the Church of the Brethren during World War II.

The Brethren Peace Position

1. The peace position was still Biblical. The church held that all war is out of harmony with the teachings of Christ.

2. Annual Conference resolutions declared that "all war is sin" and that "the whole war system is futile." As late as 1941 the Conference said that "war is sin, unconditionally and always." This is the strongest position against war that the Church of the Brethren had ever taken.

3. The Brethren advised the young men of the church not to take any service within the ranks of the army. Even noncombatant service was held to be inconsistent with the teachings of Christ and the historic peace position of the church. The attitude of the church, however, toward members who entered military service was to be one of brotherly love and forbearance, granting them the full fellowship of the church and teaching them the peace principles of the Brethren. This was a great contrast to the strict discipline of the Civil War period.

4. The Brethren interpreted their relationship to the state as being that of constructive and creative citizenship. They recognized their obligation to work for the highest

---

[76] Personal interview with Paul French, Washington, D.C., Feb. 23, 1943.

welfare of their country and declared that they wanted to be faithful citizens. However, the Brethren held that their supreme allegiance was to God, that love for country did not mean their participation in war, and that the majority had no right to suppress the conscience of the minority. Even in wartime the Brethren wanted to serve the country in creative ways in harmony with conscience. Thus, the church before the war came indicated its willingness for its young men to serve in projects detached from the war system.

5. The Church of the Brethren took a more active part in preserving peace. Through letters, resolutions, and personal visits to lawmakers, the denomination worked toward the reduction of armaments and the passing of a neutrality law and expressed its opposition toward universal military training and peacetime conscription. The church became more of a pressure group endeavoring to influence legislation.

6. The church recognized to a limited extent the relationship of their peace principles to industrial and economic problems. Annual Conference advised the members to protest against paying taxes for military purposes, held that the church through its program of goodwill should help to relieve industrial conflicts, and declared that Brethren should apply the peace principles of the denomination to labor union practices.

7. A program of neutral relief work was outlined as a service to humanity and as a preparation for alternative service in the event of war. Relief work was carried on in Spain and China in large proportions.

The Brethren Peace Program and Activities

1. Between the world wars, the Brethren made a great many strong peace pronouncements, carried on a great

variety of peace activities, and promoted a comprehensive peace education program.

2. The peace education program, however, had the following weaknesses:

(a) There were ten changes in boards and committees dealing with peace education over a period of twenty years. No one organization had a chance to do its most effective work.

(b) There was no general supervision to see that local churches carried out the peace education program.

(c) The peace education program itself lacked a sound educational procedure. It largely consisted of preaching sermons and distributing peace literature; young people as a whole were not placed in an educational setting where their points of view were challenged through stimulating discussions. The peace education program had not prepared the young people of the Church of the Brethren for World War II.

The Brethren Getting Ready for the Coming War

The church leaders worked for peace but at the same time looked ahead and laid the foundation for the church's action in the event of war.

1. The peace statement of the Annual Conference of 1935 was presented to the secretary of President Roosevelt and to Cordell Hull, informing the government what the peace convictions of the Church of the Brethren were.

2. The advisory committee for conscientious objectors outlined a plan of action for war crises, led the church to advise against all service under military command, and listed the types of services considered to be consistent with the position of the church.

3. The Brethren, Friends, and Mennonites began to work together more closely. The Newton conference of 1935 ap-

pointed a Continuation Committee which planned co-operative activities. Two conferences were held with President Roosevelt. The conference in 1937 informed the President concerning the historic peace convictions of these denominations, but the conference of 1940 went further and made suggestions to the government regarding an acceptable program and organization for conscientious objectors in the event of war. The co-operative work of the historic peace churches laid the foundation for the formation of the National Service Board for Religious Objectors.

4. The Brethren worked with the Friends, Mennonites and others, while the conscription law was being written, to secure complete exemption for absolutists, and to liberalize the bill to read "religious training" or "belief." Absolute exemption was defeated, and the law was limited to read "religious training and belief." However, The Selective Training and Service Act of 1940 was more considerate of conscientious objectors than it would have been had the peace groups not worked with the lawmakers. For the first time in history those opposed to war in any form by reason of religious training and belief could be assigned to work of national importance under civilian direction.

5. The National Service Board for Religious Objectors was formed at the suggestion of General Hershey and because the many peace groups had to have a central organization with which to deal with the government. Through a gentleman's agreement with Selective Service, the National Service Board operates the C.P.S. camps and the peace churches are the administrative agencies for this board. The administrative agencies agreed to finance Civilian Public Service camps because asking the government to finance them meant government-operated camps. The Director of Selective Service is officially in control of the camps but he has delegated a measure of authority for the time being to

the National Service Board. At the outset of the draft it seemed that Selective Service officials wanted a fair and just administration of the law.

6. The philosophy of Civilian Public Service is that of co-operation with the state in working out mutual problems. Although the Brethren oppose conscription, when it comes they prefer to render creative service to the state in harmony with conscience, rather than being obstructionists and doing nothing! The Brethren are in reality saying to the state that if they are allowed to render service according to conscience, they will sacrifice and pay for it.

The Church of the Brethren after two hundred thirty-five years has moved from non-co-operation with the state to that of co-operation in working out a program of service for conscientious objectors.

Chapter IX

GENERAL SUMMARY AND BRETHREN PHILOSOPHY OF THE RELATIONSHIP OF CHURCH AND STATE

The History and Position of the Church of the Brethren Regarding War

The Brethren are a religious minority group, German in origin, whose founders took the position that war was contrary to the spirit and teachings of Jesus. The chief factors which made the early Brethren a peace people were the taking of the New Testament as their rule of life, the sufferings resulting from years of warfare in Europe which made them hate war, the persecutions suffered at the hands of church and state in Germany, the influence of the Pietists who emphasized spiritual devotion as well as nonresistance, and early contacts with the Mennonites and Quakers. The Church of the Brethren was founded in an atmosphere of Bible study and the New Testament was the church's only creed.

The Brethren followed the Mennonites to Germantown, Pennsylvania. For many years these people lived sheltered lives under the peaceful Quaker government. The two outstanding Brethren during the colonial period were the Christopher Sowers, the printers at Germantown. They worked for peace with the Indians and constantly printed articles on peace in their periodicals. The church took the position that neither Brethren nor their sons should go to the muster grounds. The church members were non-associators during the Revolutionary War and took no part in the military defense of the country. They paid the taxes demanded of them but stood unitedly against military service.

For seventy-five years following the Revolutionary period

the Brethren had no schools, educational periodicals or outstanding educational leaders. They became a frontier people living in an exclusive fellowship. New enlightenment for the church came with the revival of printing around 1850. The "Gospel Visitor" helped to create an interest in education and missions. Annual Conferences between the Revolutionary and Civil wars made strong pronouncements declaring that Christ forbade his followers to participate in war activities.

The Brethren were opposed to the Civil War and did not want the Southern states to secede from the Union. They were strictly an antislavery people. The church members in the South suffered more than those in the North because the Northern government was more stable. The Brethren were well united against bearing arms and only a few entered the army. Those who did lost their church membership. Some of the church members hired substitutes in the early days of the war but the church preferred the payment of taxes in lieu of military service. However, the members lived under the constant threat of the law being repealed. There were many fines and imprisonments among the Brethren.

Between the Civil War and World War I some who had been soldiers united with the church. The Annual Conference asked them not to attach themselves to the Grand Army of the Republic. Peace pamphlets were printed indicating that the peace point of view of the church was still founded upon the New Testament. The first peace committee for the denomination was appointed in 1911 but for twenty years prior to that time no outstanding Conference declaration had been made on this subject. The peace committee had no funds and therefore was unable to carry out any extensive program. The church had been active in building colleges and extending its foreign mission program, and peace education was a minor emphasis prior to World War I. The denomination had taken its peace position for granted. And since the Civil War something had happened to the church. Young people were going to high school and college, church members were taking an active part in community life, the old exclusiveness of the church had passed, and the church was no longer strictly disciplining its members. The character of the church had changed and it had not adjusted its teaching program to the new conditions. The Brethren were not prepared for World War I.

The Brethren opposed the entrance of the United States into the first World War. Since the draft law of May 18, 1919, exempted Brethren from only combatant service, the leaders of the church were confused as to whether to recommend that young men accept noncombatant service or to refuse all military service and take the consequences. Most of the leading Brethren in the early part of the war advised noncombatant service, but some did not. The disillusioning experiences in military camps, the pressure of army officers for Brethren to take army service, the statement of an army general that there was not any such thing as noncombatant service in the army, and the widespread feeling in the church that the Brethren should clarify their position, led to the calling of the special Conference at Goshen, Indiana, January, 1918. This Conference took a stricter position, advising against wearing the military uniforms and any service in the army. This statement had to be recalled from the mails and the officers of that Conference narrowly escaped prosecution by the government. The statement had some influence in the church but the change of church position came too late to stop an increasing number of Brethren from taking noncombatant service. The majority of drafted Brethren entered noncombatant military activities, but there were some regular soldiers and a few army officials in the church membership. Several hundred young men refused all army service and were held in detention camps and later furloughed to farms. Sixteen Brethren were sent to prison.

World War I was followed by a strong revulsion against war among the Brethren. Practically every Annual Conference for twenty-five years made strong peace pronouncements. The Conference went on record declaring that all war is sin and that church members should take no part in it whatsoever. Church committees outlined the types of service which were and were not consistent with the historic peace position of the church. The Mennonites, Friends, and Brethren went twice to President Roosevelt and to other government leaders informing them regarding the peace principles of the churches and asking for their cooperation in the event of war in working out the problem of the conscientious objectors. Strong peace programs for the denomination were outlined and approved but there were several outstanding weaknesses which prevented them from becoming effective. First, there were too many changes made in the general organizations responsible for peace education. In twenty years there were ten changes in boards and committees. Second, there was no general supervision to see that local churches carried out the peace teaching program. Third, there were very few discussion groups which placed the young people in an educational setting.

Brethren leaders opposed the coming of military conscription and worked with the Friends and others to liberalize the draft bill so as to include conscientious objectors of all churches, to provide Civilian Public Service for those opposed to noncombatant military duties, and absolute exemption for those opposed to all service under conscription. The securing of absolute exemption failed but through the efforts of the peace groups a more liberal law was realized. The National Service Board was formed because General Hershey wanted to deal with a central body and it was necessary for the church to deal with the government co-operatively.

The most consistent thing regarding the Brethren's opposition to war throughout the history of the church has been that war is contrary to the teachings of the New Testament and the spirit of Christ. The most inconsistent thing has been the almost complete failure of the church members to apply the peace position to financial, economic and industrial problems. Nowhere in Brethren history have the church members protested very vigorously against the payment of war taxes.

The Position of the Church of the Brethren Regarding the State

When the Church of the Brethren was founded in 1708, church and state were united in Germany, and separation from the established church meant breaking with the state. The earliest known statement regarding the state which influenced Brethren thought was the "Confession of Faith" by Christopher Hochmann. Hochmann believed that civil government was divinely sanctioned by God and that Christians should submit to civil authority unless the laws of government conflicted with the Christian's conscience and God's Word. The Brethren were dissenters only when they felt that the will and Word of God were being transgressed. The early church leaders wanted their position regarding the state to be entirely Biblical but they had difficulty in harmonizing the thirteenth chapter of Romans with their peace convictions. Since Romans 13 stated that governments were "ordained by God, to punish evildoers and protect the good," they thought that the state according to the nature of its responsibilities might have to use force, while the Brethren with their nonresistant principles could not. To them the church belonged to the kingdom not of this world. This dualistic conception continued through the Civil War period. The Brethren believed that the New Testament taught that they should pay the taxes required of them. They paid heavy taxes and fines for exemption from military service. Their opposition to war was confined more to the overt acts of warfare than to the whole war system. There was a basic inconsistency in the Brethren peace position during the first one hundred fifty years of the church's history. If it was wrong for Christians to fight according to the New Testament, and right for the government when necessity compelled, the leaders of government were sometimes forced not to be Christian.

The Brethren gradually changed this conception of the state following the Civil War. James Quinter wrote in the "Gospel Visitor" that the principle of civil government is ordained of God but not all laws are thus ordained.

Because of the influence of the Industrial Revolution, and the development of printing, education and missions within the church, the Brethren gradually took more interest in the affairs of the state and by World War I they were generally voting. The Annual Conference of 1917 committed the church to a constructive patriotism and a loyal citizenship of genuine service to the country. The members of the Church of the Brethren were asked to make extra sacrifices for the relief program out of gratitude for the government's exemption of the Brethren from combatant military assignments.

Following World War I the church declared that all war was wrong both for the state and for individuals. The Brethren stated that they loved their country, desired to be loyal citizens, and were willing to serve her highest welfare;

but they held that when the demands of the country conflicted with the teachings of Christ, their supreme allegiance was to Christ.

The church opposed the coming of conscription. But after it came, the church leaders took the position that the peace testimony of the church and their constructive citizenship could be better expressed through a program of civilian service within the conscription system than by refusing all service. Civilian Public Service has been worked out co-operatively with the government. The National Service Board operates upon the basis of co-operation, goodwill, and cultivation of understanding. The Brethren moved from a complete break with the state in Germany, and non-co-operation with the state during the Revolutionary and Civil wars, to co-operation with the state in working out a mutual problem.

How the State Dealt With the Brethren As a Religious Minority Group

The early history of the Church of the Brethren is one of persecution. The Peace of Westphalia did not grant religious freedom to minority groups. Since Germany was divided into provinces, the status of minority groups depended upon the attitude of the ruling prince. The original Brethren went to Schwarzenau because it was a refuge for religious dissenters. Prince Henry made the Brethren pay a head tax, and Alexander Mack probably used most of his wealth paying these taxes for the church members. Persecution drove the Brethren from Schwarzenau to West Friesland, and from Marienborn to Creyfeld. Arrests, fines and imprisonments for church members were common. Finally, for the sake of religious liberty the Brethren came to America.

After the Quakers lost control of the Pennsylvania Assembly there was increasing criticism of nonresistant people. According to the Pennsylvania law they were required to pay an equivalent to the time spent by associators in military service. The Brethren aimed to be neutral, but since they would not fight for the colonies, they were accused by many people of being in sympathy with the British. The Oath Law of June 13, 1777, was aimed directly at non-associators. The Council of Safety of Pennsylvania ordered personal estates and effects of inhabitants who had aided the enemy to be seized and sold. Some Brethren suffered the loss of their property, including Christopher Sower, the printer, whose property was confiscated and whose printing press was destroyed. Sower himself suffered severe humiliation and persecution. The destruction of the Sower printing press removed the leading educational light among the Brethren and probably set the church back seventy-five years.

At the beginning of the Civil War eight states granted exemption from military service to members of the historic peace churches upon the payment of an equivalent, an almost equal number placed the whole matter in the hands of the legislatures, and other state constitutions were entirely silent. During the Civil War it was necessary for the Brethren to work first with their state governments and then with the Federal government and the Southern Confederacy. Every law which recognized the Mennonites, Friends and Brethren came after serious work on the part of these churches with leading congressmen. The Brethren in the North each paid $300 for exemption from the army and remained on their farms. In the South there were many changes in the law. At first drafted church members paid $600 to $1,500 each for substitutes. Later they could secure exemption under the Virginia law for the payment of $500 and 2 per cent of the assessed value of their taxable property. Still later the law of the Southern Confederacy allowed exemption for Brethren through the paying of $500 each into the public treasury. But in spite of these taxes, which were paid at a great sacrifice, the Brethren lived under the constant threat of the law's repeal. President Davis needed men and he recommended that the exemption law be repealed. The change in the law came near the end of the war, but many church members because of their uncertain status under the government had moved westward, escaping across the lines into Northern territory. There were many arrests and imprisonments among the Brethren but the greatest blow to the church was the killing of Elder John Kline, whose activities in getting church members exempted from army service brought upon him increasing criticism and a martyr's death.

The draft law of the first World War was patterned somewhat after that of the Civil War. It recognized only members of the historic peace churches and granted exemption from only combatant service. There was no consideration for the absolutists and no work provided, until near the end of the war, for those who would not accept army service. The President did not define noncombatant service until March, 1918, and for months conscientious objectors lived in the constant uncertainty as to what would be required of them. Conscientious objectors were under the continual pressure of army officials and both the army and the War Department followed the deliberate policy of getting as many conscientious objectors as possible to accept army assignments. The government was confused regarding how to handle the conscientious objector problem. There were many court-martial proceedings and sincere Christians were convicted by army officials who did not understand them. The farm furlough plan was not inaugurated until the summer of 1918. Before that time those who refused army service were held in detention camps where idleness was not wholesome for young men. The punishments for religious objectors in prison were frequently severe until developing criticism caused the government to issue an order against it. Neither the government nor the Church of the Brethren showed any far-sighted statesmanship in providing for the protection of the consciences of those who were opposed to participation in war.

The first draft of the conscription bill prior to World War II likewise recognized only members of the historic peace churches and granted exemption from only combatant service. Leaders of the Friends, Mennonites and Brethren worked with the lawmakers to liberalize the bill, to include conscientious objectors of all churches, to obtain complete exemption for absolutists, and civilian work for those who would not enter the army. While it was not possible to secure absolute exemption, the law recognizes conscientious objectors upon the basis of "religious training and belief" regardless of their religious denominations and provides for "work of national importance under civilian direction" for those opposed to both combatant and noncombatant military assignments. A more liberal law is the product of the efforts of peace leaders working with the government.

It should be noted that every gain in behalf of a more liberal law for conscientious objectors, throughout the history of the Church of the Brethren, has come through the repeated efforts of the churches bringing their claims to bear upon the government. The church cannot depend upon the government of itself to provide an adequate recognition for those opposed to war. The church of necessity must shoulder the responsibility. Nowhere in the history of the Church of the Brethren has the government taken the initiative to provide adequate protection of conscience.

The Brethren Philosophy Regarding the Relationship of Church and State

We see that the early Brethren leaders recognized the necessity for an orderly civil government. They supported the state by paying the taxes required of them and by obeying all laws which did not conflict with their religious convictions. The Brethren, however, changed from non-voting to a recognition of their citizenship obligations and a direct participation in the affairs of the state. The dualistic concept of early Brethren thought, that the church belonged to the kingdom of God, and the state to the kingdom of this world, and that the state might have to wage war which the church according to the teachings of Jesus could not do, changed until the Brethren applied their peace principles to the state as well as to the individual and the church. The Brethren moved from the Mennonite position, which is that of living as guests in a country, toward the position of the Society of Friends—that of accepting responsibilities for citizenship.

The present philosophy of the Church of the Brethren regarding the relationship of its members to the state may be stated thus:

1. There is a higher authority than that of the state which the Christian should obey. This higher authority is the will of God as expressed in the New Testament and centered in the ethics of Jesus. The conscience of the individual church member regarding war is respected, but as far as the church is concerned, the rightness or wrongness of the individual's participation in war does not depend upon the individual's conscience, but upon the ethics of Jesus. The Church of the Brethren asks its members to live according to the teachings of Jesus expressed in the Sermon on the Mount.

2. The Brethren, also, recognize their citizenship obliga-

tions. They love their country and want to work for its highest welfare. They hold that love for country does not mean hatred of other peoples, and that the highest welfare of this country must be consistent with that which is best for humanity everywhere. The Brethren apply the ethics of Jesus to the state as well as to the church and believe that war for the state is wrong and destructive of the most precious values. The use of force by the state, according to the Brethren, should be nonviolent and should not destroy personality. The use of goodwill, co-operation, and the conference table, the cultivation of understanding among other peoples, and dealing with other nations upon the basis of downright fairness, are the methods the Brethren would have this country substitute for the sword and material force. The members of the church accept their responsibility to be faithful citizens and to do what they can toward creating the kind of government which will allow the values of peace and goodwill to be realized.

3. The Brethren, as members of a church asking allegiance to Christ, and as citizens of a state participating in government, are caught in a conflict between the demands of a conscripting state and the claims of the church. In this conflict the denomination holds that the Christian should be true to the higher loyalty centered in the teachings of Christ. The Brethren believe *that the state is a means* toward helping to provide for the welfare of the people *and not an end,* that personality is the central value in the universe, that the human conscience should be free, that the religious and moral convictions of minorities are valuable in a democracy, and that even in war the consciences of those opposed to war should be respected by the government. As a minority group, the Brethren believe in working through democratic means for a recognition of the rights of minorities. Even though conscription is

considered to be wrong, the Brethren prefer to render creative service to the state within the conscription system rather than to do nothing.

4. In working out the problems caused by the conflict between a conscripting state and a peace church, the Brethren hold that co-operative relationships with the state are necessary. In this co-operation the separation of church and state is assumed. The Church of the Brethren believes in a free church and that the state should not dictate to the church. Historically, when the state conscripted or persecuted the church members, the Brethren met the situation through emigration. Now emigration is practically impossible. The attitude of the church members toward the government has changed. The church is meeting the problems related to conscription and war through co-operation with the government in the working out of mutual problems. It is co-operation with stubborn resistance on the part of the church groups when the agencies of conscription try to exercise more control over the consciences of those opposed to war, and co-operation with the state through a general organization representing many pacifist groups. The united efforts of pacifist groups make possible a more powerful influence upon the government. However, the co-operative relationship with the government in the program for conscientious objectors has involved some compromise for the peace churches. The Civilian Public Service camp directors have administered the regulations of Selective Service. The Brethren claim that it is a justifiable compromise in that consideration has been gained for conscientious objectors through this procedure.

There are dangers in the present relationship of the peace churches to the government. The state may increasingly try to dictate to the churches. In order to avoid becoming a tool to carry out the will of a conscripting state, and also to continue their historic opposition to war, the historic peace churches must maintain their readiness to break with the state whenever the rights of conscience are not respected. It seems clear that minority religious groups opposed to war should co-operate together in their dealings with the state. It also appears that these co-operating minority groups working co-operatively with the state in outlining and administering a program for conscientious objectors may be setting a pattern for future church and state relationships in dealing with those whose consciences forbid participation in war. However, the philosophy of co-operation with the state which is motivating minority peace groups should be subjected to critical evaluation. Out of the experiences of World War II further light may come upon the problem of church and state relationships for the historic peace churches.

PERTINENT PROBLEMS

Even though this study stops short of a consideration of World War II, five outstanding problems present themselves for consideration by the Church of the Brethren:

1. How far will the church members be faithful to the church's peace position during World War II?

2. How far will it be possible for members of a religious minority group like the Brethren to maintain their peace convictions under conditions of widespread war propaganda, heavy social pressure and increasing government control of life, without forming an exclusive church fellowship and practicing strict denominational discipline?

3. What kind of a peace education program should the Church of the Brethren create and carry on in order to teach the children, young people and adults the church's historic peace position?

4. Have the historic peace churches been gaining or los-

ing ground in the struggle with the state for the recognition of the consciences of those opposed to participation in war? Is the present pattern of church and state co-operation in solving mutual problems a valid one for future church and government relationships?

5. How far will the disillusionments which follow World War II prove an impetus for a strong peace education program within the church?

As these lines are being written there are signs that the disillusionments are coming.

BIBLIOGRAPHY

Brethren Publications

Brumbaugh, Martin Grove. *A History of the Brethren.* Elgin, Illinois: Brethren Publishing House, 1899.

Cassel, Abraham H. *History of Sower's Newspaper.* Unpublished document in the handwriting of A. H. Cassel. Philadelphia: Pennsylvania Historical Society, Sept. 1, 1885.

Cassel, Abraham H. *Memorandums of Meetings, Texts, and Sermons. Also Extracts from Christopher Saur's Diary, Besides Anecdotes and History of the Ancient Brethren.* Unpublished book in original handwriting. Philadelphia: Germantown Historical Society.

Cassel, Abraham H. *The German Almanac of Christopher Sower.* Philadelphia: The Pennsylvania Magazine of History and Biography, Vol. VI, 1882. Pennsylvania Historical Society.

Correspondence of the Brethren Service Committee with directors of Civilian Public Service camps, Selective Service officials, and the National Service Board for Religious Objectors. Files of the Brethren Service Committee. Elgin, Illinois: Brethren Publishing House.

Flory, John S. *Literary Activity of the Brethren in the Eighteenth Century.* Elgin, Illinois: Brethren Publishing House, 1908.

Foundations for the Peace Position of the Church of the Brethren. (Pamphlet). Brethren Service Committee. Elgin, Illinois: Brethren Publishing House, 1942.

Funk, Benjamin. *Life and Labors of Elder John Kline.* John Kline's diary. Elgin, Illinois: Brethren Publishing House, 1900.

Gospel Visitor (Bound Volumes), 1858-59, 1860-61, 1862-63, 1864-65. Printed in Columbiana, Columbiana Co., Ohio.

Historical Sketches, Anecdotes, Etc. Compiled by A. H. Cassel, and in his handwriting. Cassel Library, Juniata College, Huntingdon, Pennsylvania.

Laws Affecting the Historic Peace Churches. Authorized by the historic peace churches, May 26, 1941, and compiled by J. B. Martin and N. M. Bearinger. Publisher not given.

Letters from Brethren boys in army camps. Unpublished letters furnished to the writer by Merlin C. Shull. Elgin, Illinois: Brethren Publishing House, 1942-43.

Long, K. G. *Attitudes of the Brethren in Training Camps During the World War.* Unpublished B.D. thesis. Chicago: Bethany Biblical Seminary, 1939.

Mack, Alexander. *Rechten und Ordnungen des Hausen Gottes.* 1774. Translated: *A Plain View of the Rites and Ordinances.* Contains the memoirs of Alexander Mack, Senior, and an introduction by Alexander Mack, Junior. Mt. Morris, Illinois: Brethren Publishing House, 1888.

Moomaw, B. F. *A Dialogue on the Doctrine of Non-Resistance.* Singer's Glen, Virginia: Joseph Funk and Sons, 1867.

Original Letters of Christopher Sower. Huntingdon, Pennsylvania: Cassel Library, Juniata College.

Report of the Director of Civilian Public Service, Elgin, Illinois: Brethren Service Committee, Brethren Publishing House, January 15, 1943.

Sanger, S. F., and Hays, D. *The Olive Branch.* Elgin, Illinois: Brethren Publishing House, 1907.

Servicegrams. Releases of the Brethren Service Committee. Elgin, Illinois: Brethren Publishing House.

The Brethren's Encyclopedia. By Elder Henry Kurtz. Published by the author at Columbiana, Ohio, 1867.

The Brethren Family Almanac. Bound Volumes, 1872-1880, 1881-1890, 1891-1900, 1901-1910, 1911-1920. Elgin, Illinois: Brethren Publishing House.

The Brethren's Tracts and Pamphlets. Vol. I. Elgin, Illinois: Brethren Publishing House, 1900.

The Gospel Messenger. Weekly church paper. Elgin, Illinois: Brethren Publishing House, 1917, 1918, 1939-43.

Thurman, W. C. *Non-Resistance, or The Spirit of Christianity.* Charlottesville, Virginia, 1862.

Yearbook, Church of the Brethren. Elgin, Illinois: Brethren Publishing House, 1943.

Zigler, D. H. *A History of the Brethren in Virginia.* Elgin, Illinois: Brethren Publishing House, 1908.

German Publications

Broadsides by Christopher Sower. (Printed in German.)   Philadelphia: Pennsylvania Historical Society.

Cassel, A. H.   *Von dem Familien Buch des Alten Christopher Sowers.* Unpublished book in the original handwriting. Philadelphia: Germantown Historical Society.

Der Hoch-Deutsch Americanische Calendar, 1740-1800. Bedruckt bey Christoph Saur, Germantown, Pennsylvania. These were personally examined by the writer. Huntingdon, Pennsylvania: Juniata College Library.

Der Hoch-Deutsch Pennsylvanische Geschicht Schreiber. Printed at Germantown, Pennsylvania. A great many of the issues from 1742 until 1752 are in the Rare Book Collection of the Pennsylvania Historical Society, Philadelphia.

Ein Geistliches Magazien. Bedruckt bey Christoph Saur, 1764. Germantown, Pennsylvania. Monthly magazine. The issues for one year are found in the Library of the Pennsylvania Historical Society, Philadelphia.

Geschichte des Christlichen Lebens in der rheinisch-westphalischen evengelischen Kirche von Max Goebel. Coblenz, in commission bei Karl Badeker, 1852. Vol. II. Vol. III printed in 1860.

Glaubens Bekenntniss, bey Ernst Christoph Hochmann. Bedruckt bey Christoph Sauer, Germantown, Pennsylvania, 1743.

Pennsylvanische Berichte, 1754-61. Printed in Germantown, Pennsylvania. Monthly paper. The issues for the years 1746-47, 1749-52, are in the Rare Book Collection of the Pennsylvania Historical Society, Philadelphia.

Government Documents

Acts of the General Assembly of the State of Virginia. William F. Ritchie, Public Printer, 1861. Richmond, Virginia.

American Archives. Fourth Series, Vol. VI. 1775-76. By Peter Force, Washington, D.C., March, 1846.

Colonial Records. Vol. XII. Harrisburg, Pennsylvania, 1853.

Colonial Records. Vols. II, III, IV, VI, VII. Harrisburg, Pennsylvania.

Colonial Records. Pennsylvania, 1776-1779, Vol. II. Harrisburg: Printed by Theo. Fenn and Company, 1852.

Bibliography 337

Confederate Statutes at Large. First Congress, Sessions I, II, and IV. Chapters 31, 45, and 65. Richmond, Virginia: J. M. Matthews, Editor.

Congressional Globe, 38th Congress. Vols. 63, 64, 68, 69. By John C. Rives. Washington, D.C.: Printed at the Congressional Globe Office, 1863-65.

Congressional Record, House of Representatives. Vol. 57, Pt. 4, 65th Congress, 3rd. Session, February, 1919. Washington, D.C.: Government Printing Office, 1919.

Congressional Record, 76th Congress, Third Session, Vol. 86. Washington, D.C.: Government Printing Office, 1940.

Executive Minutes, Pennsylvania Archives, 1794-1796. Ninth Series, Vol. II. John R. Hood, Department of Property and Supplies, Harrisburg, Pennsylvania, 1935.

German Baptist Brethren (Dunkers), Census of Religious Bodies, U.S. Department of Commerce. Washington: Government Printing Office, 1936.

Hearings Before a Subcommittee of the Committee on Military Affairs, United States Senate, Seventy-Fourth Congress, Second Session, on S.3309. Washington: Government Printing Office, 1936.

Hearings Before the Committee on Military Affairs, United States Senate, Seventy-Sixth Congress, Third Session, on S.4164. Washington: Government Printing Office, 1940.

Hearings Before the Committee on Military Affairs, House of Representatives, Seventy-Sixth Congress, Third Session, on H.R. 10132. Washington, D.C.: Government Printing Office, 1940.

High-School Victory Corps, Federal Security Agency, U.S. Office of Education. Washington, D.C.: Government Printing Office, 1942.

"High-School Victory Corps." Printed in Education for Victory. Washington, D.C.: United States Office of Education, January 15, 1943.

Journal of the Congress of the Confederate States of America, 1861-1865. Vols. I-VII. Washington: Government Printing Office, 1905.

Journal of the House of Delegates of the State of Virginia for the Sessions of 1861 and 1862. Richmond, Virginia: William F. Ritchie, Publisher.

Kellogg, Walter G. *The Conscientious Objector.* Introduction by Newton D. Baker. New York: Boni and Liveright, 1919.

Kilty, William. *The Laws of Maryland, 1799-1818.* Vol. III. Annapolis, Maryland: Printed by J. Green, Printer to the State, 1820.

Official Records of the Union and Confederate Armies. Washington: Government Printing Office, 1897-1901.

Pennsylvania Archives, First Series, Vols. 5 and 6, 1777-1778. Philadelphia, Pennsylvania: Printed by Joseph Severns and Co., 1853.

Pennsylvania Archives, First Series, Vols. V, VI, XII, 1776-1777, Philadelphia, 1854. Fourth Series, Vol. VI, Harrisburg, 1901. Second Series, Vol. XVII. Harrisburg, Pennsylvania.

Pennsylvania Archives, Sixth Series, Vol. XII, Harrisburg, Pennsylvania, 1907. Vol. XIII.

Richardson, James D. *A Compilation of the Messages and Papers of the Confederacy,* Including Diplomatic Correspondence (1861-1865). 2 Vols. Nashville: U.S. Publishing Company, 1905.

Selective Service in Peacetime. First Report of the Director of Selective Service, 1940-41, by Lewis B. Hershey. Washington: Government Printing Office, 1942.

Selective Service Manual. Second Edition, January 15, 1943. Washington: Government Printing Office.

Selective Service Regulations. April 11, 1941. Washington, D.C.: Selective Service System.

Shambaugh, Benjamin F. *Messages and Proclamations of the Governors of Iowa.* Vol. II. Iowa City: Published by the State Historical Society of Iowa, 1903.

Statement Concerning the Treatment of Conscientious Objectors in the Army. Prepared and published by direction of the Secretary of War, June 18, 1919. Washington: Government Printing Office, 1919.

Statutes at Large of the Provisional Government of the Confederate States of America. Richmond, Virginia: Edited by James M. Matthews. R. M. Smith, Printer to Congress, 1864.

The Federal Register, May 22, 1942, June 13, 1942, March 11, 1942, January 23, 1943. Washington, D.C.: Government Printing Office.

The National Defense Act. Approved June 3, 1916. Washington: Government Printing Office, 1924.

Thorpe, Francis Newton. *The Federal and State Constitutions.* Vols. I, II, III, IV, V, VI, VII. Washington: Government Printing Office, 1909.

United States Statutes at Large, Vol. 12, Sessions II and III, 37th Congress. Boston: Little, Brown and Company, 1863.

United States Statutes at Large, Vol. 13, 38th Congress, Session I, 1863-65. Boston: Little, Brown and Company, 1866.

Votes of the Assembly. Vol. I 1682-1707. Printed and sold by B. Franklin and D. Hall, Philadelphia, Pennsylvania.

Votes of the Assembly. Vol. III. 1726-1744. Printed and sold by B. Franklin and D. Hall, Philadelphia, Pennsylvania.

Votes of the Assembly. Vol. IV. 1744-1785. Printed and sold by Henry Miller, Philadelphia, Pennsylvania.

Votes of the Assembly. Vol. V. Printed and sold by Henry Miller, Philadelphia, Pennsylvania.

Votes of the Assembly. Pennsylvania Archives, 1753-1756, Eighth Series, Vol. V. Harrisburg, Pennsylvania, 1931.

Votes of the Assembly. Pennsylvania Archives, 1771-1776, Eighth Series, Vol. III. Harrisburg, Pennsylvania, 1935.

Votes of the House of Representatives of Pennsylvania. Vol. II. 1707-1726. Printed and sold by B. Franklin and D. Hall, Philadelphia.

Votes of the House of Representatives of Pennsylvania. Vol. VI. 1767-1776. Printed and sold by Henry Miller, Philadelphia.

Minutes

Full Report of Annual Conferences, 1915-1918, Bound Volume. Chicago: Bethany Biblical Seminary.

Minutes of the Annual Conference, Church of the Brethren, 1938-42. Elgin, Illinois: Brethren Publishing House.

Minutes of the Annual Conferences of the Church of the Brethren on War and Peace, 1935-1940. Board of Christian Education. Elgin, Illinois: Brethren Publishing House.

Minutes of the Annual Meetings, Church of the Brethren, 1778-1909. Elgin, Illinois: Brethren Publishing House, 1909.

Minutes of the Annual Meetings, Church of the Brethren, 1910-1937. Bound Volume. Chicago: Bethany Biblical Seminary.

Minutes of the Board of Religious Education, Church of the Brethren, September 25, 1928, to November 10, 1942. Elgin, Illinois.

Minutes of the Brethren Service Committee, Elgin, Illinois, 1940-43.

Minutes of the General Sunday School Board, Church of the Brethren, June 6, 1911, to July 3, 1928. Elgin, Illinois.

Minutes of the National Service Board for Religious Objectors, 1940-43. Washington, D.C.

Minutes of the Peace Commission, Church of the Brethren, 1933-34. Elgin, Illinois.

Other Publications

America's Pacifist Minority. Addresses delivered at the Chicago Conference of Conscientious Objectors, November 15, 1941. Distributed by the Mid-West Fellowship of Reconciliation, 740 Rush Street, Chicago, Illinois.

Cyclopaedia of Biblical, Theological, and Ecclesiastical Literature. By John M'Clintock and James Strong. Vol. X. New York: Harper and Brothers.

Falckner's Curieuse Nachricht von Pennsylvania, A.D. 1700. By Julius F. Sachse. Printed for the author, Philadelphia, 1905.

Friedman, Robert. "Spiritual Changes in European Mennonitism, 1650-1750." Reprint from the *Mennonite Quarterly Review,* January, 1941.

Hartzler, J. S. *Mennonites in the World War.* Scottdale, Pennsylvania: Mennonite Publishing Company, 1922.

Liberty Bell Leaflets—Leaflet No. 4, *Charter of the Province of Pennsylvania, Granted by Charles the Second of England to William Penn, in January, 1682.* Edited by Martin G. Brumbaugh and Joseph S. Walton. Philadelphia, Pennsylvania: Christopher Sower Company, 614 Arch St., 1898.

Official Statements of Religious Bodies Regarding the Conscientious Objector. Compiled and published by The Department of International Justice and Goodwill of the Federal Council of Churches, 297 Fourth Avenue, New York City.

Page, Kirby. "Nineteen Thousand Clergymen on War and Peace." Published in *The World Tomorrow,* May, 1931. Bound Volume XIV. New York: The World Tomorrow, 52 Vanderbilt Avenue, 1931.

Page, Kirby. "20,870 Clergymen on War and Economic Injustice." Published in *The World Tomorrow*, May 10, 1934. Bound Volume XVII, No. 10.

Pennypacker, Samuel S. *Historical and Biographical Sketches.* Philadelphia, Pennsylvania: Robert A. Tripple, 1883.

Releases of the Friends War Problems Committee, 1942-1943. Philadelphia, Pennsylvania.

Richards, Henry. *The Pennsylvania German in the Revolutionary War, 1776-1783.* Vol. 17 of the Pennsylvania German Society Publications. Lancaster, Pennsylvania, 1908.

Rupp, I. D. *An Original History of the Religious Denominations at Present Existing in the United States.* Harrisburg, Pennsylvania: J. Y. Humphreys, 1884.

Rupp, I. D. *A Collection of Upwards of Thirty Thousand Names of German, Swiss, Dutch, French and Other Immigrants in Pennsylvania from 1727 to 1776.* Philadelphia: Leary, Stuart & Co., 1898.

Schaff-Herzog's Religious Encyclopedia. Vols. I-III. New York: Funk and Wagnalls, 1883.

The Autobiography of Benjamin Franklin. The World's Greatest Literature. The Spencer Press, 1936.

The Conscientious Objector. A paper published at 2 Stone Street, New York. The issues of November, 1942; December, 1942; and February, 1943.

The Encyclopedia Britannica. Eleventh Edition, New York, 1910. Vol. XI.

The Four Freedoms. Franklin D. Roosevelt, January 6, 1941. Office of War Information. Washington, D.C.: Government Printing Office.

War and the Bill of Rights. New York: American Civil Liberties Union, 170 Fifth Avenue, January, 1942.

Wright, Needles Edward. *Conscientious Objectors in the Civil War.* Philadelphia: University of Pennsylvania Press, 1931.

Year Book of American Churches, 1941 Edition. Benson Y. Landis, Editor. New York: F. C. Vinguerie, Publisher, 37-41 85th St., Jackson Heights.

Publications of the National Service Board

Civilian Bonds for Religious Objectors. Civilian Bond Committee of the National Service Board for Religious Objectors, Washington, D.C., 1942.

French, Paul Comly. *Civilian Public Service,* National Service Board for Religious Objectors, Washington, D.C., November 1, 1942.

Proceedings of the Assistant Directors Training Institute of the National Service Board for Religious Objectors, November 9 to December 1, 1942.

Report of the Proceedings of the Civilian Public Service Conference Held at Winona Lake, Indiana, September 1 to 3, 1941. National Service Board for Religious Objectors.

The Conscientious Objector Under the Selective Training and Service Act of 1940. National Service Board for Religious Objectors, Washington, D.C., July 1, 1942.

The Reporter. Published semi-monthly by the National Service Board for Religious Objectors, Washington, D.C., 1942-43.

Rare Books and Papers

A Brief State of the Province of Pennsylvania. (Thought to have been written by Cross.) Printed for S. Bladon, in Pater-Noster-Row, London, 1755. (In Rare Book Collection of the Congressional Library.)

Captain Ashmead Papers. Rolls of his company, 1777 to 1778. (In Rare Book Collection of the Pennsylvania Historical Society.)

Cassel, A. H. *A Short Sketch of the Life of E. C. Hochmann.* A typed and undated manuscript. University of Pennsylvania Library.

Chronicon Ephratense. A history of the Community of Seventh Day Baptists at Ephrata, Pennsylvania, by "Lamech" and "Agrippa." S. H. Zahm & Co., Lancaster, Pennsylvania, 1899.

Day, Sherman. *Historical Collections of the State of Pennsylvania.* Philadelphia: Published by George W. Gorton, 1843.

Edwards, Morgan. *Materials Toward a History of the Baptists in Pennsylvania.* Vol. I. Joseph Cruxshank, Philadelphia. Book undated. Found in the Rare Book Collection of the Pennsylvania Historical Society, Philadelphia.

Genealogical Chart of the Sower Family. In possession of Albert Sower, Philadelphia, Pennsylvania.

Jones, U. J. *History of the Early Settlement of the Juniata Valley.* Philadelphia: Published by Henry B. Ashmead, 1856.

Minute Book of the Founding of the Church of the Brethren in Philadelphia. In possession of Roland Howe, Philadelphia, Pennsylvania.

Pemberton Papers. Vol. II (1755-1757). *Article Written by Christopher Saur, Jr., for the Gazette on His Father's Death,* September 25, 1758.

Peter's Papers. Vol. IV. 1755 to November 1757. *Extracts From the Germantown Newspapers Published by Christopher Sower.* Pennsylvania Historical Society, Philadelphia.

Proud, Robert. *The History of Pennsylvania.* Vols. I and II. Zachariah Poulson, Jr., Philadelphia, Pennsylvania, 1798.

Sachse, Julius Friedrich. *The German Sectarians of Pennsylvania* (1742-1800). P. C. Stockhausen, Philadelphia, 1900.

Sachse, Julius Friedrich. *The German Sectarians of Pennsylvania* (1708-1742). P. C. Stockhausen, Philadelphia, 1900.

Scription to Henry Mill's Company. The Ashmead Scrap Book. Pennsylvania Historical Society, Philadelphia.

Seidensticker, Oswald. *German Pioneers in Pennsylvania.* Unpublished work of Professor Seidensticker. Germantown Historical Society, Pennsylvania. Probably written between 1870 and 1890.

SECONDARY MATERIALS

Abrams, Ray H. *Preachers Present Arms.* New York: Round Table Press, 1933.

Ankrum, Freeman, *Alexander Mack the Tunker and Descendants.* Scottdale, Pennsylvania: Herald Press, 1943.

Applied Nonresistance. Papers read at the Mennonite conference on Applied Nonresistance, Goshen, Indiana, April, 1939. Scottdale, Pennsylvania: Mennonite Publishing Company, 1939.

Beidleman, William. *The Story of the Pennsylvania Germans.* Express Book Print, Easton, Pennsylvania, 1898.

Bicentennial Addresses. *Two Centuries of the Church of the Brethren.* Elgin, Illinois: Brethren Publishing House, 1908.

Blough, Jerome E. *History of the Church of the Brethren of the Western District of Pennsylvania.* Elgin, Illinois: Brethren Publishing House, 1916.

Bosley, Harold. "The Federal Council Declares War." Published in *The Christian Century,* January 13, 1943.

Bowman, Paul H. *Creative Citizenship.* Statement presented on behalf of the Church of the Brethren before the Committee on Military Affairs of the House of Representatives, July 30, 1940. Brethren Service Committee, Elgin, Illinois, 1940.

Brandt, H. A. *Christopher Sower and Son.* Elgin, Illinois: Brethren Publishing House, 1938.

Brown, William Adams. *Church and State in Contemporary America.* New York: Charles Scribner's Sons, 1936.

Cassel, D. K. *History of the Mennonites.* Philadelphia: Globe Printing House, 1888.

Clark, Elmer T. *The Small Sects in America.* Nashville, Tennessee: Cokesbury Press.

Diffenderffer, Frank Reid. *The German Immigration into Pennsylvania.* Part II. The Redemptioners, Lancaster, Pennsylvania, 1900.

Dove, Frederick Denton. *Cultural Changes in the Church of the Brethren.* Elgin, Illinois: Brethren Publishing House, 1932.

Encyclopedia of Religion and Ethics. By James Hastings. Vol. X. New York: Charles Scribner's Sons, 1925.

Falkenstein, George N. *History of the German Baptist Brethren Church.* Lancaster, Pennsylvania: The New Era Printing Company, 1901.

Faris, John T. *Old Churches and Meeting Houses in and Around Philadelphia.* Philadelphia: J. B. Lippincott Co., 1926.

Flory, John S. *Builders of the Church of the Brethren.* Elgin, Illinois: The Elgin Press, 1925.

Flory, John S. *Flashlights from History.* Elgin, Illinois: Brethren Publishing House, 1932.

Francis, J. Z. *The Church of the Brethren in Lebanon County.* Lebanon County Historical Society, 1916.

French, Paul Comly. *We Won't Murder.* New York: Hastings House, 1940.

Gillin, John Lewis. *The Dunkers.* New York: 1906.

Graeff, Arthur. *The Relation Between the Pennsylvania Germans and British Authorities.* (1750-1776.) Norristown Herald, Norristown, Pennsylvania, 1939.

Gray, Harold S. *Character Bad.* New York: Harper and Brothers, 1934.

Heckler, James Y. *Ecclesianthem Or a Song of the Brethren,* Embracing Their History and Doctrine. Lansdale, Pennsylvania: A. K. Thomas and Co., 1883.

Heckman, Samuel B. *The Religious Poetry of Alexander Mack, Jr.* Elgin, Illinois: Brethren Publishing House, 1912.

Henry, J. M. *History of the Church of the Brethren in Maryland.* Elgin, Illinois: Brethren Publishing House, 1936.

Historical Society of Pennsylvania. Vol. **XXIV.** Published by the Historical Society, Philadelphia, Pennsylvania, 1902.

History of the Church of the Brethren of the Southern District of Ohio. By the District Committee. Dayton, Ohio: The Otterbein Press, 1921.

History of the Church of the Brethren of the Eastern District of Pennsylvania. By the Committee appointed by District Conference. Lancaster, Pennsylvania: The New Era Printing Company, 1915.

Hocker, Edward W. *Germantown.* 1688-1933. Germantown, Pennsylvania, 1933.

Hocker, Edward W. *The Founding of the Sower Press.* Germantown Historical Society, 1938.

Holsinger, H. R. *History of the Tunkers and the Brethren Church.* Oakland, California: Pacific Press Publishing Co., 1901.

Howe, Roland L. *The History of a Church,* Lancaster, Pennsylvania: Lancaster Press, Inc., 1943.

Jones, Rufus M. *A Service of Love in War Time.* New York: The Macmillan Company, 1920.

Kaufman, Edmund George. *The Development of the Missionary and Philanthropic Interest Among the Mennonites of North America.* Berne, Indiana: Mennonite Book Concern, 1931.

Keeton, Morris T. *Should CPS Camps Continue?* Unpublished article. Brethren Service Committee, Elgin, Illinois, 1942.

Klein, Walter C. *Johann Conrad Beissel.* Philadelphia, Pennsylvania: University of Pennsylvania Press, 1942.

Kurtz, D. W. *Ideals of the Church of the Brethren.* General Mission Board, Elgin, Illinois, 1933.

Kurtz, D. W. *Nineteen Centuries of the Christian Church.* Elgin, Illinois: Brethren Publishing House, 1914.

Kurtz, D. W. *The Church and State.* A pamphlet, Board of Christian Education, Elgin, Illinois, 1936.

Ludwig, Emil. "The German Mind." *Atlantic Monthly,* February 1938. pp. 255-262.

Macgregor, G. H. C. *The New Testament Basis of Pacifism.* The Fellowship of Reconciliation, New York City, 1936.

Memorial Services. Bishop Christopher Sower. Germantown, Pennsylvania, January 1, 1899. University of Pennsylvania Library.

Miller, D. L., and Royer, Galen B. *Some Who Led.* Elgin, Illinois: Brethren Publishing House, 1912.

Miller, J. E. *The Story of Our Church.* Elgin, Illinois: Brethren Publishing House, 1942.

Miller, J. E. *Stories from Brethren Life.* Elgin, Illinois: Brethren Publishing House, 1942.

Moomaw, D. C. *A Cloud of Witnesses.* Ashland, Ohio: The Brethren Publishing Company, 1925.

Moomaw, D. C. *Christianity Versus War.* Ashland, Ohio: The Brethren Publishing Company, 1924.

Moore, J. H. *Some Brethren Pathfinders.* Elgin, Illinois: Brethren Publishing House, 1929.

Neuman, Albert Henry. *A Manual of Church History.* Vol. II. Philadelphia, Pennsylvania: American Baptist Publication Society, 1903.

Noffsinger, John Samuel. *A Program of Higher Education in the Church of the Brethren.* Teachers College, Columbia University, New York City, 1925.

Ogden, Galen. "Chronological Bibliography of Books of Brethren Authorship—1800-1941." Published in *Schwarzenau,* Vol. III, Number 2, January, 1942. Alexander Mack Historical Society, 3435 Van Buren Street, Chicago, Illinois.

Oswald, John Clyde. *Printing in America.* The Gregg Publishing Company, 1937.

Palmer, Albert W. *Victory For Humanity.* Article printed by the Churchmen's Committee for a Christian Peace, 740 Rush Street, Chicago, Illinois, 1942.

Pennypacker, Samuel W. *The Settlement of Germantown and the Beginning of German Immigration to North America.* William J. Campbell, Philadelphia, Pennsylvania, 1899.

Rupp, I. D. *History and Topography of Northumberland, Huntingdon, Mifflin, Centre, Union, Columbia, Juniata and Clinton Counties, Pennsylvania.* Printed at Lancaster, Pennsylvania, 1847.

Seidensticker, Oswald. *First Century of German Printing in America, 1728-1830.* German Pionier-Verein, Philadelphia, 1893.

Sharp, S. Z. *The Educational History of the Church of the Brethren.* Elgin, Illinois: Brethren Publishing House, 1923.

Sharpless, Isaac. *A Quaker Experiment in Government.* Philadelphia, Pennsylvania: Alfred J. Ferris, 1898.

Sharpless, Isaac. *Quakerism and Politics.* Philadelphia: Ferris and Leach, 1905.

Sharpless, Isaac. *Two Centuries of Pennsylvania History.* J. B. Lippincott Co., 1900.

Smith, Henry C. *The Mennonites of America.* Scottdale, Pennsylvania: Mennonite Publishing Company, 1909.

Smith, Henry C. *The Story of the Mennonites.* Berne, Indiana: Mennonite Book Concern, 1941.

Sweet, William Warren. *Religion in Colonial America.* New York: Charles Scribner's Sons, 1942.

Sweet, William Warren. *The Story of Religion in America.* New York: Harper and Brothers, 1930.

Snider, Harold. *Does the Bible Sanction War?* Grand Rapids, Michigan: Zondervan Publishing House, 1943.

The Churches and a Just and Durable Peace. The Christian Century Press, 1942.

Thomas, Norman. *Is Conscience a Crime?* New York: Vanguard Press, 1927.

Van Doren, Carl. *Secret History of the American Revolution.* New York: The Viking Press, 1941.

Walker, Williston. *A History of the Christian Church.* New York: Charles Scribner's Sons, 1922.

Walker, Williston. *The Reformation.* New York: Charles Scribner's Sons, 1901.

Walton, Joseph S., and Brumbaugh, Martin G. *Stories of Pennsylvania.* New York: American Book Company, 1897.

Wayland, J. W. *A History of Rockingham County, Virginia.* Dayton, Virginia: Reubush-Elkins Co., 1912.

Wayland, J. W. *The German Element of the Shenandoah Valley.* Charlottesville, Virginia: The Michie Company Printers, 1907.

Wertenbaker, Thomas Jefferson. *The Founding of American Civilization, the Middle Colonies.* New York: Charles Scribner's Sons, 1938.

West, Dan. *Brethren Community Service.* Board of Christian Education, Elgin, Illinois, 1943.

Weygand, Cornelius. *The Dutch Country.* New York: Appleton-Century Co., 1939.

Winger, Otho. *History and Doctrines of the Church of the Brethren.* Elgin, Illinois: Brethren Publishing House, 1919.

Wood, Ralph. *The Pennsylvania Germans.* Princeton, New Jersey: Princeton University Press, 1942.

Zerfass, S. G. *Souvenir Book of the Ephrata Cloister.* Lititz, Pennsylvania: John G. Zook, Publisher, 1921.

Ziegler, Jesse H. *The Broken Cup.* (Three Generations of Dunkers.) Elgin, Illinois: Brethren Publishing House, 1942.

Zigler, M. R. *Religious Liberty.* Pamphlet printed by the Brethren Service Committee, Elgin, Illinois, 1942.

INDEX